HERO OF THE UNDER-GROUND

JASON PETER

A MEMOIR **WITH TONY O'NEILL**

HERO OF THE UNDER- GROUND

 ST. MARTIN'S GRIFFIN ＊ NEW YORK

www.stmartins.com

Design by William Ruoto

THE LIBRARY OF CONGRESS HAS CATALOGUED THE HARDCOVER EDITION AS FOLLOWS:

Peter, Jason, 1974–
     Hero of the underground / Jason Peter with Tony O'Neill.—1st ed.
     p. cm.
     ISBN-13: 978-0-312-37576-8
     ISBN-10: 0-312-37576-X
     1. Peter, Jason, 1974– 2. Footabll players—United States—Biography.
3. Heroin abuse. I. O'Neill, Tony, 1978– II. Title.
     GV939.P476A3   2008
     796.332092—dc22
     [B]
                                                              2008012364
     ISBN-13: 978-0-312-56103-1 (pbk.)
     ISBN-10: 0-312-56103-2 (pbk.)

First St. Martin's Griffin Edition: July 2009

10 9 8 7 6 5 4 3 2 1

CON-TENTS

vi   Contents

ACKNOWLEDGMENTS

To my family, thank you for never turning your back on me, I never lost your support and I could not have gotten through this nightmare without you. Mom, I'm sorry for keeping you up all night waiting for that dreaded phone call; the last thing I would ever want to do is to hurt you. Ashley, words can't express the regret I feel for the years I stole from our relationship. To my incredibly beautiful wife, Sarah, you brought my world into focus and truly taught me how to live life. As a son, a brother, and a husband, I know it's not possible for anyone to have been surrounded by people who have more forgiveness, compassion, and love than all of you. I love you all!

—Jason

Heartfelt thanks to Michael Murphy for working so tirelessly to make this book happen, also to George Witte and everyone at St. Martin's Press for doing such a great job. Thanks to Jason Peter for being so honest and fearless in telling his story without the usual BS. Special, special thanks to my wife, Vanessa, and my daughter Nico for their love, support, and, most of all, for putting up with my insanity.

—Tony

If winning is the only thing, then the only other thing is nothing—emptiness, the nothing of a life without ultimate meaning.

—TOM LANDRY, HALL OF FAME COACH OF THE DALLAS COWBOYS

Myths & legends die hard in America. We love them for the extra dimension they provide, the illusion of near-infinite possibility to erase the narrow confines of most men's reality. Weird heroes & mould-breaking champions exist as living proof to those who need it that the tyranny of "the rat race" is not yet final.

—HUNTER S. THOMPSON, HALL OF FAME–WORTHY JOURNALIST, AUTHOR, AND FREE SPIRIT

A NOTE TO THE READER

This is my true story. However, some names and details have been changed.

HERO OF THE UNDER-GROUND

1

ARE YOU THE GUY?

I WASN'T AFRAID OF DEATH.

How could I be? I lived under death's shadow every day. When you swallow sixty Vicodin, twenty sleeping pills, drink a bottle of vodka, and still survive, a certain sense of invulnerability stays with you. When you continually use drugs with the kind of reckless determination that I did, the limit to how much heroin or crack you can ingest is not defined by dollar amounts but by the amounts your body can withstand without experiencing a seizure or respiratory failure. Yet at the end of every binge, every night of lining up six, seven, eight crack pipes and hitting them one after the other *bam! bam! bam!* every night of smoking and snorting bag after bag of heroin . . . after all of that, when you still *wake up* to see the same dirty sky over you as the night before, you start to think that instead of dying, maybe your punishment is to live—to be stuck in this purgatory of self-abuse and misery for an eternity. Sometimes you start to think that death would come as a blessed relief.

I found myself contemplating death again. Only this time I wasn't going to leave it to chance. I was going to buy a gun, load the thing, place the barrel in my mouth, and blow my fucking brains out.

I sat on my parents' sofa as I pondered this. All I needed was a gun.

And all—

Of my problems—

Would be—

Solved.

This had all started the night before. It started in the way that life-shattering events, like suicides or murders, usually begin, with something so small, so meaningless, that it is almost comical.

It started with an argument over a television program.

Diane had been on my last goddamned nerve, ever since we had driven from my apartment building in New York to my folks' house in New Jersey. They were out of town and had asked me stay there to watch the house and look after the dogs. Our heroin habits were again out of control, so we talked it over and decided that we would take the opportunity to kick dope. The plan was this: We would take a small amount of heroin with us. Week one, I would start to kick. Diane would use enough dope not to get sick so that she would be able to look after me and get me through the worst of the physical symptoms. Then, when I was feeling better, Diane would kick, and I would nurse her back to health. It seemed like a simple, obvious plan.

What could possibly go wrong?

Doctors will tell you that kicking heroin is like having a severe flu. They will reel off a list of symptoms: runny nose, runny eyes, muscle aches, stomach cramps, fever, the chills, insomnia, diarrhea, nausea . . . I mean, it doesn't sound like a walk in the park, but it's hardly as bad as having your vertebrae crushed under a 300-pound offensive lineman, right?

Well, as any addict can tell you, doctors—for all of their good intentions—really don't know shit. Comparing heroin withdrawals to the flu is like comparing getting hit by a truck to falling off a tricycle. I don't care how severe your flu is, it's unlikely that you've seriously considered throwing yourself out of a window, just to make the screaming in your head go away and the agony in your body stop. Heroin withdrawal is the nearest thing to hell that the living ever get to experience.

We barricaded ourselves in my parents' house. I had gotten a prescription for a new drug called Subutex from one of my doctors, a little white tablet that dissolves under the tongue. Supposedly it would help with the withdrawals. I also had Xanax to help me sleep. Diane carried the heroin and cocaine, and I resigned myself to a very unpleasant seven days.

By the time I reached day three, the huge flaw in my plan became apparent. Withdrawal sickness tends to come to a peak around the third or fourth day. You are vomiting, shitting yourself, your body is twitching and spasming so hard you can involuntarily throw yourself out of bed. You feel like you have white hot sulfur in your veins instead of blood, and your brain is literally screaming out for some heroin to take the pain away.

As all this was going on, in would walk Diane, high as a fucking kite. Her pupils like pinpricks. Slurring her words. And I knew that in her purse there was enough shit to take all of my pain away. All I had to do was ask.

You see, the relationship with Diane was not exactly an equal partnership. I knew that at the end of the day, if I asked her, she would have to give it to me. Because she knew that if she pissed me off too much and I kicked her out, she would be left with nothing, except a drug habit she had no way of being able to support.

Diane had been a dancer when I met her. A truly beautiful girl with a body that could drive a man insane. She was also a very sweet, kindhearted person. She came into my life like so many of the others—we met at a club, we exchanged messages, and one day she turned up at my apartment with two or three other girls to party. Only Diane never left when the party was over. She stayed, and at this point we had been together for just under a year.

She had changed. I had changed her, I suppose. There was no way that someone could live with me, could be around me for such an extended period without changing. When you live with someone who is high literally seven days a week, twenty-four hours a day you either leave . . . or you adapt. Diane adapted. When I met her she used drugs—maybe a little crystal meth when she danced, or coke recreationally. Normal people stuff. The stuff that is happening in homes and clubs all over the country at this very moment. After a year, however, Diane was snorting as much heroin and smoking as much crack as I was, and I was supporting her habit. Without me to continue funding her drug habit, Diane would be completely screwed.

It was during this attempt that I realized that maybe Diane didn't want us to get clean. After all, it's an old story—if you take the drugs away from a relationship like this, often there is nothing left in their place. Maybe a part of her worried that if we weren't high all of the time, I wouldn't want her around anymore. It would have at least required a huge period of readjustment. Outside of getting high, we didn't have much in common.

At some point during the third day I had managed to hold down enough Xanax that I passed out in a dark, dreamless sleep. I don't know how long I was out. An hour? Two? Maybe only a matter of minutes. Soon something started to bring me around . . .

Then I smelled it.

Something familiar.

Something dragging me out of my cocoon of sleep.

I started to become aware of my surroundings again. The duvet that I was wrapped in, soaked through with my sweat. The aches in every inch of my body. The relentless fucking daylight burning into the back of my eyelids.

And the smell.

That fucking smell.

With a groan of disappointment, I woke up fully. I was curled in a fetal position. I didn't know how long I'd been asleep. I became aware that Diane was sitting on the edge of the bed next to me. I gingerly turned around.

"What the fuck . . . ," I gasped, "are you doing?"

She turned and looked at me. In her hand was a large square piece of aluminum foil. A pipe fashioned from foil hung casually from her lips. Her bleary, stoned eyes looked at me quizzically, before she fired up the lighter and carried on smoking heroin, right there, in the same bed where I was trying to get clean.

"What the fuck are you doing, Diane?"

She exhaled plumes of white smoke from her nostrils, and took the pipe from her mouth.

"I'm staying well, Jason! So I can look after you. How are you feeling, baby?"

I was furious with her, but too sick and weak to argue. Instead, I told her to give me the fucking dope so I could get well, too. I swear she looked relieved when I finally caved.

This sudden change in our plans necessitated a trip back to New York. Once I was using heroin again, I realized we needed more. More of everything. We drove back to the city that night to have coke and heroin delivered to the apartment.

My connections were always ready to deliver. It's pure economics. I was everybody's best customer, and there is no better working model for capitalism than the relationship between a dealer and his customer. If I called at 7:00 in the morning and he was dropping his kid off at school—he made sure I got my drugs first. Late for his mother's funeral? He made sure I got my drugs first. So within an hour of making the call I had five eight-balls [⅛ ounce] of cocaine and three bundles of heroin sitting on my coffee table.

It was too late to drive back to Jersey. We decided to stay home, and we started our usual routine. I cooked up the cocaine with bicarbonate of soda to make freebase. We put the TV on, began to furiously smoke crack and snort heroin, the same thing that we had been doing daily for the past twelve months.

A woman, in tears, was screaming at her boyfriend, about how she was going to keep her baby no matter what. I noticed Diane staring at the screen intently.

"Fuck," I laughed. "I tell you. Diane . . . If you ever got pregnant we wouldn't be keeping that baby."

It was an innocuous enough comment, I thought. After all, we were heroin addicts with out-of-control crack habits. We weren't exactly the models of stability. Whatever I was expecting from Diane, it wasn't the reaction that I got.

"How do you mean?"

"I mean what I say. If you ever got pregnant, you wouldn't be keeping that baby!"

"What the fuck do you mean *you wouldn't be keeping that baby,* Jason?"

"You're a fucking junkie, Diane! So am I! What . . . You're saying you'd keep it if you got pregnant?"

"I couldn't get rid of my baby," Diane told me quietly.

"What, you'd rather have a baby born addicted to fucking crack than get an abortion? Listen to what you're fucking saying!"

"Fuck you!"

Then Diane lost it. She started screaming about how I didn't love her. How I was taking away her right to choose. How I was a controlling asshole. She hadn't slept in days, and we were both loaded on dope and crack, and with our psyches so fragile the argument quickly escalated. I screamed at her that she was crazy if she thought that she was ever having my baby. She told me that I was crazy if I thought I could tell her what to do.

"Fine!" I yelled at her. "Then we aren't having sex again, *period!* Not until the both of us clean up!"

With that Diane stormed into the bedroom and slammed the door shut.

It was a ridiculous argument. It wasn't as if Diane getting pregnant was at all likely. At the beginning of our relationship it had been all sex; but that soon fizzled out as drugs became the focus. Sometimes when she got high Diane would get horny, but the last thing I wanted to do was have sex. To keep her happy, once in a while I would cut down on the drugs, pop a Viagra, and we would screw, but there were so many chemicals in my bloodstream that even this was an extremely rare occurrence. When you have been doing crack for a while, it becomes the least sexual drug you can imagine. The very idea of touching another person, or doing any-thing that would divert your attention away from the pipe, is un-thinkable.

I sat and fumed. Fucking bitch! She was acting crazier and crazier. The crack was making her unstable. All it would take was a wrong word out of me and she would be in tears, screaming, throwing things. In my eyes, I was the stable one. I sucked on the crack pipe angrily and contemplated throwing her ass out on the street.

After an hour I checked in on her. She sat at the desk by the bed, furiously writing a letter, with the pipe next to her. She was so high and so angry, her eyes looked like they could pop right out of her skull. When you're high on crack you get into manic bouts of activity like this. I decided to leave her to it. I went back to the TV room and carried on getting loaded.

I couldn't concentrate on the screen. I started to cook more crack, using a large dessert spoon to dump the cocaine and the bak-ing soda into. At every step of the process—adding the water, cook-ing up the coke, draining off the water, drying the base cocaine—I would stop to smoke some more of the previous batch. My hands trembled from the effect of the coke.

Schhhhttttt!

I heard the noise maybe a half hour after the crack was cooked. I immediately realized that it was the sliding door leading to the fire escape. *What the fuck was she doing?*

It was 4:00 in the morning. My building was one of the more exclusive in New York City. I counted Matt Damon among my neighbors. The heads of multimillion-dollar corporations lived here. As I stormed into the bedroom I caught a glimpse of Diane, crack pipe and torch in one hand, letter in the other, disappearing up the fire escape.

My blood ran cold. My mind still reeling from the crack I had been smoking, I started to realize just how messy this could get. One of my big-shot neighbors hears Diane stomping about on the fire escape, thinks somebody is trying to break into their apartment, and calls the cops. I mean, Jesus, I could see the headlines:

EX-NFL PLAYER JASON PETER ARRESTED IN HIS MULTIMILLION-DOLLAR CRACK DEN

"Diane!" I hissed. "Get the fuck down!"

"Fuck you!" she yelled back. "Leave me alone! You don't love me!"

I saw her climbing unsteadily up the fire escape. Oh Jesus, it got better and better. I could hear her muttering to herself up there about what an asshole I was. The girl was so high and so hysterical that there was no reasoning with her. I tried a different tack.

"Diane, baby," I pleaded, "come down. Let's just talk."

"Fuck *you*, Jason!"

Goddamn it. Any minute now, lights were going to start coming on all over the building. If one person called 911, this whole house of cards was going to come tumbling down around me.

"*Diane!*" I hissed, louder this time. "*If you don't get the fuck down here RIGHT NOW, so help me God, I'm gonna lock you out on this fire escape! Now I'm going inside! If you aren't in here in TWO FUCKING MINUTES, I am locking the door!*"

Fucking bitch! I was suddenly gripped with the drug-fucked certainty that if I didn't get away from the apartment right this minute I was going to be spending an extended period in a prison cell. I opened the door, and as I did so I heard a noise above my head.

Crunch!

Diane had either dropped or thrown the crack pipe down and it shattered into fragments on the escape. Tiny shards of glass tinkled as they fell through the cracks and started to settle. I could see them twinkling like frost on the metal walkway. I pulled the door open, and stepped back into the relative safety of my apartment. I thought about locking the door and then decided against it. My concern for Diane's safety was fading now, and my survival instinct kicked in.

There was no way in hell I was gonna do time because of her tantrum. I was going to split, whether she decided to stay on the fire escape or not. My heart pounding, my adrenaline levels pumped to insane levels, I started to throw my clothes into a bag.

I grabbed all of the drugs in the place. I stashed the cocaine in my pockets. I looked at the heroin. I had three bundles left. Every time I heard a siren outside on the street, I thought that the cops must be showing up at my building already. In a moment of idiot genius I decided to flush the heroin. After all, if I walked outside and the cops were waiting, I could deal with being busted with coke. There is something acceptable about coke. I mean, shit, 90 percent of Wall Street does coke. It's a success drug. I think people are more taken aback when they find out that rich people *aren't* doing coke.

Heroin is a different matter. People don't think of good times when they think of heroin. They think of junkies, passed out in the gutter, stealing for their next fix, shooting up with dirty needles . . . I figured I could handle a coke bust, but not a heroin bust. The smack would have to go.

I stood over the toilet, and threw one bundle in the bowl. *Plop!*

Don't worry, man, I told myself. *You'll be cool. You can buy some more as soon as this shit blows over.*

I threw the second bundle into the bowl. I'm now looking at what amounted to three hundred dollars floating in my toilet, like the world's most expensive turd. One bundle left.

**JASON "JUNKIE" PETER, EX-NFL PLAYER,
BUSTED LEAVING APARTMENT WITH HEROIN
AND COCAINE. FAMILY EXPRESSES SHOCK,
DISGUST.**

Cursing, I placed the last bundle back in my pocket with the coke and flushed the rest of the dope before I had time to change my mind. I'd just have to take my chances with the cops. I needed

the heroin more than I needed the peace of mind. I picked up my
bag and headed for the door.

"Where the fuck are you going, Jason?"

I turned, and there was Diane. I hadn't even heard her come in.
Her eyes looked crazed. In this light, I could see the toll the drugs
were taking on her. She looked thinner, hollowed out almost. And
her eyes. There was something terribly vacant about her eyes. She
was still clutching the torch and the letter like her life depended on it.

"Away, Diane. I'm going away."

"Where are you going? Answer me!"

"I told you! Away! I'm done! I'm done with all of this bullshit!" I waved my hand around the apartment. "This shit is making
you crazy! You're acting like a fucking lunatic! I'm out, Diane. Do
what you need to do, but I'm out of here!"

I saw her mind turning the situation over.

"You can't go," she said quietly.

"Oh yes I can."

I knew that she was worried about the drugs. She knew I had
them on me. The last thing she wanted was for me to storm out
right then and leave her with no drugs. It was a survival mechanism
on her part, but I was in no mood to negotiate. With a scream Diane
launched herself at me, and started trying to punch me and claw my
face. Now, I'm 240 pounds, and 6'5". If I was that kind of guy I
could have knocked her on her ass. But she still tried anyway. She
was going for my bag. I let her have it. She ripped it open and
started throwing my clothes out on the floor in a vain attempt to
find the drugs.

"They ain't there. I flushed the fucking drugs, Diane! They're
gone! Here!" I dug around in my wallet and took out a bunch of
twenty-dollar bills, and threw them at her. They drifted down all
around her, like confetti. Diane just stayed on the ground, her breath
ragged, with the contents of my bag and the scrunched-up twenty-
dollar bills vomited all around her. She looked like she was about to
burst into tears.

"The fucking candy store is closed!" I spat. "I'm going . . . and when I get back you'd better be gone."

I left her like that. I ran down the stairs, still convinced that the cops must be on their way. It was 4:00 A.M. and I was cracked out, sweating. The whole incident had spun me out completely. I heard my heart pounding in my ears, and felt the cold sweat trickling down my back.

Outside of my building taxis were loitering to pick up the stragglers from the night club next door. I wrenched a door open, and the driver—an older Indian guy—almost jumped out of his skin when he saw a sweating, brawny crackhead with eyes bulging and a shaved head jump into the back of his cab. Like in a bad movie I looked at him and yelled, "Drive!"

"W-where you want to go?"

"Anywhere, man! Just fucking drive!"

We headed uptown, cruising the streets of New York at 4:00 in the morning. After the initial rush of crack you are left with a pretty unpleasant sensation. Your adrenaline levels and heart rate are pushed way up. The pleasurable aspects start to fade quickly. Then you find yourself in full-on fight-or-flight mode. You start to get a little tweaked. Everything carries the air of threat. Sudden noises seem loud and malicious. You mind is reeling, and paranoia floods in. My mind started to turn on me.

What if she dies, my mind said. *What if she fucking jumps? That note was obviously a suicide note of some kind. If she throws herself out of a window, or slashes her wrists, and the cops show up to see that you've fled the scene . . . you do the math. Heroin and crack-addicted football player kills his girlfriend and flees the scene . . . tries to make it look like a suicide. It'll be an open-and-shut case. You'll get the fucking chair, asshole, and it will take more than Johnnie Cochran to save you.*

You need an alibi.

You need to cover your ass.

So, spurred on by crack logic, I started talking to the cabdriver.

"Listen, man, something bad is happening in my apartment.

My girlfriend . . . I think she's going to hurt herself . . . I don't know . . . she's fucking crazy. She's all cracked out, up on the fire escape, I think she wrote a fucking suicide note . . ."

I could tell the old guy behind the wheel was getting more and more freaked out. What I was doing was patently insane, but I carried on anyway.

"Look. I need a receipt. A receipt with the time on it. And if anything happens I need your word that you'll tell the cops I was in your cab at—hey, what time is it? Four? Four fifteen? Look I need you to tell me that you'll tell the cops that I didn't do anything, OK?"

I carried on in this vein for a while. The driver would look back at me in the mirror for a second before meeting my manic gaze and looking away quickly. He probably thought I was some kind of psychopathic murderer. Every so often he would say, "Oh yeah?" or "Really?" and I started to get the impression that he was being very careful not to antagonize me. We pulled up at an ATM and I withdrew as much cash as I could. I didn't want to use my card when I got to a hotel. Maybe the cops could trace it. It seemed as if the whole city was buzzing with a malicious energy. I imagined the cops out there with their computers and their tracking devices and their hi-tech equipment all trying to nail me, for a crime I hadn't commited. I jumped back in the cab and told the driver, "OK, head to the Hudson Hotel."

On the way there, the cabbie started gently asking questions. I answered a few of them before I started to get wary that he was probing me for too much information and I clammed up. Twisting around to look out of the rear window I noticed that the same car had been behind us for a few blocks now. Shit, maybe they were on to me already. I turned back around. After a few seconds I looked again.

Still behind us. Shit.

When we pulled up outside the Hudson Hotel, I handed the cabbie the money, which he accepted with nervous hands. I took my receipt and his assurances that he would testify on my behalf if Diane showed up dead. Then with a squeal of tires he split, as if the devil himself was getting out of his cab.

I stepped into the deserted lobby. I walked straight for the escalator. I fought the urge to look over my shoulder. At any moment I expected a strong, steady hand to land on my shoulder. "Going somewhere, buddy?"

I stood on the escalator and watched the empty lobby for clues as I was carried farther and farther up. I rode the thing up to the top and then rode another straight down. Back at the lobby, I walked out into the night in an effort to evade anybody who might have been tailing me. I hurried to a yellow cab waiting for a pickup outside of the hotel and got in. As we drove to our next destination, I made sure I kept my mouth shut.

I started hitting hotels, in an effort to find a place for the night. What I needed to do was get a room, bolt the door, and get high. Get so high that I could just turn off the screaming voices in my head for a moment. In the back of my mind I knew that the wreckage of my life would still be there when the drugs wore off, but at this point I didn't care. Whether Diane was alive, dead, or something in between, my overwhelming need was for the temporary oblivion of drugs. I needed to be high as a motherfucker.

I started making the rounds. All of the fancy hotels. I started to find that I had a problem. No one had a room. The first time it's bad luck. The second time, too. But after hitting four hotels and asking for a room and being told that there were no rooms, on a Monday night, I started to get worried. I was shoving handfuls of cash in people's faces, begging for a single room, a double, a fucking penthouse suite, *anything!*

Nothing.

Zip.

Something was up.

Someone was calling all of these hotels ahead of time and warning them that I was bad news! That I was a drug-crazed woman killer on the run from the law! I started ducking into hotel bathrooms, and taking little snorts of coke to try to delay the crash, but with all of the stern-faced desk clerks repeating, "Sorry, sir, we have no vacancies," my paranoia could no longer be reined in.

They're on to you, asshole. Your money is no help to you now.

They know what you did. The cab driver probably called ahead to tell them you were some kind of lunatic as soon as you stepped out of his cab.

You've been red-flagged.

You're screwed!

I practically ran from the last place into a waiting cab. As I opened the door and jumped in, panting and trembling from the effects of the coke, I swear the cabbie asked: "Are you the guy? The guy with the girlfriend in the apartment?"

That kind of floored me. As we drove off, I started to imagine how it was going down. The first cabdriver got on his radio and alerted all of the other cabbies that a manic, brick-shithouse skinhead got into his cab and started talking about killing his girlfriend. I mean, shit, I'm not hard to pick out from the crowd. I imagined this radio network chattering with voices all conspiring against me.

I tried to get the guy off topic.

"Me? Nah, you're thinking of someone else! I'm from North Carolina . . ." I started in, "I'm new in town. You know where the action is? Where can I get some pussy around here?"

"Um . . . well, it's 5:00 in the morning, man . . . Everything is closed."

"Yeah . . . yeah, right!"

Shit. Shit, shit, shit.

I tried one more hotel and got turned away. Maybe it was the disconcerting effect that a cracked-out man-mountain can have on the concierge of a nice hotel at 5:00 in the morning that led to the lack of a room, but at the time it all became one giant, head-spinning conspiracy between the cabdrivers, the cops, and whoever else. I was getting desperate.

I walked past the cabs outside of the hotel and started wandering

the street. The last cabdriver's comments had really bothered me.
Did he really say that? Did he say something else and I heard what I
was expecting to hear? No, fuck that, I had heard it as clear as day:
Are you the guy?

I needed to stop using the cabs outside of the hotels. Maybe
those guys were watching me. I needed to find a cab from the street.
After a couple of blocks, I hailed one.

"Take me to the Soho Grand."

We drove in silence.

Pulling up at the Soho Grand I tried to calm myself. My stomach churned. I got out and made my way to the front desk. I forced
an inviting smile to my face but it must have seemed a hideous, terrifying grimace.

I'm sorry, sir. We have no vacancies.

I gave up. There was nothing else to be done. The Soho Grand
has a huge lobby, imposing and cavernous. The feel is rustic, stone
and steel. You can *hear* things in there. Voices echo and bounce off
the walls. Walking down the staircase toward the exit I heard the
concierge speaking into a phone or a walkie-talkie. His words echoed
down the staircase, following me like a flock of bats.

OK.

He's

Coming

Down

Now.

I staggered out to the street. It was 5:00 in the morning. There
were cabs waiting outside of the hotel. I started to feel nauseous. I
could see cars lingering farther down the street.

Calm down.

Be cool.

But I couldn't. I could feel eyes on me, burning holes through
me from the windows of cars. I was being watched. I was being followed. Maybe they'd found Diane's body already. Maybe she'd splat-
tered herself all over the sidewalk. Oh Christ.

I didn't want to get back into a cab again. I needed to be out-side, away from people. I started walking back to Lafayette and Astor. I needed to see what was happening back at the apartment. I kept my head down and started pounding the sidewalk. *Just keep walking. Don't look. Just keep walking.*

Up on Broadway I started to notice people on the streets. They were just hanging around. White guys, reading papers, drinking cof-fee. Bums maybe. They were dressed in a perfectly nondescript manner. They had the smoothed over, anonymous look of cops. I counted them . . . one, two, three . . . Crossing the street I came up to a DON'T WALK sign. Even though the streets were pretty much de-serted I stood on the sidewalk until the light changed. A part of me was convinced that if I stepped onto the street before the walk sign appeared they would rush me, screaming, "Down! Down! Down!" pointing guns at my head.

Shit. I should have dumped the drugs I was carrying with me. I cursed Diane again, and my own rookie stupidity. It seemed incon-ceivable that only two hours ago I was in the safety of my own home, pipe in my hand, without a worry in the world. Now I was walking the streets of New York, with what seemed like half of the city's undercover cops trailing me, possibly a dead girlfriend, and enough drugs in my pocket to get me hit with intent-to-supply charges.

I noticed the bastards following me somewhere along Broad-way. I heard a noise behind me, and when I turned to look there were two kids on my tail. Too young to be cops. They looked like punks, snitches maybe. They were keeping pace with me, talking be-tween themselves, but looking up every so often. I picked up my speed. So did they. They were trailing me. The cops' very own tracking device. I knew that the game was gonna be up any second now. I took my cell phone and started desperately calling the apart-ment. I needed to know that she was alive.

No answer.

I tried again.

No fucking answer.

Oh shit. If she's dead, I'm fucked for sure.

On the opposite side of the street, a guy was walking virtually alongside of me. I looked back, and the kids had fallen back a block or so. But the guy across the road looked like trouble. Older guy, white, buzz cut. He wasn't even being discreet. Just tailing my ass. I punched in the number again and dialed. I was waiting to cross Houston onto Lafayette.

Ring.

Ring.

"Jason?"

I stood still and let the relief seep into my body. "Oh Jesus, Diane! Listen, I'm on my way back—"

"No! Fuck you, Jason. I don't wanna see you."

"Shut up! Shut up and listen! I'm being followed! There are cops on my tail! Hide anything you can, clean the fucking apartment! I'm coming up. Something crazy is going on. Get ready to leave the fucking apartment and get rid of anything incriminating."

I hung up. I stopped, and looked around enjoying the relief for a moment. I was on top of the world, a winner. They couldn't pin shit on me! Triumphantly I raised the phone over my head and yelled over to the cop on the other side of the road and anyone else who wanted to hear: "*She's alive! She's alive! You wanna speak to her? Huh? 'Cos she's alright!*"

Back at the apartment I stashed the drugs in the bathroom. Diane was confused, but still pissed at me. I insisted she come downstairs with me to get coffee, so that the cops would see that she was in one piece and leave us alone. We stepped out into the 5:30 A.M. murk, and I gave her a big theatrical hug for everybody's benefit. I could see cops everywhere . . . lurking in the shadows, parked in the unmarked van across the street. The bricks and concrete of the city seemed to glow with a malevolent energy. As I hugged Diane she hissed, "You are an asshole," and I kept my grin as wide as possible.

After sitting at the twenty-four-hour Starbucks across the street for a while, nursing coffees, we saw the sun slowly appearing over the buildings. As the darkness faded and light crept into the city streets, so the threat and terror of the previous night started to dissipate. My stomach growled. I felt beaten up and tired. I was starting to crash from the coke, and my hand trembled a little as I tried to stir my coffee. I could see no one on the streets except for regular people . . . commuters, bums, kids . . . It was over.

At the apartment I started to get jittery again. Diane was still stalking around me silently, incandescent with rage. I thought I heard something, and started checking the apartment.

Crunch! Crrrrunch!

It was coming from the fire escape. Someone was creeping around out there, crunching the glass from the broken crack pipe underfoot. I briefly considered smoking more crack, then gave up. I took some Xanax and fell into bed. I left all of the lights burning and the windows open. I wanted whoever was creeping around on the fire escape to see. My last thought before drifting into a dreamless sleep was "If she kills herself . . . I want them to see I did nothing . . . They won't pin shit on me . . ." Then I was gone.

I woke up with the afternoon sun streaming through the window. Something was on top of my chest. I opened my eyes and saw Diane, passed out, snoring softly on top of me. I eased my way out from under her and stood.

The place was in chaos. I felt awful. My lips were dry, cracked, and covered with spots of dried blood. My mouth tasted like shit. I still felt the last vestiges of terror from the night before. All I knew was that I had to get away from this place and never come back. This million-dollar apartment had become a cave, a trap, a place of darkness. I knew I had to leave, right now, or things were only going to get worse. I was standing on the precipice of a complete free fall into insanity.

Driving back to Jersey I called my younger brother and a few of my friends and left them similar messages.

"It's Jason. Listen, something happened last night. I don't want to get into it, but . . . look—just be ready to bail me out if something happens, OK? Please, just be ready to bail me out.

"I'm sorry."

That's how I found myself contemplating suicide in my parents' house. I knew that there was no other option for me but death. I would never be able to quit, not so long as there was cocaine on this planet. After four futile attempts at rehabilitation, I had come to the conclusion that I was beyond help. The twelve-step recovery program that everybody seemed so determined to push on me was next to useless. After leaving rehab I would attend maybe one or two meetings. Sitting in a circle of ex-addicts complaining about their lives, thanking God for sobriety, holding hands and praying . . . it just wasn't me. If anything, I left those places more desperate to get high than before I walked in.

If I carried on living, my years would be spent in this state of abject desperation, sucking on a glass stem praying for a moment of oblivion, before my mind started in on me again. I considered the way I had been acting last night. Wandering the streets with enough drugs in my pocket to send me down for years. Blabbing to anyone who would listen about my crackhead girlfriend and her possible suicide. Seeing undercover cops everywhere. I was losing my fucking mind.

I was a mess. Everyone knew it. It seemed cruel to keep up this charade and put my family through all of this bullshit. If I just put a gun in my mouth and pulled the trigger, maybe it would be better for everyone.

The whole next day I alternated between fits of uncontrollable sobbing and hours of snorting cocaine to stave off the crash. My heart pounded in my chest, my extremities were ice cold. The cocaine made no difference. I wanted to die. I couldn't stand to live this life anymore.

I was sitting there, zombified by the cocaine, when I heard a car pull into the driveway. I recognized the vehicle straightaway. It was

Aunt Lee. My first reaction was to hide. Pretend I wasn't there. I couldn't deal with her right now. I was coked out of my mind, in tears, semipsychotic . . . I couldn't let her see me like this.

She could see that my car was here. She'd know I was hiding. It was stupid to think that I could lie to her, but a part of my brain was still screaming orders at me even as I reluctantly walked to the back door to let her in.

Run!

Run, you fucking idiot!

She'll see what a mess you are! She'll start trying to talk you into cleaning up again! Four times in rehab, Jason, this one isn't going to be any different! You're just gonna let them down again . . .

Don't answer the door!

Don't—

I was afraid to open this door, because I knew what was waiting on the other side was more than just my aunt, more than just another family member who would be saddened and disappointed to see poor Jason, who once had all of the potential in the world, lost in the midst of his latest, endless, downward spiral.

I pulled the door open, and stood facing my Aunt Lee. If she was shocked at my appearance, she was good enough not to let on. She smiled warmly and said: "It's good to see you Jason. I've been terribly worried about you."

Just looking into Aunt Lee's face I felt that I was about to start crying again. I knew that if I started crying, I would not be able to stop. I wished I could be a child again, so Aunt Lee could look at me with real pride, or joy, or anything except for the mixture of sadness and worry that she showed now. For a brief, insane moment, I considered barging past her, getting in my car, and driving away as fast as I could. Instead I fought back my tears.

"Come in, Aunt Lee. I missed you."

2

THE FIRST HIT IS FREE

I DON'T BELIEVE IN PREDESTINATION, FATE, OR any of that stuff. I believe that we each write our own story. I spent a lot of time talking with therapists, doctors, my family, and myself trying to work out what it was inside of me that made me the way I am. I don't believe in predestination because it takes the blame and the control away from me and places it in the hands of unknown forces. The reason that so many of my attempts at recovery ended in catastrophic failure is my total refusal to accept the concept of powerlessness. An admission of powerlessness is a prerequisite in the all-pervading Alcoholics Anonymous concept of recovery. This outlook is embraced with the same zeal and fervor in the United States as the concept of a flat earth once was. The day that I accept I am powerless over anything is the day that I surrender all control over my life and place it in the hands of others.

The word "surrender" has so many negative connotations; it's hard for someone who played a deeply physical and competitive sport like pro football to even consider anything like surrendering. Maybe surrender was what I had always been afraid of. The concept of surrender was more terrifying than that of dying. But by opening the door, and letting Aunt Lee in, I knew that surrendering was exactly what I was doing.

I suppose I am telling you a love story. This is the story of the two great loves of my life. Maybe "love" is the wrong word. Maybe

I should say the two great *obsessions* of my life: football and pharmaceutical-grade drugs. The thing is, when you get close enough, it's pretty hard to distinguish the two.

I come from a family of football players. My older brother, Christian, went away to Nebraska to play college football before a National Football League career with the Giants, the Colts, and the Bears. I was fifteen years old when Christian left the house. By that time my body had already begun to grow and develop so that I had great speed, as well as bone-crunching power. My younger brother, Damian, also possessed a football player's physique and a God-given aptitude for the sport. When we played sports together as kids, it would get seriously competitive. Noses bloodied, legs bruised, and egos hurt. Despite being younger than us, Damian seemed to have that extra *something* when it came to football. Call it a gift, or what-ever, but we all sensed that Damian was going to make his mark on the world playing for the NFL.

I got my first taste of competitive sports when I was six years old. Our family would spend the summer at the Jersey Shore in the Peninsula House Beach Club, and I would take part in the interclub swim meets. Mom would wake us up at 6:00 A.M. so we could make practice, and my brothers and I were all strong swimmers. The entire family would spend the summer at Peninsula House: my brothers and I, Mom, Aunt Lee, and my cousins. My father—along with my uncle Markus—spent most of his time at his restaurant, the Fromagerie.

The swim meets became important to me because my father was a sports fanatic. On Sundays we would spend the day with him, and he would be especially proud when I pulled out a blue ribbon that designated a first place finish. I understood that my father's restaurant was the reason that we had a nice house, and were able to spend our summers at a beach club on the Jersey shore, and I never resented him for the time he put in there. On the occasions that I would see him in the Fromagerie I would be awed by the idea that my father owned and ran all of this. Excelling at sports became my way of making him proud of *me*.

When I was around nine I started to take soccer more seriously, and because of practice began to spend less of my time at the beach club. The idyllic years of Peninsula House came to a close after the summer of 1986, when the place was destroyed in a fire. My taste for sports and competition grew, and by the time I reached high school it became obvious that football was my calling. Like my older and younger brothers, I had the Peter physique.

I went to Middletown South High School in New Jersey, and my coach, Robert Generelli (or Coach G as we used to call him), didn't immediately recognize that I had potential. In my junior year I was unlike my older brother in that I hadn't hit my growth spurt yet, but the next year the Peter genes kicked in and I filled out to a 6'4", 235-pound frame. I began to turn heads and seriously consider a career in football. My life in high school revolved around playing for our team, the Eagles, and mentally and physically preparing to get into a college that had a top athletic program. Academics were not my thing. I remember sitting at my desk during math or English, and the nauseating feeling of ice-cold panic when called upon to answer a question. In front of a classroom, tripping over my algebra or geometry I was clumsy, faltering, hesitant, unsure. Stepping out on the field to play for my high school football team I was exactly the opposite. I was fearless, cocksure, and confident. Other kids may have been able to do math, write long and lyrical essays about Shakespeare or Whitman, or recall the names of past presidents with infuriating ease, but when I was in my uniform, standing under the Friday night floodlights, I was the king of all I surveyed.

Those nights were the only time in school when I was unquestionably the best at what I did. I never, ever wanted to let go of that feeling of power. So I knuckled down: I trained, I practiced, I pushed myself relentlessly, and I turned my developing body into a machine capable of running faster, inflicting more damage, and hitting harder than anyone else on the field. I willed myself into becoming a football player.

Christian was the first of us to get recruited, and through him

I learned a lot about college football. He would get letters in the mail what seemed like every other day—from colleges in Alabama, Florida, Georgia—and he would pass them on to me. I pored over each of them, fascinated, reading about how all of these places wanted my brother to come and play football for them. Feeling the buzz in our home over Christian's recruitment spurred me on. I wanted to get those same letters, I wanted to be the best, I wanted to play big-time college football!

In the end Christian opted for Nebraska. Before his recruitment the only college teams I knew anything about were Notre Dame and Michigan. Those teams were always on television. One of my earliest memories of college football is thinking that I wanted to play for Michigan because they had the coolest uniform.

Later, Notre Dame would recognize in my brother Damian what Christian and I had known all along: He had something really special. I remember one particularly surreal day seeing Lou Holtz, the Notre Dame coach at the time, on ESPN declaring that my brother—my fucking *brother* Damian!—was maybe the best offensive lineman that Notre Dame had ever recruited. He had recently been made a *USA Today* All-American, and to watch him play the game was heart-stopping. Poetry. In the same way that people say Mozart came out of the womb writing symphonies, Damian Peter seemed to have been created with an innate ability to play football. Damian's sudden successes were like something out of a movie, too perfect to be true, and there was a real sense of excitement in our house that summer before Damian was due to leave.

When the time came for me to go to Nebraska, even though I would be leaving home, I would have my big brother at the other end of the journey waiting for me. I learned about Lincoln, Nebraska, from Christian, who whetted my appetite for college on his regular calls back home. He told me that there wasn't a hell of a lot to do in Lincoln other than play football, but the football was so good that it was more than enough. I learned about the various players and the coaches, especially the legendary head coach Tom Osborne, and most of all the fans. Christian told me breathlessly on many occasions about how crazed the fans were. "The most loyal, most crazy bunch of motherfuckers you've ever seen," he told me. "I mean, Jason, these people would *die* for this team!"

That was enough for me. I went on my first recruitment trip to Nebraska in February of 1992, during my senior year at Middletown South.

My first impressions of Nebraska came through the window of the airplane as we descended into Lincoln. I could see nothing but brown. Browned fields, vast expanses of brown earth, and in the desolate acres between farms a sea of brown broken up only by the occasional shrinking patch of mid-February snow. No signs of people anywhere, only a lonely farmhouse and a single stretch of asphalt. Then, off in the distance, at last I spotted Lincoln: the small, proud city that revolved around Memorial Stadium. I would soon learn that the city's psychic geography orbited the stadium as much as its architecture did.

How completely different the lifestyle here was from my own upbringing in New Jersey. Back home the only thing that separated towns was a line on the map, the 12,000 home-owners in Red Bank practically sharing backyards with the 14,000 people in neighboring Eatontown, while in Nebraska what separated towns were thirty or so miles of nothing but cornfields. On one of my first days there the coaches were driving me around when we came to a railway line. We stopped as the gate descended, the bell began tolling, and then the train began to roar past us. We sat there for what seemed like fifteen or twenty minutes while miles and miles of shuddering, clanging steel whooshed past us, seemingly never ending, drowning out all conversation in the car. All I could do was sit there and marvel at the scale of it, and wonder when exactly the fucking thing was gonna finally pass us.

I noted also, in quiet amusement, the difference in the temperament of the people in Lincoln. Unlike the twenty-four-hour traffic jams on the Garden State Parkway or the Jersey Turnpike, here people allowed each other to cut in and out of traffic, and when they did so, they didn't honk their horns or scream at each other to go fuck their mother. Here was a place where people didn't get caught up in the bullshit of having the best pair of sneakers, the biggest house, the flashiest car. Lincoln was made up of real, honest-to-God down-home American folk, the kind of folk I had only seen on the television before. The place had a certain allure, and during that very first visit I felt it begin to get under my skin.

The coaches took us to the best restaurants in town, and later the player escorts would get us into the wildest college parties. And the girls! Oh Christ, they were like something from some cheerleader sex fantasy. Agape I watched them with their blond hair tied back, their impossibly long legs, their ice-blue and emerald-green eyes, and their dazzling, perfect teeth, I noted the way that they fell over themselves to get close to the football guys who treated them with calculated indifference, and I realized that to get onto the team at Nebraska was to get all-areas access to the best parties, the best girls, the American fucking dream. As the season was already over I didn't get the chance to see the Cornhuskers play, but I had memorized Christian's accounts of Memorial Stadium: the roar of the crowd, 78,000 voices hoarse and steadfast, cheering on this team that was worshipped like young gods in the state of Nebraska. The thought of this sound sent shivers up my spine. It seemed to provoke something in me, and I felt a druglike rush flooding my brain. I imagined myself stepping out onto the field, and that roar, that deafening, dizzying, 78,000-voices-strong scream being directed toward me.

That was it! I was *hooked*. Nothing else in life mattered to me as much as making sure that one day the Cornhuskers uniform was on my back. That's all I wanted from life.

The big problem was the fact that there was no offer of a scholarship on the table. I had only played two years of organized football. While the coaches could sense my promise, I was still growing into my then 6'4", 235-pound body. I wanted to go to Nebraska as a scholarship player; anything else would have been an admission of some kind of failure. Christian had gotten all those letters and offers. Christian was at Nebraska on scholarship. An assistant coach at the University of Miami named Art Kehoe inadvertently changed my life. He suggested that I retake my senior year at a private academy in Connecticut called Milford Academy. When my parents researched it, we discovered that this was indeed a possibility so long as I didn't graduate Middleton South. Armed with this knowledge, from my second semester on I rarely attended classes. I started hitting the gym with the express aim of conditioning my body and making myself irresistible to my college of choice, the Nebraska Cornhuskers. Not surprisingly, most of my teachers failed me at Middletown South, and the following year I started at Milford Academy.

In those days Milford Academy was a hellhole, and the time I spent there was miserable. The dorm rooms were freezing cold and decrepit. It wasn't unusual to wake up in the middle of the night to the sensation of cockroaches as big as mice scuttling across your bed-sheets. The kids were tough, the teachers ambivalent, and drug use and violence common. Gangs of kids would hang around smoking weed before football practice, and fights would often be settled with knuckledusters and even the threat of guns. We called the guy who worked in the cafeteria "Lurch," and it seemed that every day he would have some kind of weeping, infected wound on his fingers that he would try to mask with crusty-looking duct tape. My only focus was on getting into college, and what time I didn't spend studying to pass my classes, I spent in the gym. The place was a breeding ground for a lot of young talent, but you had to mentally rise above the pitiful surroundings. When the football season started, I had bulked up to 6'5" and 265 pounds and was more determined than ever to play big-time college football. I now found myself in the position of being able to go to whatever college I wanted on scholarship, and I was now rated the number-one recruit in the whole Northeast. In one year of hard work in the weight room, I had effected a 180-degree turn in my fortunes. In July of 1993 I joined Christian at Nebraska as a scholarship student.

Before playing even a down of college ball, pain control was essential. Sitting out of games or missing training sessions with a pulled muscle or a bruised rib cage was not an option. I learned from Christian that a football player had to be tenacious, balls to the wall, a fighter. So in my freshman year, when I hurt my knee during practice and limped from the field to the team doctor's office, I knew I needed to recover quickly. The doctor checked out the knee and determined that the damage wasn't serious. He handed me six white, oblong pills to help me get through the night.

"These are Lorcets," he told me, "to control the pain. These will fix you right up."

He was right, they did fix me up. I took two after practice, and not only did they mask my aches and pains for a while, they lifted my mood to the point that for the next couple of hours I was bubbling over with euphoric good cheer. I was filled with benevolence and goodwill for everyone. The sky seemed bluer, clearer, and more beautiful than I had ever noticed before. Although it would be grossly mistaken to say that this was the beginning of an addiction or anything approaching it, it is fair to say that this was my first inkling that maybe my metabolism reacted to painkillers in a more extreme way than other people's did. I was susceptible to the Sickness, be it a spiritual sickness, as the mainstream recovery industry would have us believe, or a genetic weakness, as some scientists argue. All I knew was how much better life looked when you saw it through the haze of opiates.

At that point I never thought of painkillers as something you could abuse. My ignorance of them was total. Painkiller abuse wasn't the media hot topic it is now, and to me they were just medicine, albeit medicine with a pleasant aftereffect. I didn't know that addiction to painkillers was even possible. Drug addiction didn't feature in my world. Drug addiction was something that happened in the bad parts of town back home in New Jersey, a furtive, underground world that I was no part of. I wouldn't need to take another painkiller for at least another year, and for the moment I forgot about them totally. As I went through my paces on the field of Memorial Stadium I had bigger things on my mind than getting high on pills. I had a vocation in life, an honest-to-God calling. I worshipped at the altar of college football, and the more involved I got, the greater my love for the sport grew.

My younger brother's college career was due to begin the following year. For Damian, going to play for the legendary Notre Dame was a dream, a culmination of all of the hard work and dedication that he had put into the game. He had the whole fucking world at his feet, the number-one lineman in the country, according to Coach Holtz the "best lineman" ever recruited to Notre Dame, and it seemed that with continued hard work and careful application of that natural talent on the field, Damian had in his grasp the kind of future that hundreds of thousands of football-loving kids can only ever dream about. Once I left home I followed every step of his progression with the devotion of a true fan. We all knew that Damian was on the precipice of something really special.

It was two weeks before Damian was due to start his scholarship at Notre Dame when my mother called me in Nebraska, sobbing and hysterical, to give me the news of the accident. And just like that, everything changed.

Christian and I were getting ready for workouts when we heard the news. My mother called us and from the moment I picked up the phone I had a sick feeling in my gut that something was terribly wrong. She couldn't even get the words out before the sobbing started. Great big, heaving sobs that hit me with an almost physical impact even over the phone.

"Damian . . . It's Damian . . . There's been an accident . . ."

And then she lost it. I heard her wailing, lost in despair. My father took the phone from her.

"Jason," he said, and his steady voice reassured me for a moment, but as he continued to speak I began to hear it crack, too. Terrified and uncomprehending, I listened to my father crying for the first time in my eighteen years on this earth.

The next morning Christian and I left behind our summer classes for a grim, wordless flight back to New Jersey. Two nights before Damian had been over at his friend Greg's house, enjoying their family pool with a couple of others. He dived into the pool, just as he had done a thousand times before, and in a freak accident he hit the slope in the pool and broke his neck. Paralysis didn't set in immediately—he managed to reach the surface for long enough to gurgle "Help," before he sank back to the bottom. Greg was a lifeguard and managed to drag Damian's 300 pounds to the surface, and swim him down to the shallow end. Their friend Brian got a pool lounger underneath Damian's limp body. Amid the screams and the panic, the ambulance arrived and rushed him to a local elementary school where he was airlifted to University Hospital in Newark.

An old family friend, a high school football coach named Ken Parker, met Christian and me at the airport. We embraced and walked silently to his car. His face was a mask of worry and fatigue. He tried to smile when he saw us, but it seemed forced, painful.

On the ride over he tried to prepare us for what was coming.

"Your brother is very badly hurt. University Hospital has the best trauma center in New Jersey, and they're doing all they can. These doctors are the best . . . but he sustained a very serious injury."

"Will he be able to walk again?" Christian asked quietly, and my blood ran cold hearing such a thought expressed out loud. Coach Parker's response did nothing to make me feel better.

"They don't know yet."

Christian turned to me, and seeing me silently staring off into space he whispered, "Bro. Hey, bro, are you still with me?"

I snapped out of it. I was thinking about the games of football we used to play in the backyard. How even as children, Damian's feet seemed to move so fast you couldn't see them. I felt like I was going to vomit again.

"Yeah. I'm here."

"Listen, we have to be strong. I don't want to see you bawling like a goddamned baby in there. Damian doesn't need that shit. He needs us to be strong, OK?"

"Yeah, I know. I know."

I glanced over at Christian during the rest of the ride to the hospital. He was silent, and his face betrayed none of the anguish I knew he felt. Damian and Christian always had a special bond. Christian felt extra protective of Damian. Maybe it was because Damian was the youngest. But when our sibling rivalry bubbled over into blows, Christian would always wade in to the defense of Damian. My older brother was the toughest motherfucker I knew, but since we got the phone call it was as if the life had gone out of him a little. He had a faraway look in his eyes that I had never seen before, and it unnerved me.

Walking through the sterile, institutional corridors to Damian's room, we ran into our aunt Lee, and cousin Lauren. Aunt Lee was probably the closest adult to all of us besides Mom and Dad. She was a regular fixture at our house, our babysitter when we were kids, and our confidante as we grew older. In a way, Aunt Lee had as much of herself invested in Christian, Damian, and me as she had in her own children. She looked exhausted. We barely talked, but rather gave each other a long, heartfelt hug, and that was all it took. I was sobbing like a baby, saying over and over, "*Aunt Lee . . . aw, Jesus, why did this happen? Why did this happen? Is he going to be OK?*" and Aunt Lee held my head and tried to comfort me, still sobbing herself.

Afterward Christian pulled me aside and hissed, "Calm the fuck down, Jason. You need to be a fucking man! Hold it together, for chrissake!"

I took a minute to calm myself, and then we took the long elevator ride up to see our brother.

Damian was in a big private room. The rest of the family had left so that Christian and I could be alone with him. As Mom and Dad slipped out, heads down, I noticed that for the first time they seemed old, frail almost. I felt Christian pause slightly when we walked into the room, and he choked back a curse or a sob. Damian was lying flat on his back, with the sheets pulled up over his entire body. All we could see was his face, shell-shocked and uncomprehending of the card that fate had dealt him. It was encased in a halo, a steel hoop with four rods, which held his neck together and looked like some kind of medieval torture device. An IV snaked out of one arm, and he was attached to a catheter. He looked so fucking fragile. My brother, the All American, the athlete, the gifted, tenacious destroyer of all who got in his way, looked as brittle and as ephemeral as an ice sculpture. We walked over to him and Christian whispered, "Aw, fuck, Damian!" and all of our talk of being strong, of acting like men, of putting on a brave face evaporated in the face of Damian's injuries. We cried like babies. The three of us cried for Damian, for his pain, for his fear, the tears not just an expression of sorrow but a monstrous cocktail of sadness, anger, and fear.

Christian sat at one side of Damian, and I at the other, and we each held one of his hands in ours. His hands were warm, but terribly limp and heavy. They hung there, useless and motionless. I squeezed his hand and whispered, "Damian, we're going to get through this. Do you hear me? We are going to get through this and it is going to be OK." Damian's eyes turned toward me, a terrible resignation crossed his face, and he told me through gritted teeth, "I can't even feel you touching me. I can't feel anything. I'm fucking . . . *trapped* . . . in here . . . I don't want to be trapped in a useless fucking body, Jason! They don't even know if I will regain any feeling whatsoever! My fucking life is *over!* It's *over*, Jason!"

We comforted him the best we could, tried to reassure him, and sometimes the three of us just sat there in silence, looking at but not seeing the lame shows on the TV screen, or we simply stared into the impenetrable whiteness of the walls as if they could offer any kind of answer. But despite my reassurances to my brother, I was having a hard time reassuring myself that anything would be the same again. My faith in the basic justness of life had taken a hit that it would never fully recover from.

At one point it really seemed as if Damian would never recover.

Everybody was numbed by the turn of events. We would try to keep up the charade of cheerfulness, but a part of the family died when Damian had his accident. The uncertainty was a huge strain, and I started having terrible thoughts about the future. It even crossed my mind that Damian might ask me to kill him, if he were to remain paralyzed for the rest of his life. I suppose that's what I imagined I would want if the situation were reversed. As we approached the forty-eight-hour mark following his accident, the doctor informed the family that in most cases if there is no return of sensation and movement by that point, then the damage was probably permanent. He offered my parents the chance to sign Damian up for an experimental drug called Sygen. As with all experimental drugs, we were not told if Damian would be getting the drug or the placebo, but figuring they had nothing to lose, Mom and Dad signed him up. The medical staff immediately began administering the drug, and we waited breathlessly to see if it would cause any reaction.

Within a couple of hours of Damian's receiving the treatment, feeling and movement slowly began to return to his extremities. The family acted as if we had won the lottery. Even the tiniest shard of hope was leapt upon and taken as a sign that everything would be all right again. Above all else, we desperately needed to believe that.

With the tentative signs of recovery brought about by the Sygen, Damian's state of mind began to improve. But it was still early, and we had no clue whether Damian would be able to walk, pick up a fork, or do any basic physical activities unaided. Back at home I would sit up late sometimes, and from upstairs listen to my father's heartbroken sobs in the small hours of the morning. A part of me wanted to go downstairs and hug him, tell him that I loved him and that Damian was going to be OK. But I knew that no one could promise that, not the doctors and certainly not me. I let my father work through his grief in private, the way I know he wanted to deal with it.

Christian returned to Nebraska, at Damian's insistence, the following week. It was Christian's junior year, and it was very important to his career that he return to play for the Cornhuskers. I remember he didn't want to go, but Damian told him, "If the situation were reversed, you would tell me to go. You know you would. Don't make this worse for me by fucking your life up over this shit, too!"

I stayed on for two months. I was just beginning my second year, so it wasn't as urgent that I return to Nebraska straightaway. When he was strong enough, Damian was moved to the Kessler Rehabilitation Center to continue his recovery, and every morning for the next month I would drive over to do his rehabilitation with him. The center had earned a degree of fame as the place that Christopher Reeves went to following his accident. If anything, the accident seemed to bring the family even closer together. Damian fought for his recovery with a determination that was way beyond his years. I would be bubbling over with pride as I watched him fight for each inch of movement that his body allowed him.

He didn't want the nurses taking him to the toilet or giving him sponge baths. It weirded him out too much, and so I took on those duties. On a good day, having to wipe my brother's ass or sponge him down would have the pair of us in hysterics. On a bad day, I would have to fight to hold back tears. But the weeks I spent caring for my kid brother strengthened our bond in ways that I cannot even articulate. Even now, thinking about that period fills me with a mixture of pride and grief. There is something heartbreaking and terrifying about a young man, at the peak of his physical fitness, reduced by a simple accident to a level of total helplessness. That fear would weigh heavy on my own mind later in my career.

When I returned to college, Damian was living at home again, still in his halo, but now able to walk for short distances unaided, something the rest of the family and I had feared we would never see. Damian showed a fighting spirit that I think is quite rare, and I often wondered if I would have coped as well as he did. It would have been so easy to give in to grief and despair, especially for someone whose entire life—whose entire future at that point—was tied to a sport he would never again be able to play.

But I'm not telling you this as some kind of feel-good tale of my brother's noble struggle to overcome the odds. The reason I am telling you this, is because of what happened next.

The whole time that Damian had been in the hospital, Lou Holtz never picked up the phone to see how he was doing. Not once. There were a couple of calls from the assistant coach, but nothing from the man who had actually recruited my brother. Nebraska coach Tom Osborne, on the other hand, called several times despite the fact that Damian wasn't one of his players. Damian returned to Notre Dame following his recovery and started the grim task of attending football practice from the sidelines. Day after day, he walked on to the field and watched the team that he was almost a part of going through its paces. Here was this eighteen-year-old kid in a neck brace, getting a glimpse of how things could have turned out. Only now, he was a spectator instead of a participant. I don't know whether I could have handled that, but somehow Damian did.

And Lou Holtz, the same guy who had stood in front of those TV cameras and declared that Damian Peter was maybe the best offensive lineman that Notre Dame had ever recruited, he was there, too. When Damian stood in the stands, watching the team that he should have been a part of going through its motions, not one person—not Lou Holtz, not the offensive line coach, *nobody*—even came over to talk to him. He was for all intents and purposes frozen out, ignored, discarded. I suppose in doing that Lou Holtz gave us all a forewarning of what life in the game can be like. When you put on your team colors, you are no longer a person—you are a cog in a machine. That is how a team operates, and that is what wins games. People are discarded in this game when their usefulness is at an end. It's a harsh lesson to learn when you are eighteen years old, with a broken neck, trying to figure out just what the hell you are going to do with the rest of your life, but a lesson all the same.

That said, even though he did let us in on one of football's dirtiest secrets, I still wouldn't turn down the opportunity to spit in Lou Holtz's motherfucking face. Each Saturday in the fall when Holtz makes his jovial, dumb-ass remarks on ESPN, I hope he knows that there's at least one family on the other side of the screen, the Peter family, that knows what a piece of snake shit he really is.

Damian became increasingly unhappy at Notre Dame, and eventually, and with the help of Tom Osborne, he switched over to join Christian and me in Lincoln.

You know, when you are eighteen years old you don't spend a lot of your life worrying and wondering about how things are going to turn out. That is the age when you are able to live in the moment completely. But Lou Holtz's dismissal of my brother foreshadowed a lot of stuff that would happen to me when my own body started to show the signs of the abuse I heaped upon it in my quest to be the greatest defensive tackle I could be. Football is a tough game, and although I didn't know it yet, in a matter of years I would be facing crippling injuries of my own. I would, one day, be as useless and dispensable to the game as Lou Holtz made my brother feel that morning.

As welcoming as the Nebraska fans and the people of Lincoln were, I still felt like an outsider. From the way I dressed to the way I spoke, I didn't exactly fit the Nebraskan lifestyle. I'd still have to stop and think when after buying my groceries the cashier would ask if I wanted a "sack" to put them in. I know it might sound stupid, but sometimes I even missed how tightly wound the people were in New Jersey. Here everybody just seemed so goddamned friendly all of the time that it creeped me out. Two people would be going for the same parking spot, and one would immediately concede, wave, and smile at their opponent, before driving off to look for another space. Back home, that same incident wouldn't have resolved until someone pulled out a tire iron and threatened to put the other guy in the emergency room.

For my first year at Nebraska, I was a red shirt. This meant that I wouldn't play any games for the entire season. Instead, I trained every day and prepared to earn my spot with the Cornhuskers. I had to earn the respect of the older guys on the team, and even though I was a prized recruit and the younger brother of a future team captain, no exceptions were made for me. I had to do the same petty, menial shit that every other red shirt had to do. Going to the sprawling cafeteria and bringing the older guys their food. Enduring the friendly taunting and name-calling with good-natured cheer. Typical locker-room stuff.

Having an older brother on the team meant that I didn't have to go through the social adjustment phase that many have to endure at college. Through Christian I had a ready-made social circle— sophomores, juniors, and seniors. Looking back, it's fair to say that my experience as a freshman was vastly different from that of many of my teammates. Also, by the time I got to Nebraska, Christian was already a fixture on the team: the inspirational leader and a big man on campus. This was something of a double-edged sword. As a result, for a lot of my first year I was known as "the other Peter" or as "Christian's little brother." While I was proud of everything that my brother had achieved at Nebraska, there was no way in hell that I would settle for being known as Christian's kid brother. I spent the entire first year preparing to make my own mark in the world of Cornhuskers football.

When I arrived, I did so with Dave, my best friend from back home, in tow. Dave wanted to play big-time football, and when the offers of scholarships started flooding in after my year at Milford Academy, Dave wanted to come with me. We pored over my offers together, imagining ourselves still best friends and teammates through college. Before we left for Nebraska, Dave—who was not what you would call an exceptional student—had been accepted to Georgia Tech, Miami, and a bunch of other great football schools. But he knew in his heart, as I did, that it would be Nebraska we would eventually attend. For the first six months Dave and I lived on campus, then we moved in with Christian and were later joined by Christian's friend Brian "Nunzy" Nunns. The four of us were inseparable for the whole first year, until Dave realized he was odd man out. Unlike Christian, Brian, and me, it would be virtually impossible for him to have any real role on the team given the amount of exceptional talent already gunning for every position in the starting lineup. After freshman year, he decided to transfer to Salve Regina, to join his older brother.

Our off-campus house really was a home away from home. Christian was a good friend of Dave's older brother, and Dave and I had been tight for many years. The place didn't feel like your typical sports-guys house. Christian had posted a lot of pictures of vineyards around the place, or exotic-looking wine boxes and tableware—all of which had accumulated in our father's life in the restaurant business. We were also lucky in that Christian was something of an obsessive when it came to cleanliness. I'm sure that most people's imagining of what was going on in the Peter house at Nebraska would be along the lines of *Animal House* or spring-break type debauchery and squalor, but it was quite the opposite. As much of a man's man as Christian was, he wasn't afraid of dusting and polishing, nor making demands that Dave and I "move your goddamned feet off of the coffee table!" With the arrival of Brian Nunns, the house found its comedy relief. He became a whipping boy for the other three of us, for Brian was a big guy and the butt of a lot of jokes. A lot of the time he responded simply to the call "Hey, fat fuck!"

Christian brought Nunzy into the house and vouched for him. I already knew who he was: an offensive tackle, not exactly some- one who blended in with the crowd. He weighed around 320 pounds, most of it between his neck and his hips. His enormous body was perched on top of two stick-thin legs, making him resemble an os- trich egg on stilts. Even worse was the fact that he was a hip-hop fanatic: he walked hip-hop, he talked hip-hop, and he certainly dressed it. With his gold chains, tentlike Tupac T-shirt, and "yo, yo, yo!" mannerisms, he seemed to me like some unholy combination of Humpty-Dumpty and Vanilla Ice.

But Christian was right about Nunzy. He was a great guy, with a lot of heart. He was from Nebraska, and had always dreamed of being a part of the Cornhuskers. Nunzy didn't have that natural gift for football that the star players had, but he got to the position he was at through sheer determination and hard work. He played Corn- husker football for the right reasons: a love of the team. Although he never made it past the second team, and I suppose in his heart he knew that he would never be a starter or an All American, Brian still loved the shit out of playing for the Huskers. As a kid who grew up in Nebraska worshiping football, contributing in any way to help the team win was all he cared about.

We teased Nunzy relentlessly, and Nunzy gave as good as he got. To an outsider, it may have seemed that Nunzy was the low man on our totem pole, but the truth was that Nunzy was one of the only people I trusted in Nebraska, a true friend. He would eventually live with all three of the Peter boys, and the three of us considered him one of our own.

The teasing was never malicious. If anybody else tried to hassle Nunzy, he knew that Christian and I both had his back. It was simply the kind of roughhousing and name-calling that we indulged in at home. I suppose it was our way of preserving our own identities in this new and alien landscape. Because it is the truth that Nebraska is a long fucking way from New Jersey. Not just in miles.

Red shirting was a fun time for me, in all. It was an adjustment phase. Although there was pressure to perform from the team coaches, most of the pressure being applied to me came from me. It was a period in between my football life and regular college life: I was a staple at the parties that football guys threw, I practiced hard and studied hard, but since we were not allowed to wear the uniform until our sophomore year, in a way it was as if I wasn't on the team at all.

A bigger concern to me was the academic rigor of life as a student at Nebraska. If I could have, I would have done nothing but play football my whole time there. But there was the other side of college to deal with. I started off as a business major simply because I didn't have any better ideas. On arriving at college I found that due to my cheating on the math placement test, I had ended up being placed in an advanced calculus class. I sat there with an uncomprehending look on my face as the teacher opened her briefcase and began the class in what may as well have been a foreign language. I looked over to my classmates, all of whom seemed to be nodding sagely and making copious notes. The more I tried to follow what was being said, the more the words swam around in my head until I found myself staring vacantly at a spot a few feet above the teacher's head, where a fly was crawling lazily across the wall. When the class was over, I went straight to my academic counselor begging to be placed in another class.

I was a C student. I did what I had to do to get by. Being on the team helped. There always seemed to be some young, pretty girl on the tennis team willing to let me cheat off her in class, and a whole lot more out of class. My inclination was to choose the biggest classrooms, where I could hide among the students, become invisible behind my desk, and beg, cheat, or (if all else failed) study my way to an acceptable grade that would allow me to play for the team.

It was in my sophomore year that my career in college football really started. Up until then, the most I had seen of the games was when the team played at home and the red shirts were given tickets to sit in the stands. It was here that I really started to focus my attention on the team's strategies and strengths. I knew that Tom Osborne, the Nebraska coach, was treated almost as a saint among the Nebraska faithful. Although I didn't know a lot about the lore of college football at the start, through Christian I learned quickly that Tom Osborne was *the* man in Nebraska. In fact, the first few times that I spoke to him, I suddenly found myself nervous and stuttering. But he had an easy kind of calm about him, and a way of making you feel comfortable within moments. By the time I started on the Cornhuskers defense alongside Grant Wistrom, we had developed an almost father-son relationship. I think he recognized in me a quality that he believed to be essential for success in the team—total commitment at all times. Tom Osborne not only was a great strategist and coach, he was a people person. No one on the team had a bad thing to say about him, which is pretty incredible given the amount of pressure the coaches routinely put on the players. Years later, Tom Osborne would use this skill as a orator and a crowd pleaser to forge a highly successful career in the equally tricky world of politics; from 2001 to 2007 Osborne has represented Nebraska's Third Congressional District in the House of Representatives.

It's fair to say that the pivotal event of my sophomore year was meeting the man who would later become my best friend, my confidant, my housemate, and my teammate, Grant Wistrom. I know it may sound strange to hear me describe Grant as my brother, when I had an older brother at Nebraska and would later have a younger brother there, too; but maybe a better description would be that Grant was almost like my twin. As has often been the case with twins, from such parallel beginnings, our lives would take vastly—and devastatingly—different courses.

At first, I was prepared to dislike Grant Wistrom intensely. He came with an incredible pedigree. While I had arrived at Nebraska as a prized recruit, Grant had one up on me in that he was also—like Damian once upon a time—a *USA Today* high school All American. So I had heard his name, even before training camp began in 1994. While I was excited that there would be another great defensive player on the team, I felt that some of the buildup that Grant was receiving was a little premature. There was no way in hell I was gonna allow people to talk about the Nebraska defense that year without mentioning the name of Jason Peter, whatever accolades Grant Wistrom had earned up to this point.

I didn't have much to do with Grant at first. I saw him out on the field in training camp. This was the two-week period when all the new players were put through their paces, when we drilled endlessly, ran till we puked, and sat through endless strategy meetings with team coaches whenever we were not out on the field, basically a time when we lived 24/7 at Memorial Stadium. First off, there was really not a lot of time to talk. There was also an unspoken agreement that if Grant wanted the respect of the other players he would have to earn it. I suppose Grant's successes played against him a little bit, because everybody was extra hard on him. There was no way that he would be allowed to waltz onto the team and take over.

He was a tall, skinny-looking bastard. That was my first impression of him: He was 6'5" and weighed only around 220 pounds—virtually an anorexic by defense standards. I heard that he came from

Webb City, Missouri, a town that Grant would later tell me had a population of less that 10,000.

While some of the older guys, in Christian's class, would put Grant through the typical freshman ribbing—holding him down to shave his head, or issuing vague threats to "watch yourself" to keep him on his toes—I didn't take part. I was still only a sophomore and not in a position to do that to him in the hierarchy of college football life—but I watched him. We did have brief conversations both on the field and off, but it wasn't until after training camp that I started to get to know Grant Wistrom.

The first thing that impressed me was his incredible dedication to the game. Grant always went all out, whether practicing or playing. You could tell that he loved the game more than life itself. And he was good! Despite my feelings of rivalry, there was not much to pick apart on the field. That motherfucker was fast, and strong, and not afraid of getting hurt. He earned the team's respect.

I also respected the way he dealt with the older guys. If you show the least sign of weakness, your first year at college can be hell. Sometimes you would see guys taking the threats and the roughhousing personally, and it would make their beginning year at college so much harder. Grant took it all, never lost his cool, and never lost his focus on why he was there. I saw a grudging respect make its way through the older guys, too. After a while there seemed to be an acceptance of Grant that was almost universal. Instead of being the spoiled football prodigy that many suspected when he joined Nebraska as part of the starting lineup, now people seemed to agree: *That Wistrom kid is alright. And shit, he can play like a motherfucker.*

The Nebraska training table was a blatant symbol of the separation between the athletes and the rest of the students. It was a special lunchroom where only athletes could eat, located under the stadium. The table, back in those days, was unbelievable. We would get served only the best food there: filet mignon, crab legs, lobster, you name it, they served it. In fact, the training table at Nebraska was so extravagant that it was partially responsible for the NCAA rule changes that came into effect after I left college. This bullshit decision hinged on the fact that supposedly Nebraska athletes had an unfair advantage because other schools could not afford to feed their athletes the same quality of food. So after the do-gooders at the NCAA got done, everybody was forced to eat the same, crappy food, but back then, we were treated like royalty and acted accordingly.

There was a section of the training table where the same twelve defense players always sat. This group consisted of the biggest, baddest, and toughest motherfuckers on the Nebraska D-line, back in a period where our defense was regarded as one of the best in the country. As I was still a freshman, the only reason I was even allowed to eat with these guys was because I was Christian's brother. Other freshmen avoided the table, because they knew what would happen to them if they got too close. The D-line acted like a gang on the field and off of it. If you fucked with one of us, you were fucking with all of us. If you sat—or even walked—too close to our section of the table, you would receive threats that would make you want to leave the college that night. Maybe someone would throw some food at you, and make no mistake you would be the one cleaning it up. We had a fearsome reputation in the school.

It was after my freshman year, when I was about to be starting as a defensive tackle, that I looked around the table and began to realize just how isolated I was. I barely knew anybody who started the same year as I did. All of my close friends were Christian's friends, and they would be leaving when Christian did. Very soon, I would be enjoying the power and the privileges of my seat at this table alone, whether I liked it or not.

This was still on my mind the next day when I found myself in the lunch line next to Grant. I asked him if he wanted to sit with us. I'd hung out with Grant a little at this point, both on and off the field, but I really didn't know him. I knew I respected him. I knew that he wasn't afraid to stick his finger in someone's eye, or twist their nut sack hard when he was at the bottom of a pile. I felt that

Grant and I were cut from the same cloth. He accepted my invitation, and from that day on Grant never sat anywhere else.

We soon became inseparable. It became something of a running joke on campus: Where you see one, you see the other. In a couple of years it would become a story for sportswriters. We were two of the best players on the team; we dominated the field and were as relentless as a pair of rabid pit bulls. There was an almost instant understanding between us: We laughed at the same shit, scoped out the same girls, and pushed each other to new heights of brutality on the field.

To make it easier, Grant was immediately accepted by Christian and the other guys on the team. They saw the same qualities in him that I did, and he slotted into our clique with ease. When Damian later joined me at Nebraska, he and Grant also became great friends. Over the years Grant became a de facto member of the Peter clan.

Our friendship was cemented on the field of Memorial Stadium. We spent a lot of time together practicing and playing. There is something about being on a team with another player, especially when that player has the same all-or-nothing attitude toward the game that you do: It creates a bond that lasts a lifetime. The life of college football is intense, brutal, and exhausting. Nobody understands the pressures put on you at such a young age, except your teammates. Some people, who have the natural talent, the natural physique, don't have the mental dedication to the game. Grant—although he was indeed a skinny bastard—had that. It was poetry to see him take down guys twice his size, get up, and keep on running.

The more I got to know Grant, the more surprised I was by our similarities. On the surface we were opposites: He considered me something of a city boy, while I often poked fun at his country accent and way of dressing. I was on average a C student, while Grant sailed through academically. Nevertheless, the parallels ran deep: We were both middle children. Our parents, although geographically far apart, seemed very close in their way of raising us. We both had fathers who were dedicated to our athletic careers. We both had strong mothers who we felt attached to. We both were raised to respect our elders, work hard, succeed at whatever we chose to do. Our ages also brought us together. Arriving at Nebraska, I was surrounded by Christian's friends, but having someone my own age around me helped. Because we were too young to drink in Nebraska, it wasn't always possible to sneak into bars, so it was essential to have a friend with whom you could go crash the college parties.

One of the unique pressures of being a college football player was the scrutiny from the press and the public, especially in a city—in a state—where college football is a religion. We were held up to be role models, examples, leaders, and celebrities. That's a lot of pressure for an eighteen-year-old kid who just wants to play football.

Sometimes the added attention brought good things into our lives. One of the warmest memories I have about college was when I met a kid called Kendall Chalmers. He was a six-year-old boy from Lincoln, who was the biggest fan of the Cornhuskers. He had recently been diagnosed with leukemia, and was due to start his chemotherapy. Kendall's family had heard about the defense's ritual of shaving our heads before each game, and it was arranged for Kendall to come see the defense before the Nebraska-Baylor game.

When you saw this kid, so young and facing this life-threatening illness, you just wanted to pick him up and tell him that everything was going to be OK. But I wanted to be careful not to patronize him. He hung out with us that day in the training room, and then took part in our pregame ritual of head shaving. He really wanted to lose his hair on his own terms, since he had heard that the chemo would probably cause his hair to fall out anyway. He blew my mind. He was such a sweet kid, and he reminded me of my brother Damian in a way: the fact that he showed complete bravery in the face of odds that would make most people quit. When we gave him his very own black shirt, that honored symbol of starting status on the Nebraska defense, he beamed. Grant and I were beaming, too.

"Bald and beautiful Kendall," somebody laughed. "Just like us!"

When stuff like that happened, it made you realize just what this team meant to people, and what a force for good the team could be within the community. We kicked the opposition's asses the next game twice as hard, and speaking for myself, a part of me did it for Kendall.

But there were downsides to the attention, too. Being on the team at Nebraska made you a de facto celebrity whether you liked it or not. Everybody knew your name, your face. It caused problems. Being a star player only intensified the problems. I can only liken it to what being George Clooney in Los Angeles must feel like. Sure, the attention from the women was great. I was like a kid in a goddamned candy store. Although sometimes you'd be out celebrating and you'd catch a whisper in the bar: "Colorado is gonna kick your ass."

You'd get this shit every so often. I had to learn to deal with the negative shit, just as I had to learn to deal with the adoration heaped on the Cornhuskers by their rabid following. It broke down like this: A bunch of girls wanted to fuck you. A bunch of guys wanted to be you. And some guys, they just wanted to fight you.

It was laughable. The guy who said Colorado was going to kick our ass was a squirrelly drunk, leaning back against the bar with a thumb tucked casually into the waistband of his jeans. He was drinking with a smattering of his jackass friends. One of them laughed when he said it, the others fell quiet in anticipation. Was there going to be blood? Would I rise to the bait? I knew, and I suppose they knew, even the punk who said it knew, that if I wanted to I could put the prick in the emergency room without breaking a sweat. Besides, that was half the fun. If I bit, and broke the guy's jaw, he'd be straight over to his lawyers complaining about how an out-of-control Cornhusker attacked him in a bar and screaming about compensation. If I backed down, he had bragging rights to his broken-down friends and anyone else who would listen that Jason Peter, one of the big bad Nebraska Cornhuskers, was too scared to take him on in a man-to-man fight. He could laugh and yuk it up over pints of light beers, playing the big man for a while. Either way I couldn't win. I kept my mouth shut, and I kept walking.

The last time I had been in an honest-to-God fight was following a game when my buddy DJ, Grant, and I were out celebrating in a bar where we liked to hang out. As we arrived, the owners, Marie and Angie, two lesbians who ran the place with an iron fist, were tossing out a screaming drunk. The guy was purple-faced and hurling abuse at them. Angie, the more physically intimidating of the two, had him by his collar and was not deterred by his furious screams. As the three of us approached the door, the other trio, exiting, kind of ran into us.

"You motherfucking dyke bitches!" the guy screamed, as Angie finally let him go, now that he was on the street. "Touch me again and you're dead!"

Angie smiled with the practiced neutrality of those who spend their lives in bars and dealing with out-of-control drunks.

"Go home," she suggested.

The three of us fanned out to let the guy pass, and he did take a couple of steps away from the women, but then stopped, as if forgetting something, maybe his wallet or his cell phone. He snapped his finger, took a long drag on his cigarette, and turned again, wobbling on unsteady heels. He looked at Angie and spat on the ground.

"*You fucking whore,*" he growled. "*Nobody talks to me like that!*"

He made a grab for Angie, and as he did so, I lunged for him, grabbing him by the collar and spinning him around. I hadn't had a drink yet, I was stone-cold sober, but I was still rushing from the excitement and the aggression of the game.

"You weren't gonna hit a woman, were you?" I asked, shooting him a grin. "I'd listen to Angie and go home, man."

He looked me in the eye. I could see it happening. His brain turning over, struggling to place my face through a sea of alcohol and brain cells pummeled into submission by Miller Light and Johnny Walker Black. Then his eyes narrowed and he smiled. He didn't say a word, but then again he didn't need to. My face was regularly in the sports section. All eyes were on me, for good or for bad.

The drunk's face radiated hostility. "*Look who we have here,*" his face said. *"Mr. fucking big-shot football player! Just couldn't resist playing Prince Charming to a couple of mouthy fucking dykes, huh?"*

I let him loose, and as I did so he carefully enunciated the words "Fuck you!" as he lifted his cigarette and flicked the glowing stub through the air, directly at my face. It hit me in the eye, and when I looked up again I knew that there was no turning back.

It took DJ and Grant both to restrain me, after I had smashed the guy to the sidewalk with a full-force right hook that collapsed his legs underneath him. When he hit the ground with a grunt, I kicked him in the guts as hard as I could before I felt four strong hands pulling me back and DJ's urgent voice in my ear hissing, *"Stop it! Stop it! He isn't fucking worth it, Jason!"*

I stopped and looked around, and the guy was trying to get to his feet. Angie looked over to me, and beckoned the three of us into the bar. We followed her downstairs to a back room.

"You boys want a drink?" she asked.

"Oh hell yes!"

She set us up in the little stockroom with beers and spirits. She hung out for an hour or so, drinking with us and laughing about the look on the guy's face when I clobbered him. Soon enough, though, the call came. The extension rang, and Angie picked it up.

"Uh-huh. OK. I'll be right there."

She put down the phone and looked over to me.

"It's the police. They're upstairs. I'll be right back."

Nothing came of it. Angie said something to the cops, and the next day the incident was forgotten. I spent a few anxious days wondering if there would be a call to the team, but it never came. I figured that if it did, all I had to tell then was that I was only trying to stop the guy from attacking a female, but once he sobered up I guess he decided not to pursue the complaint.

After that, I learned to keep my mouth shut and my fists to myself. For the rest of my time in college I was not involved in any fights or trouble of any kind.

I saved my anger for Saturdays, and then I unleashed it furiously on the ground of Memorial Stadium. I knew that the odds were this same asshole would be in the stands, his voice hoarse, screaming and egging me on. Life on the team was always entertaining.

There was a lot of pressure to perform. We had a winning history, and a lot of talent on the team. In the 1996 season, though, our chances of winning the championship were frustrated early on. The second game, against Arizona State, we were beaten. That took the wind out of our sails and sparked in me a furious anger and depression that lasted for days. I knew that the team had been sleeping, and there was no one to blame but us. It was my first real taste of defeat, and I hated it. I swore that I would never be made to feel that lousy again.

We all knew that at the level we were playing at, it would be tough to have a shot at the title, even with only one defeat. Most of the teams that won national championships had undefeated records. We fought our asses off, and clawed our way up to being ranked third in the nation by the end of the regular season. We were coming off an emotional win against "ass-kicking" Colorado in late November, which we played in driving sleet and snow. The game had been a dogfight, and we came out of it on a high. All we had to do was beat an unranked University of Texas in a Big 12 Championship game to make it to the Sugar Bowl. Mentally, we were already there. On game day, we were caught asleep at the wheel.

I can hold my hand up and say that the defense was a mess that day. The real problem was that we underestimated our opponents. To us, it was a foregone conclusion that we would kill Texas and effortlessly go on to the bowl game at New Orleans. The Texas team had nothing to lose, and they simply hit harder than we did. We were disorganized and unfocused and we lost the game, 37–27.

Our dreams of taking the championship were gone. The mood of disappointment and frustration in the team—and in the entire state of Nebraska—was palpable. I didn't leave the house for anything more than to attend classes and football practice. The guilt and the anger were too much. I sensed that the real problem with the 1996 team was one of leadership. Though we had a technically strong team, and an experienced team, we didn't have leaders willing to grab the team by the throat. I had watched my brother Christian carefully during the '95 season. To this day, I can't imagine anyone better at doing the job of firing up the players than Christian: He had a gift for it; he could have easily been a general in the army. After Christian got done, the team was possessed, ready to kill and fucking maim out there on the field. He would shout and scream, smash things over his head; I mean, he was a *lunatic.* Nevertheless, everybody bought in to what he was saying. It was magic. The team captains in the 1996 season had a much more laid-back approach. They were strong players, but they were missing that certain something, that fire, that rage to succeed. Grant and I tried our best to get people motivated, but as juniors it was difficult. We couldn't call a team meeting without stepping on the current captains' toes. The disappointing season impressed upon me the need for strong leadership, no matter how talented the team might be. This revelation, after the defeat in 1996, laid the seeds for Grant and me to take over the team our senior year.

After Christian graduated, it was natural that Grant would move off campus and live with us. He fit right in. I teased him for being a "skinny country boy"; Grant cracked up every time he saw me wear my leather jacket ("Hey, city slicker!" he'd laugh. "Goin' for a manicure?") and both of us laid into big old Nunzy with gusto.

Grant didn't tease Nunzy as hard as Christian and I did. Grant was one of those rare people who could be an animal on the field, but was a genuinely nice guy off of it. When Grant got involved in pranking Nunzy, it was usually because I was egging him on and taking the initiative. That's not to say Grant was always the innocent.

Ring-ring!

   Ring-ring!

   The phone in the house was ringing even more than usual that day. There were a lot of calls coming in for Grant and me from agents, and also from the girls who were hanging out at the house over the weekend. Even Nunzy was reaping the fruits of being associated with the Huskers, and had been hidden away in his room since coming home the night before with a skanky drunk girl he had picked up in one of his many favorite bars. It was Sunday afternoon and Grant and I were tired, hungover, and watching a really bad kung-fu movie in a daze. The goddamned phone kept ringing relentlessly. I saw on the caller ID that it was Nunzy's current girlfriend, Dinah.

Dinah was a hot girl, but she had a temper. When she and Nunzy would argue, she would curse him out like a sailor, throw punches, plates, whatever. It was pretty entertaining to watch. I suddenly felt evil, picked up the phone, and silently waved to Grant to make sure he was listening.

"Oh, hey, Dinah!" I yelled. "How's it going? Brian? You know, I just spoke to him; he said that you should come over. He's just jumping in the shower, and he wanted to see you . . . Uh-huh. Yeah. OK, cool. See you soon."

Grant was laughing when I hung up.

"She'll be here in like fifteen minutes," I told him.

"Jason, that's fucked up!" he grinned, and we slapped palms.

Dinah showed up right on cue, and Grant let her in, chitchatting with her.

"So where's Brian?" she asked.

"He's downstairs, in his room. He's waiting for you."

As Dinah left we scurried over to the top of the stairs to eavesdrop. We heard Dinah knock and then try the door. It opened, and we could hear slow, romantic music drifting out of the room, a moment of shocked silence and then—

"Motherfucker! What the fuck are you doing?"

"Dinah? What the—"

"Youbastardi'mgonnakillyouyasonofabitch!"

Grant and I were dying! Suddenly there was a loud crash and we heard Nunzy yelping in pain. We ran back to the couch when Dinah started to stomp up the stairs.

She was incandescent with rage, literally shaking as she told us: "That fat piece of shit! I walk in and he's butt naked lying on top of some crack whore! Well, she can have him! We're done! That fucking bastard!"

Before she stormed out, Dinah yelled down the stairs: "*Do you hear me, bitch? You can keep that fat fuck, and his little cock!*"

Ten minutes later Nunzy emerged with a big red mark on his forehead, hustling the pissed-off and confused girl he was with out of the door, promising her, "Yeah, yeah, I'll call you!"

Then he grabbed three beers and collapsed onto the couch with us. Grant and I were still crying with laughter.

"What happened to your head?" Grant managed to say.

"Dinah threw one of my boots at me. It bounced off my fuckin' forehead and broke my lamp. You know something, you guys are fucked up! That wasn't cool!"

I tried to say something, but all I could do was keep on laughing. Nunzy tried to keep up the façade of being furious, but he was smirking, too. We cracked open our beers and soon the three of us were laughing about it together. Stuff like this happened every single weekend.

After school let out for the summer and I returned home, I discovered what had been going on with Damian. He wasn't happy at Notre Dame, and without a spot on the football team anymore, he felt that he had no real reason to remain there. It took a couple of phone calls, and some string pulling by the Cornhuskers hierarchy, but by the beginning of the 1997 season, Damian had transferred to Lincoln and was living with Grant, Nunzy, and me.

The 1997 season at Nebraska would prove to be one of the most important of my life. It was the year that Grant and I became team captains, and we decided to forge the defense in our image. After my junior year in college, following our Big 12 championship loss, we heard a lot of talk from agents about skipping our senior year and going for the NFL draft a year early. They looked at Grant and me and saw dollar signs. We considered it. It was the subject of more than a few late-night, hushed conversations in the house. When the agents would get one of us on the phone they'd be doing the hard sell straightaway.

"Jason, baby! You AND Grant . . . you are definite first-round picks! There's no question. My advice to you is that you should go now, while the will and the momentum is there. There's no point waiting, I'm telling you! I've been in this business a long time, kid."

There was something about the agents that always gave me the creeps. Their friendliness was so transparently forced that sometimes it made my skin crawl to talk to them. Most of them weren't even that good at bullshitting. This was a career-making—or a career-breaking—decision. I knew that beyond the money they stood to make off us, the agents didn't really give two shits about our careers.

It was tempting just to go for it. The success with the Cornhuskers had created a kind of alternate universe, a fantasyland that both Grant and I lived in. We ate steak and lobsters for lunch. The hottest girls tripped over themselves to be with us. We were lauded as heroes in the press, and we couldn't walk the streets of Lincoln without being stopped by well-wishers and autograph hunters. Now people were telling us that we could go pro. That we'd be millionaires. Household names. That kind of stuff is seductive when you're twenty-one years old.

"Do you think they're right?" I whispered to Grant one night over beers, "I mean about being definite first-round picks?"

Grant shrugged. "They seem pretty sure."

"I'm not sure that it would be the smart thing."

Grant nodded. His gut instinct was the same as mine.

"We need to talk to someone."

We went to Tom Osborne. I feared that maybe he'd be hurt, or offended by the idea that we were even considering leaving the team a year early. On the contrary, he was more than willing to help us out. As we sat in his office, telling him about the agents' calls, he laughed.

"You know that those agents would step on their own mothers to make a fast buck, right? That's just the nature of the business. I can make some calls, get an idea of where you guys would really go if you were in the draft. How does that sound?"

So we let Nebraska do some research. It turned out that the agents, for all of their reputation for hype, were not far wrong. The general feeling seemed to be that we would indeed be first-round picks, although late picks. The ball was back in our court.

As Grant and I talked it over, there was one thing we kept coming back to: the team that we had sweated blood for, and had not won the championship.

"Jason, you know that we could take that championship next year. With us as captains we can't lose. You do know that, right?"

"Right."

One of the things the agents kept bringing up was injuries.

"What if one of you boys takes a fall next season? What's that going to do for your NFL chances? Why are you going to risk that to play for a college team?"

Grant raised this prospect again. I told him what I told the recruiter: "You only get injured when you don't play hard. If you don't half-ass it, you don't get hurt. And this isn't just any college team. This is *our* team."

Grant nodded. "So you're with me?"

"Yeah. We'll fucking do it. We're gonna win the championship."

We grabbed our beers, and clunked the cans together with a newfound sense of purpose.

"We're gonna win the championship."

COOKING THE RUSH

4

BOOM, boom. Boom, boom. Boom, boom.

My heart is pounding in my chest, thudding against my rib cage like a half-starved rat trying to escape a garbage can. The blood roars in my ears. Breath is tearing in and out of my coiled body. Adrenaline has turned me into a machine, pure function, pure aggression, an invulnerable fucking cyborg. Endorphins send shivers of pure pleasure down my spine, into my feet, roaring like an el train though every nerve ending.

I am so fucking high right now, even God himself better not dare get in my way.

It is November 15, 1997, and I am a senior All-American defensive tackle on the field for the Nebraska Cornhuskers, for my final game in front of the home crowd in the storied Memorial Stadium. The drug that I am at this very minute half insane with is the potent cocktail of my own testosterone, machismo, and adrenaline-fueled aggression, stirred with the fanaticism, pride, and adoration of screaming ticket holders and poured into a glass that seats 78,000, plus nearly 100 jacked-up players on each team.

This most addictive of rushes has been building steadily since yesterday's pregame warm-up, through the movie the coaches took us to on Friday night . . . one with plenty of guns and explosions and car chases . . . every heart-pounding *boom!* augmented by a pack of guys in the auditorium hollering and howling for blood . . . hoarse-voiced and ready to kill—maim—destroy.

The rush has been building through the defense's pregame ritual of shaving heads—when I held the razor to Grant and Grant to me—the hair that has sprouted since the last game falling on the bathroom floor. In silence I feel Grant pushing the electric razor over the contours of my skull, I focus on the white tiles as my dark hair drifts down toward it. I inspect his handiwork in the mirror. With my hair shorn I am a fearsome sight, and I grin at my reflection.

"You ready, Wistrom?"

"Do it, man."

Grant gets into position, and I click the razor into life again, while a flinching freshman stands by, not daring to complain about the mess we are making in his bathroom, as the last vestiges of the old Grant float to the floor. The kid knows better than to interrupt this ritual, this symbol of our devotion to each other, the game, the team. When the hair comes off, so do the last trappings of our life off the field, and we become warriors whose soul purpose is to destroy any poor motherfucker on the field not wearing a Nebraska red jersey.

The mind-numbing, stomach-flipping rush has been building through the Bible reading next morning, where I sit steadfastly in the same seat, the same position as always, so that God can look down on me and recognize what a bad-ass he created.

The rush is building through the team meeting, where Coach Osborne gives our pep talk. He holds himself with stoic quiet firmness. He never has to yell, to scream, to throw chairs. The team hangs on his every last word.

"You are representing more than just yourself out on that field . . .

"You are representing your team . . .

"You are representing your school . . .

"You are representing an ideal . . ."

He reminds us to dig deep. That we are so close to closing out a perfect undefeated season, but that complacency could destroy us. To leave no stone unturned . . .

The rush continues to build as the team splits into offensive and defensive meetings. Charlie McBride holds the defensive meeting. Charlie shows his emotions a lot more than Coach Osborne. His voice rises into impassioned oratory as he urges us to remember that we are playing for the team, our loved ones, that we have the weight of the Nebraska fans—the greatest fans in the world—on our shoulders, and we carry the weight of their hopes and expectations. The opposing team's strategy is discussed and ruthlessly pulled apart. We have the tools, now we have to get to work.

Boom, boom. Boom, boom. Boom, boom.

There is time to contemplate the game on the ride to the stadium on the defensive bus. The offensive bus is like something you'd expect the Rolling Stones to ride in on their way to Madison Square Garden. Our bus is closer to the bus they might have taken to Altamont. It is old, creaky, few modern luxuries . . . but it keeps going, and it is built like a tank. I like our bus. It is like our defense. It may not be the fastest, but it has heart, and it gets the job done. Our defensive players have that balls-out blue-collar mentality that renders the luxuries of the game completely obsolete. We go up against technically stronger, technically faster players and come out on top because we bite harder than they do. We sweat blood to win. We break bones, tear muscles, and rip cartilage apart to win.

We'd are the toughest, the hardest-working, and the most ferocious defense, maybe in the history of college football.

About two miles before we hit the stadium, it will start.

Boom, boom. Boom, boom. Boom, boom.

We see the fans all making their way to the game, every one of them wearing the team color—red. The Nebraska fans are some of the craziest, most devoted fans on the planet. They worship their team; their love of football turns us into idols, into modern gladiators, fighting to the death for the honor of Omaha, Osceola, Hastings,

Wahoo, and the thousand other towns of Nebraska. Fans pour in from all over the state, and as our bus pulls into Memorial Stadium the crowds are already gathering, tailgating, celebrating, ready to kick the shit out of the opposition. They used to call Memorial Stadium the Red Sea. I don't have to explain why. I make sure I am the last man off the bus, as always. We players all have our rituals: One guy I played with in the NFL prior to each game used to pick up his new pair of cleats, and kiss each shoe in turn for each of his family members. Getting off the bus last is one of mine.

Inside the stadium Coach McBride talks to the defense after watching a compilation of video highlights of the previous game. The tension and the aggression in the room are so powerful I can almost taste it. This is a different Coach McBride than the more deaconlike man who told us to play for our team and our families back at the hotel. Now Coach McBride is a man slobbering adrenaline and possessed, like the rest of us: "Are you going to let these fucking punks come into our stadium—our home!—and make us look like a bunch of pussies?"

"Hell fucking no!"

"These assholes want to make you look like a bunch of jackasses in front of your home fucking crowd! Are you going to let these pricks *humiliate* you like that? Huh?"

"Fuck no!"

"You gotta hit these cunts hard and hit 'em fast. Don't let 'em get up once you knock 'em on their asses! No prisoners! No holding back!"

"Yeah!"

"We're gonna see if you boys have got the real shit flowing through your veins tonight instead of motherfucking Kool-Aid!"

Then silence, as we get our ankles taped. My heart rate is increasing, climbing . . . I am safe in the knowledge that on my right is Grant Wistrom, a player I know is as serious and strong as I am. I know for a fact that if the opposing players make a break down his side of the field, Grant will pulverize those motherfuckers before they take two goddamned steps. I also know that I have my patch of turf completely covered. It is not just bullshit bravado to say that we are probably one of the best defensive teams in the history of college football. At this point in the season we are undefeated. Aside from Grant and me, our defense boasts Mike Brown, a safety who will later play for the Chicago Bears, cornerback Ralph Brown, who will play for the New York Giants, Eric Warfield, the team's secondary cornerback, who will go on to a six-year career with the Kansas City Chiefs and the New England Patriots, and Jay Foreman, the son of NFL legend Chuck Foreman, who will be a linebacker for the Houston Texans. That kind of raw talent is why there is so much media focus on this team. The 1996 season had been a disappointment, because we didn't get the championship. We have unfinished business—for the team, for the college, and for ourselves. We aren't walking away from Nebraska until we make sure this team goes down in the history books.

Jerry taped me up. He is the same guy who always tapes me up. Jerry is in his late forties with a mustache and a hint of gray in his hair and—though he isn't an athlete himself—he loves the shit out of sports. If I ever have a kid who goes on to play for Nebraska, Jerry will probably still be there, taping him up. He kept his ear to the ground, read all of the sports columns, and sometimes would say out of the corner of his mouth: *So-and-so has been talking up a whole storm of shit about what he's going to do to you guys out on the field today.*

Oh yeah?

Yeah. Make sure that asshole pays.

Oh, I'll do that, Jerry.

He continues in silence. The training room is pretty quiet, except for the faint noise from the outside of thousands of fans baying for blood. When I am done Jerry shoots me a grin and says: *Go get those sons of bitches.*

Walking into a locker room is like walking into church. There is no talking, complete silence. This is a place for contemplation. Walking up to the locker I look over my uniform, laid out before me like the

ceremonial dress of some medieval warrior. The rush is building . . .
building . . . we are tantalizingly close now . . . every cell of my body
is screaming out for release, like some hideously delayed orgasm . . .
my head and my heart pounding in perfect unison . . .

Boom, boom.

First the left hip pad is strapped into place.

Then the tailbone pad.

Then the right hip pad.

Boom, boom.

Then I pull the pants on, adjusting myself just so.

I slip the undershirt over my head, and wriggle it into place.

Boom, boom.

Sitting on the bench, I put both shoes on before lacing them
up. When they are in place, I lace them—first the right and then the
left—good and tight, enjoying the feeling of constriction. I take a
roll of tape and tape the laces down, firm. My routine never changes.
It is as important a part of the high as what happens next.

Boom, boom.

I walk back into the training room, to tape my hands and fingers. I do this myself. It has to be done just right. Too loose, and the
tape is worthless. Too tight, and your fingers will start to go numb. I
have gotten this down to a fine art. Not even the hushed conversations that are going on in the training room threaten to disturb my
focus, and I stride back into the tomblike silence of the locker room.

Boom, boom.

I put the shoulder pads in place, carefully. Then, silently, teammates begin to help each other roll the sleeves from the undershirts up
and under the shoulder pads. There are two specific reasons for doing
this. One is that the last thing you want during a game is some mutant
fat fuck lineman bringing you down by grabbing hold of a piece of
cloth left hanging from your uniform. The other reason is to expose
those fucking muscles you worked hard to sculpt in the weight room,
so as to strike fear into the hearts of the opposition. Let them know
the kind of maniacs they are dealing with, let them imagine how that

arm is going to feel slamming into their soft underbellies over and over again for the next two hours during the game.

Boom, boom.

The locker room is emptying out now, as the team goes onto the field to do warm-ups. A smattering of linebackers and the lineman remain. This is my last chance to grab some mental focus, to think about the upcoming battle. This is a time to focus the fear.

The fear of getting beaten.

The fear of tasting the humiliation of defeat.

The fear that maybe today, maybe just this once, the offensive lineman is going to be better, stronger, faster than me.

The fear of being made a punk, in front of my team, my brothers, my family.

Fear is a driving principle in football, maybe in life itself. The fear that causes the rabbit to flee the wolf, the fear that causes you to reach for your mother as a child when a large dog approaches. The fear that made my mouth dry and my heart rate quicken when the teacher called on me in class to answer a question in front of everybody.

As an athlete, the fear I live with is not the fear of being injured. If you play football, you will be injured. Broken bones, torn ligaments, chewed-up flesh are all a part of the game. The unexpected crunch and explosion of pain that can derail a rookie's career is something everyone who plays has to deal with. After a collision in the rookie year of my stint with the Carolina Panthers in a game against the Washington Redskins, my neck twisted agonizingly, and everything from my neck down went numb. As I lay there, I considered my brother Damian, and the broken neck that had snatched his career from him at seventeen years old. Jesus, I have had my shoulders sliced open time and time again to try and patch them back together, and always I made it back on the field to play with the same amount of brute force and determination as before. Misdirected fear can cripple a player. No, pain is not the fear of the football player; the fear of being humiliated is the most driving fear. The fear of being exposed in front of your teammates, your coaches, seventy-eight thousand fans, millions more on TV, and the exposure captured on film to be played over and over again:

Some guy was better than you. Faster than you. Smarter than you, had more will to win than you.

Shit, broken bones and torn ligaments heal. Humiliation lingers forever, always waiting in the wings of your psyche to remind you that on some critical play, in some essential game, you were found lacking. As a player, as a man, you were exposed. You didn't measure up to your dreams.

Boom, boom.

Fear is good. Fear sharpens the senses. When you aren't afraid anymore, that is when your ass is really in trouble. When you can feel fear, you know that you are still alive.

People don't like to admit to feeling fear. People who say, "I don't fear *anything*," are just confusing fear with being scared. Fear is the possibility that someone may be out there who may be better than you. Being scared is *knowing* that someone is out there who is better than you.

I felt fear before every single game I played, but I can tell you in complete honesty that I never felt scared. I walked away from every game knowing that my fears were completely unfounded.

Boom, boom.

There is a schedule on the wall, with a timetable listing when each player is to be on the field. With five minutes to go I put on my final piece of armor: the helmet.

The helmet has to fit just so. I put it on in the bathroom, where there are mirrors. I need the mirrors to ensure that the helmet is correctly in position. Every strap and buckle has to be in place perfectly to ensure a good fit. When the helmet is on correctly, a severe blow to the head will not cause the helmet to shift even a fraction. If there is some looseness there, the helmet will jolt and can easily slide down hard onto the bridge of the nose, breaking it in an explosion of pain and blood. This happens to at least a couple of guys every season.

Boom, boom.

When the helmet is in place, I look at myself in the mirror, only I am not looking at myself anymore. Jason Peter is no longer in the room. He has been absorbed, banished to some nether part of my brain. Instead I am looking at a warrior . . . the man-machine. Jason Peter, the nice guy, is gone. Jason Peter, the good son, is gone. There is, in fact, no man named Jason Peter left at all. I am not simply a man any longer. Beneath this freshly shaved head, behind the strapped and taped and fitted uniform, I have become a nameless 6'5", 280-pound block of muscle and bone—pissed-off muscle and bone—the perfect killing machine. I have no thought of past or future, just the present, in which I crave absolute mayhem. My breathing is ragged and shallow, and I can feel it building now at the base of my skull, from somewhere deep inside of me, the greatest drug that I have ever felt, some God-given natural narcotic that will never again let me be . . . like a Japanese kamikaze pilot ripped on methamphetamine and charging at the enemy's plane with a suicidal scream . . .

All I know is that I am here to destroy any poor motherfucker unfortunate enough to be wearing an Iowa State jersey on my turf, to put anyone who gets in my way into the nearest hospital. My entire body is a furious, tightly coiled spring.

Boom, boom.

Boom, boom.

Boom, boom.

Then, cutting through the rush: "Linemen! Out you go!"

Just like on the bus, I let my teammates go first . . . As I walk out of the locker room and into the tunnel leading to the field, I touch the horseshoe above the door for luck . . . and I am walking, barely aware of the sensation of my feet touching the ground . . . down the long tunnel festooned with banners and records of all of the other teams that came before this one. The whole tunnel is a reminder of the history and tradition of Husker football, and somehow this lifts us higher. From framed pictures on the tunnel walls, four previous national champion teams stare down on us, plus a record forty-six conference championships, two Heisman trophy winners, Johnny Rogers and Mike Rozier, six Outland trophy winners, thirty first-round NFL draft picks, eighty All Americans . . . When we take the field we carry the pride and glory of all these guys with us, and we walk out on that field infused with the guts and the fury of the teams that went before us. We are men with the weight of time on our shoulders, knowing that one day kids not even born yet will walk that tunnel and my name and my picture and this date will be there, part of a glorious history alongside the names Rich Glover, Dave Rimington, Dean Steinkuhler, Irving Fryar, Broderick Thomas, Jarvis Redwine, Danny Noonan, Will Shields, Zach Wiegert, Neil Smith, John Dutton, Mike Croel, and all the past Husker greats whose memory and pride I take with me through the tunnel and onto the field right now . . . The roar of the crowd is bouncing off the walls and increasing in volume and ferocity.

Walking the tunnel guys are screaming . . . getting themselves psyched up . . . I am screaming, too. As we walk out into the stadium there it is: the Red fucking Sea . . . a glorious sight . . . red, red, red, screaming faces, men, women, and children brought together from North Platte to South Sioux City all over the state of Nebraska in the pursuit of a fucking Dream, of pride in the game . . . and we are their heroes, we carry those hopes of these cities and 'burbs and small towns with a single traffic light on our twenty-year-old backs . . . and every inch of my body is covered in gooseflesh.

Walking out arms stretch out to touch their favorite Huskers . . . men who have supported the team since they were kids, and their children who hope one day to wear the sacred uniform . . . It's a full forty-five minutes before the game starts and the seventy-eight thousand person stadium is already almost filled to capacity and the roar of the crowd is deafening, dizzying . . . glorious . . .

Boom, boom.

Boom, boom.

Boom, boom.

The entire team is in the stadium now, doing warm-ups. Running, stretching, drills. The tension is building, the dizzying rush is almost unbearable now, every cell of my body is vibrating . . . The entire team runs and forms a circle on the 20-yard line so that I, their captain, can offer some words.

There is no talk of playing for our families, or our team, or playing with respect here. I am preaching to the choir. What I offer them is pure, primal aggression, one last hit of adrenaline before we go into battle.

Every vein in my body is popping out against the skin. I am screaming wildly, my eyes bloodshot and popping from my skull, my voice hoarse and ripped:

"We are the baddest motherfuckers here! And we are not going to take shit from these cocksuckers!

"This is our house! No group of cunts is gonna come into our house and try to make assholes out of us!

"We gotta destroy these pricks! Go for the kill every time! You fucking hear me?

"This is to get to the national fucking championship! This is everything we've been working for! Without this everything that went before is completely fucking meaningless! This is our motherfucking destiny!"

The words are spewing out of me faster than I can even process them. I am operating on pure, animal energy.

One!

Two!

Three! HUSKERRRRRSSSSS!

We break up into offensive and defensive groups, and on the way to the defensive warm-up with Coach McBride I am almost dizzy, as if my heart cannot pump the blood around my body fast enough to keep up with this intense state of being. We do some tackling to warm up our shoulders and some team drills. Here we are so close to the fans, we can see the joy and intensity in their faces . . . and I am so fucking jacked up I almost start to worry that I have peaked too early, but the rush keeps going and going and going . . .

When the line-ups are announced over the stadium's speakers, giant video screens project headshots of the players. Screams of appreciation accompany the announcement of each player, and when the announcer calls:

"At defensive tackle . . . a senior from Locust, New Jersey . . . Jason Peter!"

It seems that the crowd digs a little deeper, roars a little louder . . . and my stomach flips once more.

On the signal from Coach Osborne, the team heads back into the locker room to a frantic standing ovation from the crowd. Then the tension really begins to build. Everything that came before was fucking foreplay, compared to the next walk down the tunnel onto the field.

We stand in a circle, bow our heads, and begin the prayer. The seniors start it off and soon everyone joins in. We feel the electricity flowing through our bodies, through the hands of our teammates as the words hang in the eerie calm of the dressing room:

"Dear Lord,
"In the battle we go through in life, we ask for a chance that's fair,
"A chance to equal all your stripes, a chance to do or dare.
"If we shall win, let it be by the code, with our faith and honor held high . . .

Then the voices of the team drop down, to an almost whisper:

"If we shall lose, let us stand by the road and cheer the winners as they go by . . .

Then rising again:

"Day by day,
"Getting better and better . . .

Until the prayer becomes an impassioned yell on the lines:

"A team that can't be beat! Won't be beat!"

With that, we break hands. A frantic knocking on the door, and then the announcement: "Captains! You're out!"

I and the other captains begin the final walk.

Boom, boom!

Down the tunnel.

Boom, boom!

And into the arena for the final time . . . As we step out into the field, "Thunderstruck" by AC/DC is blasting from the PA, but the pounding drums and squalling guitars are almost drowned out by the furious screams of seventy-eight thousand fans crammed into the stadium, a roar that vibrates the very bones in our body . . .

We stride out onto the field for the coin toss, allowing out opponents their first glimpse of us. The motherfuckers they have been terrified of going up against since they started practice at the beginning of summer.

Boom, boom!

As we run onto the field the screams and the roars and the thump-thumping of the music, and the giant video screens flickering crazy images all serve their purpose of giving us that one, final push over the edge into a kind of ritualized ecstasy. If there is any more potent, more addictive, more unbelievable high than stepping out into the center of this insanity on a Saturday night, then I have yet to discover what it is. I imagine that this is something similar to the feeling of stepping out into battle, and the pure, naked aggression is seething out of me and I am relishing the thought of that first, catastrophic crunch of bone on bone . . . I imagine myself as a car that will smash through a brick wall at seventy miles per hour and keep going . . .

For a moment I realize that there can be nothing else for me in this world but *this*, the relentless pursuit of this most mind-blowing rush.

Beyond these frozen moments of euphoria, the rest of the world becomes flat, indistinct, a distraction.

I am Jason Peter, number 55: the baddest motherfucker on this field, in the great state of Nebraska, in this country, on the planet Earth. Hell, right now I am the baddest motherfucker in God's great universe.

And now is the moment
As the game begins,
That I am truly, devastatingly,
Alive!

JUDGMENT TIME

IT IS 1:45 A.M. THIS IS THE MOMENT THAT WE find out if all of our work, all of our sweat and pain amounted to EVERY-THING or just a big fat zero. Grant Wistrom and I are huddled together in a Miami hotel room, our eyes glued to ESPN.

It's judgment time.

January 2, 1998.

It is a hot, humid, sticky night in Miami. Hot even for Miami, while back home on the windswept plains of Lincoln, it is probably below freezing. The air is burning with electricity. I am in the dressing room, a few hours before the Orange Bowl game, and the television is playing a constant background drone of ESPN. There is an extra element of excitement to the pregame chatter tonight. For this game, the national championship is on the line. And there's a sports reporter's buffet of story lines to choose from. Coach Osborne's final game. A chance to go out a perfect 13-0. Three national titles in four years, a virtual dynasty. As I am watching the commentators talk, video images from outside of the stadium start to flash up, and there for a moment, I see the Man of the Hour arriving at the stadium, flanked by cheering crowds. The Man of the Hour is not our great and dignified coach, but America's most famous quarterback, the blue-eyed wonder, Mr. Peyton Manning, arriving at the stadium earlier in the day. It looks for all the world like images of the first GIs returning victorious from World War II.

In the lead-up to the game, Peyton's been getting equal billing to Coach Osborne and our undefeated season. After passing for over 3,000 yards and thirty-some touchdowns in his junior season, Peyton, like Grant and I, could have gone straight into the NFL, skipping his senior season. Grant and I would have been first-round picks, but Peyton would have gone first, the No. 1 pick in the draft.

Instead, just like us, he chose to return to school for his final year and try to win a national championship for his Tennessee team.

This year, he was even better. He'd passed for nearly 4,000 yards and something like 36 touchdowns. Still his team had one slipup, a loss to Florida. Tennessee comes into the game 11-1 and ranked No. 3. Unlike us, they can't win the title. Michigan has already won their bowl game to go 12-0. Tennessee is playing for pride, a solid No. 2 ranking, and to send Peyton Manning out a winner.

While I respect the man and his game, I resent the shit out of Peyton for taking any of the limelight away from my coach and my team.

I smile, knowing that within hours I am going to get my chance to break the golden boy's arms.

It's time to fuck Peyton Manning up.

This game should be about us!

We had gone undefeated, 12-0, during the regular season. With Grant and me as the defense captains, the Nebraska Cornhuskers boasted one of the nastiest defenses in the business. We closed motherfuckers down one after the other. In one three-week stretch, we'd given up a lone touchdown (6 points) and posted two shutouts. Our season *average* was scoring 51 points per game, while giving up a mere 16. Only Missouri was a close call, an overtime tooth-and-claw victory that featured the miraculous play where the ball bounced off somebody's foot and into our receiver, Matt Davison's, outstretched hands. Our fans saw that play as a sign we were destined to go undefeated. Others saw it as dumb luck, and some people were bitching about how we didn't deserve to be champions.

Well, fuck that shit. I agree with that old saying about luck and hard work. The harder I work, the luckier I get. With Coach Osborne at the reins, no one outworked the Huskers.

Coach had been at Nebraska twenty-five years, longer than any of us on the team had been alive. In all that time, he had never had a losing season. His *worst* season ever was 9-3. For most football coaches, that's better than their *best* season ever.

Coach Osborne is a godlike figure in Nebraska. There is no way our team, this team, could let him go out without a win and another national championship in his final game.

I felt Peyton Manning could have come into the Orange Bowl with the fucking Miami Dolphins and they were still not going to beat us.

Still, we couldn't take Tennessee lightly.

The same time last year, we were a highly ranked team with a shot at the national championship, playing a team, Texas, that had no national title hopes, and we got our asses handed to us.

There was no way we would allow history to repeat itself here.

I had been in a lot of pain in the games leading up to the conference championship against Texas A&M. My back had been in spasms, and I played the Colorado game in agony. The coaches gave me a few days off practice to recover for the Texas A&M game. I knew that there was a good chance that I would be off the field quickly, so I walked out onto the field intending to set the tone for the rest of the game.

On the first play of the game, I knocked their quarterback on his goddamned ass. On the third play I batted a ball down as I flew through the air. By the second defensive series I was out of the game with back spasms, but the tone had been set. The Cornhuskers dominated Texas A&M throughout, and we crushed them 54–15.

After the game, we had about a month until the Orange Bowl game, and it was decided that I should rest for two weeks to give my back the chance to recover. The week following our last victory, we found out that we would indeed be going up against Tennessee in the Orange Bowl. Playing against Tennessee meant one thing, and one thing only:

Peyton Manning.

There is really no way to exaggerate what a big deal Peyton Manning was during the 1997 season. I mean, he had been the cover boy for college football for the past two years. He represented everything that was good about college football. He didn't get drunk and act the fool. He was a clean-cut kid, the ultimate team player, the star quarterback, the son of an NFL legend, and what people loved about him most of all was the fact that he was a typical All-American boy. Peyton fucking Manning. I mean, Christ, I think every couple that had a kid in the state of Tennessee from 1995 to 1997 named him Peyton. If he had walked on water after scoring a touchdown, I don't think anybody would have blinked.

I guess that in a way I had to respect Peyton. He was loyal to his team, and he played balls-out. Still, when I heard that we were getting the chance to go up against Tennessee, Peyton Manning had a big old target on his back from that moment on.

It was amusing to me that the national media was still talking about my back injury, some commentators even going as far as questioning whether I would be able to play. With the two weeks' rest, my back was a total nonissue. Frankly, I'd have gone out there in a neck brace rather than pass up an opportunity to get my hands on Manning. You see, when people are going around saying that this guy—whoever he is—is so good he can rip apart any defense, well, that is the wrong fucking thing to be saying about our Blackshirts defense. We don't take kindly to that.

Also, when you are an elite athlete, it is your entire goal in life to pit yourself against other top athletes. I looked at this game as an opportunity. But let's not bullshit each other here: My goal was to put Peyton Manning in the hospital.

Before each game, the Nebraska defensive line had a tradition of pooling our per-diem money and taking bets on who would knock the opposing team's quarterback out of the game. The person who landed the quarterback on the stretcher would take the money home. Oftentimes no one got the money, but now and then somebody would get it all. This was the mentality of the Blackshirts defense going into this game.

It wasn't just the chance to take out Peyton Manning that was causing my heart to pound and my pulse to quicken. There was also the matter of Coach Osborne.

Coach had already made the announcement that he would retire after this game. Grant and I had been in Orlando, Florida, at an awards banquet—with none other than golden boy Manning in attendance—when Coach Osborne made the announcement. There had been rumors flying around since the commencement of the season and the grueling two-a-day practices, but this was the confirmation of what we had all feared. Our coach, the man who commanded the undying respect of the entire team, would not be with us after the Tennessee game. As soon as the awards dinner was over, Grant and I flew back and called a players-only meeting in Lincoln and talked about how we needed to send Coach out a winner.

This was the ultimate motivation. This was a man that every player on the team loved, a man we all would have taken a bullet for. His leadership had been an inspiration to all of us, and his lessons in football and life something we will all—I'm sure—carry with us until our dying days.

In layman's terms, there was no fucking way we were going to lose this game.

My heart was pounding against my ribs as the team left our hotel, to be escorted to the stadium by police. Outside of the hotel, the Husker faithful, most of whom had traveled two thousand miles just to watch this game in some crowded Miami bar, were shouting and screaming themselves hoarse. There were waves, high-fives, and screams of *Murder tha bastards!*

Grant and I had looked at each other in silent understanding moments before we walked out. This was something that had been building throughout the arduous two-a-day practices, where we pushed our bodies beyond any sane limits of endurance, through the moment that my blood brother and I were elected captains, through this whole nosebleeding black-eyed season.

"This is it. This is the chance we wanted."

"Then let's finish this story."

You get used to the insanity sometimes, playing to a stadium audience of eighty thousand every week. The Huskers fans are so dedicated, so loyal, that you get an impression of what it was like to be a Rolling Stone in their heyday. Tonight, however, on top of a capacity crowd at the Orange Bowl, there were literally millions tuning in to watch this game on TV. Every NFL coach who wasn't at the game in person would be watching at home. Football fanatics, casual fans, gamblers, drunks, kids: An entire cross section of the Great American Public would have their eyes glued to this match. People would be throwing parties, inviting friends and families around to watch. The pressure was unbelievable, unprecedented. There was the sense that history was being made. But as we got on the bus, and I took my usual spot, I had one thing and one thing only on my mind.

Peyton Manning.

Number 16.

My mortal fucking enemy. At least for tonight.

I had met Peyton before. I had no beef with Peyton off of the football field. But for now, for tonight, as far as I was concerned Peyton Manning had spat on my mother and called her a whore. Peyton Manning was gonna be carried out of the stadium in a body bag. I was relentlessly going over plays in my head, focusing, focusing, visualizing every crunch of bone, every splash of blood through shattered teeth.

For the past month I had been obsessively thinking about Peyton Manning, and the five fat fucking slobs whose job it is to keep me off of him. My mind was already on the first snap of the game, visualizing my breaking through the line of the fat fuck offensive lineman, to hunt down number 16.

He was the key to the game.

Without him, Tennessee would crumble like chalk.

We couldn't let him find his rhythm.

We couldn't give him time to throw the ball.

Every time he even *thought* about pulling his arm back, we needed to be on him—in his face—breaking bones—crushing flesh!

Those motherfuckers couldn't block me. I knew this. I'd played against guys a lot bigger, a lot faster than them. I kept whispering it under my breath, the whole way over to the stadium, ignoring the pandemonium outside, the flashbulbs, the yells, and the sirens and flashing lights.

They can't block me.

They can't block me.

They can't block me.

I could see it in my head, like a slow-motion movie playing in an endless loop. The ball is snapped. I am getting off on that ball so fast, every muscle in my body moving in pistonlike synchronicity, the offensive lineman cannot stop me, and I—*boom!*—knock him on his motherfucking ass with the paw of a bear, head-slapping those fat monstrosities, and positioning my helmet underneath the soft, exposed flesh underneath Peyton's chin strap *crunch!*

By the time I made my way off the bus, my entire body was vibrating with a nuclear concoction of adrenaline and anticipation.

In the locker room, it was the same routine as always.

The same ritualistic placing of my armor.

The same silent tape job from Jerry.

The same pounding of my heart.

The same focus, the same aggression.

Nevertheless, this time, there was an extra edge, something truly electric, like I was experiencing all of this for the first time again, like I was becoming hooked on this intoxicating, wonderful, elating drug anew. When you are playing for a national championship, it's just *different*. This truly was another level of intensity.

I knew, going out there that evening, that a lot of people were ready to crown Michigan champions. There are two polls that determine the champions—the Associated Press, and the coaches' poll. The word was that the AP poll was already set on Michigan. It was true, Michigan had had a good season, and they had played real well the last few weeks. They had played their final game the night before, finishing up their season undefeated. Some people were ready to crown them champions before we had even played our final game. I knew that a simple victory against Tennessee would not be enough: We had to dominate them, destroy them.

Aware of the hype about Michigan, Coach Osborne had been his usual, understated self. *"Boys, you need to worry about yourselves. You don't need to be worrying about what this person says or that person says. The polls are not your concern. This game is your concern."*

However, the coaches' poll was still undecided, and that was the poll that we really cared about. That was the poll voted on by people just like us. People who understood the game, guys that themselves wake up and are out on the field at 5:00 A.M. for two-a-days, guys that practiced in the 110-degree heat, their muscles screaming. Who gave a fuck about the Associated Press poll? Who gave a fuck what a bunch of journalists who had never worn a jockstrap in their lives had to say?

We knew that, besides Peyton, Tennessee had a few other good players on offense. They had a big, young running back called Jamal Lewis who we had to watch out for. There were also a few good receivers for Peyton to throw to. As much as we wanted to get to Peyton, the Blackshirts' number-one goal was to shut down the opposition's running game. To get them to pass. To make their game one dimensional. When a team gets to be one dimensional, you can shut them down altogether. When they're forced to pass, it's game on: You pin back your ears, and you go after their quarterback looking for blood.

Stepping out for the last time as a member of the Blackshirts, the last time as a part of this college, the last time under the tutelage of Coach Osborne, the last time as a teammate with my best friend and blood brother Grant Wistrom . . .

It felt disjointed—

Surreal for a moment—

As if life was moving so fast—

That my head couldn't keep up.

And then *snap*. I was back. Back in the moment. Lava pumping through my veins. This was it. No fucking around. I was here. This is life. My entire life, boiled down, condensed into one heart-stopping moment. I saw Peyton wearing the white and orange uniform of Tennessee and wondered what must have been going through his mind. When I saw him, I saw the size of him; I had a sense of why every team in the goddamned country wanted him. At 6'5" and 235 pounds, he's bigger than a lot of college defensive ends, but with a howitzer for an arm and a great mind for the game. Moreover, I also wondered if he had any idea what kind of hell he was in for tonight.

One of my burning memories of the game is the first quarter. Coach Osborne was not a man who blew his cool easily. He exuded a kind of quiet power that was more impressive than the screaming, chair-throwing pyrotechnics of some other coaches. Because when Coach Osborne actually raised his voice you knew that some pretty serious shit was going down.

We had just scored on the offense, going up 7–0. We wanted a big stop on the defense so that we could get the ball back and score again, breaking their spirit early in the game. I was standing by the sidelines getting ready to go on when I saw Coach Osborne striding down the sidelines toward me, a man possessed. He pointed to get my attention and as I turned he walked straight up into my face and screamed: *"Now, gad dongit, let's go out there and shut them down! Get the ball back!"*

To hear Coach Osborne talk like that, he might as well have said: *Get the fuck out there and shut their asses down. Get the fucking ball back so we can ram it down their fucking throats!*

Now Coach Osborne was a man of God, and not someone who ever cursed in front of me, but that's how I took it.

I nodded in understanding, and then did exactly what he said.

The very next series, our defense was a pack of raging animals. On each tackle there were two, three, or four guys flying in to make the stop. Finally, Ralph Brown slammed into a Tennessee player, causing a fumble, which Mike Rucker picked up. Just as suddenly, it was 14–0.

Our defense was playing as well as it ever had. We were all over their vaunted running game and the great Peyton Manning. In all, we picked up three turnovers in the first half. The game was put away in the third quarter. On offense, Scott Frost, our quarterback, threw exactly one pass. It was pretty much Ahman Green running left, Ahman Green running right, Ahman Green up the middle. He rushed for 206 yards, an Orange Bowl record, and was named the game's MVP.

The victory was decisive. Overwhelming. Certainly much more impressive and against a much tougher opponent than Michigan's victory earlier against Washington State. None of the Black-shirts collected the blood money for knocking Peyton Manning out of the game. Still, his coach pulled him from the game in the fourth quarter, with Nebraska leading 42–9. Peyton would have to wait another day to have his crowning moment in football. Little did I know, at the time, that my crowning moment was just passing me by.

In the locker room afterward the scene was chaotic, a mix of high spirits and high emotion. It was heartbreaking in a way, to know that this team was about to be broken up. Some of us would go on to long professional careers, some would never play again. For Grant and me there was the sense that life was just beginning, and I definitely was churning with anticipation to see what would be around the corner.

The night, however, truly belonged to Tom Osborne, who told us in a speech how proud he was of us, that we had given everything out on the field, and that even if the coaches decided against giving us the national championship, that he loved us and we were still champions. We had played everybody who had been put up against us, and we had won every time. In our hearts we knew that there was nobody better than we were.

There, in the locker room, in the aftermath of such great success, Tom Osborne officially resigned as the head coach of the Nebraska Cornhuskers. That night we all watched a great era in college football finally pass into history. Right in front of my own eyes was a legend stepping down. We were saying good-bye to a man who had done everything that it was possible for a coach to do. He had won national championships, he had coached Heisman Trophy winners, and he had sent hundreds of young guys to the NFL. We all knew what an important day this was, and everyone from the veterans to the youngest guys on the team to the equipment managers stood there and applauded him warmly, allowing the tears to come.

The news came down that the coaches would have their votes in by 2:00 A.M., and then we would finally know if we had put in all of this hard work for a championship ring, or if we had done it for nothing. That might sound like a harsh assessment, but during my time at Nebraska it was all or nothing: The only thing that decided if we'd had a successful season was whether or not we had won a national championship. I know at some schools an 11-0 season would be considered successful, but Nebraska wasn't most schools. If we didn't win that championship, well—we might as well have gone down 0-11. We set the bar high in Nebraska: If we weren't number one, we were *nothing*.

Back at the hotel, the team had a conference room to themselves to celebrate with their families. The champagne was flowing, while friendships forged in blood on the dirt of Memorial Stadium were about to be torn apart by time. Getting off the bus, we had heard the roars of the Huskers faithful in our ears, and it made me a little sad inside to know that after tonight they would no longer be cheering for me. Wherever my career was to take me, I had the sense that I would never again feel the kind of love and adoration I felt when I wore my Nebraska colors. I knew that things would never be the same.

At 1:45 A.M. Grant and I excused ourselves, so we could go back to the hotel room to watch the results come in on ESPN. Silently the whole team drifted off to watch, alone or in pairs.

When the announcer came on, the first order was to announce the winner of the Associated Press poll.

Michigan.

It was no surprise, but still I thought it was a lousy decision. Fuck the AP.

"And finally we come to the results of the coaches' poll—"

Oh goddamnit here it comes.

"And the winners are—"

Grant and I held our breath. There was the sense that all over the hotel, the entire Nebraska organization was frozen for a moment watching the announcer's mouth as he said: "Nebraska. Nebraska is number one."

Grant and I sat there in stunned silence for a moment. Then we heard the screams erupting from all over the floor. We jumped to our feet, pounded our fists on the bed, and screamed like we had never screamed in our lives. We were jumping on the beds, hugging each other; guys were running down the corridors screaming ecstatically . . . it was total fucking chaos.

Then we got dressed and rejoined our families, embracing each other, for once utterly lost in a moment. It was incredible.

I wish I could have kept hold of that feeling forever.

But there was no time to stand still. As Grant and I hit South Beach the next day, there was a slight taste of emptiness. As if once the elation passed, it left a tiny hole inside of me. A hole that unbeknown to me would begin to grow and expand until it was a gaping void. For years I would look back on this moment as being the happiest moment of my life. After a while, when I started to believe that maybe I would never be that happy again, it began to feel like a cruel joke that I should experience this dizzying peak as a young man of only twenty-one years.

These thoughts were still a long way off. At that precise moment, I had one thought, and one thought only. And that was my impending career with the National Football League.

LONELY AT THE TOP

AFTER THE TENNESEE GAME, THE NEXT BIG DATE was the NFL combine in Indianapolis. This is where the NFL invites the top two or three hundred kids out of college to test out for the NFL. They administer all kinds of tests there, both physical and mental. There are IQ tests, the 40-yard dash, the pro-agility run, the vertical jump, the bench press . . . A lot of guys come to the combine to do the physical stuff in an attempt to raise their stock and improve their draft status. It's a gamble. Some guys test out great and improve their prospects while some guys kill themselves by testing badly. After the Tennesee game Grant and I were regarded so well that it would be hard to improve our chances, so we decided to opt out of the physical workout.

Most of the big universities have a pro day where they administer the same tests as the combine. I decided to wait until Nebraska's pro day to do the tests rather than do it in the unfamiliar surroundings of Indianapolis. Prior to the combine Grant and I went our separate ways—he back to Missouri for a spell, and I back to New Jersey. Then Grant went down to Florida to do his testing while I returned to Nebraska to train at school. I had complete faith in the staff at Nebraska, for they indeed had helped me to become an All American and a top draft pick. In the 1998 draft I went to the Carolina Panthers as the fourteenth player in the country chosen, a first-round draft pick. So it was decided, my new home would be Charlotte, North Carolina.

After twelve months in Charlotte, I missed New Jersey more than anything.

When I arrived in Charlotte I rented a 2,500-square-foot condo. I had imagined in a half-assed way that I would meet a girl down in Charlotte, we'd fall in love, have kids, all of that kind of blissful bullshit. She'd be called Anne, or Joanne, and she'd be the archetypal all-American girl. Blond hair, maybe a strawberry blond, perfect white teeth. She'd know how to make apple pie. Maybe she'd be interested in sports, and she'd know how to cook, though I'd take her out to eat most nights. When I got home from practice she'd rub my back and ask me how it went. She'd cheer me on from the stands. We'd have a bunch of healthy kids running around the place. That's what I was thinking when I put the money down. *One day this will be a home. A real home.*

The condo was beautiful. It was beautiful, and vast, and after a while it was terribly, terribly lonely.

I'd wake up on a day when there was no practice, nothing to be done at all except pace the gleaming floors and wonder why the fuck I was so unhappy. It was the kind of unhappiness that turns your stomach, because when you look at your life with a dispassionate eye you realize that there is no way in hell you should feel this way. You think, "There are families living on welfare. There are people out of work and scrounging for their next meal. How dare I feel like this?"

Away from my friends and family, I felt totally isolated in Charlotte, and the apartment was probably the most potent and constant reminder of the fact. Sometimes I'd yell out my own name, just to hear the sound bounce off the walls. I'd keep the TV on so I would at least hear another human voice in the place. My teammates were mostly older guys, settled with wives and families. They had what I figured I wanted. But I never wanted it enough to go out and actively pursue it. Instead, on the rare occasions that I even wanted to go out, I'd find myself sitting in the gloom of my handful of regular strip clubs, nursing a bourbon and ice, and watching the girls dance. The clubs became my refuge from the crippling loneliness of life in Charlotte and from the bruising my ego was taking from the Panthers' seemingly unbreakable losing streak.

Losing was not something I took to easily. All of my success grew from my fear, my total abhorrence of losing. I had been lucky that defeat was not something I had to deal with often. That is, until I started playing for the Panthers.

The Panthers' losing streak came from many different factors. It was a new team, formed in 1995. It was hard to build passion for a new football team in North Carolina; shit, that's NASCAR and basketball country down there. The team was new, the sportswriters were new, and while I was there the two never had a good relationship. In fact, the relationship—especially when I was concerned—bordered on the downright antagonistic.

When you are a first-round pick, those teams are laying out a lot of money, and they are pretty much expecting you to turn their fortunes around. The Panthers had a bad year previously, giving them a top draft pick (me). There was a good feeling among the organization at first. I was being touted as one of the young bulls to lead them to the championship. I was happy at first. Everybody told me that I would love Charlotte: They have great weather there, and compared to Lincoln it's a big city. I was sure that as a Jersey boy I'd feel more at home among those surroundings than the desolate cornfields of Nebraska.

Still, I did carry with me the residual anger that I hadn't been picked higher in the NFL draft. Shit, fourteenth is nothing to complain about, but I'd figured that I'd maybe be a top-ten pick. A lot of other people, coaches, sportswriters, agents, prognosticators, had figured that too. So when I got picked fourteenth I began to fear that people would think that I'd somehow slipped. That the "experts" had seen something in me no longer worthy of a top 10. There was also, I suppose, the element of friendly rivalry between Grant and me.

Grant was my best friend in the world, but there would always be that part of me that sought to pit my strength against his. When Grant went to the St. Louis Rams as the sixth draft pick, being the fourteenth placement stung a little. Because of this, when I went down to Carolina I went down pissed off and ready to show the doubters that Jason Peter was still the baddest motherfucker in God's universe.

When I first got drafted a local Charlotte Chevrolet dealership contacted my agent and offered to loan me a car. Now, this is a pretty standard arrangement. The dealership will hand over the cars, and in exchange the player will maybe do a commercial for them, or turn up at the dealership sometime to sign some autographs. So after I had gone down to Charlotte to find a place to live, the dealership gave me two trucks—a Chevy Tahoe and a Chevy Suburban. I mean, shit, this was pretty cool. I admired the cars sitting out in front of my place, ran my hands over the gleaming contours of the bodywork and smiled. This was turning out to be a good year, I thought.

My first negative encounter with the Charlotte press happened before I had even played a game. By the time June rolled around, there was no contract signed. July, no fucking contract. This was pretty late in the year for me to be waiting for a contract. So far, all of the press had been pretty good: When they talked about the Carolina Panthers they talked about Jason Peter, the new stud to anchor the defense. The consensus among the sportswriters seemed to be that I would carry the weight of the team's expectations on my shoulders. I didn't mind that kind of pressure. I was confident of my own abilities. Nevertheless, all of that positive press was about to change.

Before the training camp began, I attended two minicamps without a finalized contract. This was my first chance to get to know my teammates, coaches, and the Panthers organization. The first minicamp took place a couple of weeks after the draft. I would take one of those brand-new Chevys down to the stadium each day. In the meantime, my agent was negotiating my contract with the team.

The camps were pretty difficult, because I had to learn an entirely new defense. At Nebraska we ran what is called a 4-3 defense. In a 4-3 defense, the defensive lineman's job is to mostly attack and penetrate, to try and cause chaos in the opponent's offensive backfield. A lineman playing a 4-3 defense can sometimes be a little lighter, but he must be strong and quick.

In a 3-4 defense, the focus is really on the linebackers. The main objective for the lineman is to keep the offensive lineman away from the linebackers, so that they are free to run and make plays. What this meant for me was that in most of my games, I would be trying to hold off two monstrous offensive linemen. I knew immediately that this was going to take a toll on my shoulders, the first rumblings of trouble from which had already started after the NFL combine. It was nothing serious at first, just a twinge, and an ache, something that would require a little extra pain control after practice, but I had the grim feeling that these little aches and pains were going to come back to haunt me one day.

Both minicamps were played without shoulder pads. The players wore helmets, but the training was always done at full speed and afterward your shoulders would be black and blue from crashing into people. Everybody was going for it, because everybody wanted to make the team. Nothing was assured at this point in the season, and people practiced balls-out throughout.

Stepping into practice the first day, I knew that it was important not to allow anyone to fuck with me. When you are a rookie player, the older guys will be looking to assert their dominance. There was one guy in particular I was keeping my eye on: a fat fuck center, who had the reputation of playing cheap and dirty. Sure enough, after one of the first plays he gave me a sharp shove in my back. Before he knew what was happening I had turned, grabbed him by the face mask, and was raining uppercuts on him.

Blam! Blam! Blam!

Suddenly the place erupted, and I was dragged off of him in about ten seconds. I was screaming that I was gonna kill that motherfucker if he touched me again. At my teammates' insistence I started to calm down, but it was important: If I didn't stand my ground early on, the veterans would have tried to walk all over me. Also, fighting in practice was nothing new to me. I must have fought at least once a day during practice in Nebraska. I'd fight with my brother, I'd fight with Grant. Jared Tomich and I would both fight the offensive guys all the goddamned time. I beat up on offensive linemen regularly. Other times I meted out beatings to the young underclassmen to teach them the ropes. Basically, I had done the same shit that this fat bastard from the Panthers had tried to do to me.

In all, the minicamps were a great experience. There was something about the camaraderie of being thrown in with a whole bunch of new guys that was pretty amazing. We would sit around when we weren't practicing and shoot the shit about college football. Because I played at Nebraska, a lot of the guys would question me about why I thought that we were so successful. Being around the guys, swapping jokes, telling stories . . . those very first minicamps, before I'd signed any contract, were some of the warmest memories I have of the NFL.

Meeting some of the all-stars, the guys who I had watched play on Sundays—that was a trip. My rookie year, we had a lot of guys on our team who had been all-stars for their whole careers. Guys like Kevin Greene, a linebacker who played with the LA Rams and the Pittsburgh Steelers. Kevin had been named the NFC linebacker of the year, and would later go on to play for the San Francisco 49ers, and even have a couple of spots as a WCW wrestler. Or Lamar Lathon, another all-star linebacker who played for the Houston Oilers before moving to the Panthers in '95. There was Eric Davis, who had been on some Super Bowl champion teams in San Francisco, and would end up being my neighbor and one of my best friends. Also Sam Mills, who had just retired as I joined the Panthers, but who stayed on as part of the coaching staff. Sam Mills was a veteran leader for the Panthers, and the only player to start every game during the team's first three seasons. A year prior to retiring, he earned his fifth Pro Bowl appearance in 1996 at the age of thirty-seven.

Sam was easily one of the greatest linebackers ever to play, only 5'9" tall, an inspirational leader and one of the nicest guys you could ever meet. Sadly, he passed away at the age of forty-five after a battle with intestinal cancer. Wesley Walls, who played in five Pro Bowls with the Panthers, was a kind of god in Charlotte. I mean, the people *loved* Wesley. He could have killed somebody and buried them under his house, and I have no doubt that people of Charlotte would have forgiven him.

So during this time I was getting to know my teammates and loving the minicamps, my agent was still negotiating my contract with the Panthers organization. After the minicamps I returned to New Jersey to continue my conditioning. My agent recommended that I not go to training camp until my contract was signed. The reason for this is simple: If you get injured in camp before your contract is finalized, that could negatively affect the contract you are offered.

"But don't worry," he assured me, "this is just a matter of crossing the t's and dotting the i's. We'll have this wrapped up in no time."

Now, risk of injury or no, it was my instinct to attend the training camp. The camps are the place where the bedrock of team unity and player relationships is laid. Jobs are won—and lost—in training camp, so to say that I was missing valuable time is a huge understatement. Still, sometimes you have to trust the people around you, be patient, and let the negotiations play out. I had a good agent, and he had been around the NFL block plenty of times. Yet with each passing day that I spent in New Jersey doing my own routine, I was getting more and more depressed and worried.

Looking at it from the outside you would figure that it shouldn't be that difficult to work out a contract with a first-round pick, but this is business, and most of the time the teams will try to low-ball the players and save money. Every team has the same amount of money each year that they are allowed to spend on their players, but how they divide it up is up to them.

I would be on the phone to my agent every day, drilling him for news.

"Look, why the fuck is this taking so long? I thought I'd be back in Charlotte by now!"

"Look, Jason . . ." My agent was well used to my frantic demands by now, and would try to placate me the best he could. "This is what's happening. The Panthers have a good amount of high-priced, veteran players, OK? So all of these guys make a healthy paycheck, you understand? So when you have a bunch of high-priced players on your team, you gotta have a bunch of low-priced players or the money is gonna run out, right?"

"Right."

"Well, each team is allowed to invite a certain number of players to training camp. As camp goes along there are fixed dates when the club has to trim their rosters down to a specific number. Now, they don't want to let go of their veteran players, so in order to sign you they have to cut a handful of low-priced guys. Right?"

"Right, but I don't see what this—"

"Well, this is the thing. If they come up with your money early on in the training camp they would have to cut so many low-priced guys that the team would have less players in camp than they are allowed. So, being smart business men, they are most likely going to wait until the final cut to get rid of those players who are taking your place in the salary cap."

"Fuck! I need to be in camp! This is not good for me, and this is not good for the team! This is total fucking bullshit!"

"It's business, Jason. This is the NFL, and you're gonna have to figure out that this is a business first, and a sport second. It's just *business*."

Christian was working with me before he was called away to start training camp with the Giants. When he left, I was still stranded in New Jersey waiting to hear when my contract was ready. I really couldn't understand how this supposed "business" could come before the good of the team. It made no sense to me. All I wanted to do was get on the field and start winning games. The idea of the "business" of football was one that I didn't understand, or want to understand.

Meanwhile, in Charlotte, the press had gotten on the story of me "holding out" for more money. If they had any understanding of how the business of pro football worked, they didn't care enough to take it into account when they wrote their articles. Within a few months I went from Jason Peter, the Great Hope for Panthers football, to Jason Peter, Just Another Spoiled Pro Athlete. Jason Peter, the greedy player fucking up the team by holding out for a contract that he didn't deserve. The articles started to appear on a practically daily basis, destroying my character and making me out to be some money-crazed asshole. And every day I would be on the phone to my agent, reading the pieces to him, demanding that I have a chance to respond to the accusations.

"It wouldn't mean anything!" he insisted. "They wouldn't give a shit! Then you'd go from being a greedy pro athlete to a whining greedy pro athlete. Just ride this out! Bad press—and good press— has a short shelf life. This is just tomorrow's recycling, Jason. We'll get the contract signed and these bastards will be getting their panties in a bunch about something else instead."

Another thing was eating away at me. Where was the Carolina Panthers organization in all of this? Why were they not talking to the press, explaining the situation? The entire organization met the barrage of negative press with a damning silence. I came from a place where the organization's first—and only—interest was the good of the players, the good of the team. When I would ask my agent this, he almost laughed at my naïveté.

"These people are locked in a contract negotiation with you! They are waiting for you to blink first. It would be stupid of them to wade into this and start taking your side. Shit, this press is great for them. They're probably hoping that you take a low offer just to make the articles stop!"

"But *they drafted me! They want me on the team!*"

"I know Jason . . . It's just . . ."

"I know. I know. It's just business, right?"

So I waited, while it ate and ate at me. I imagined what my new teammates were thinking. That I was sitting at home in the air-conditioning, while they sweated their asses off training in the 110 degree heat. That I was some spoilt, greedy son of a bitch who thought he was too good to train with his team. I used that rage to train as hard as I could, but I knew that this was the worst start I could have possibly had in Charlotte. I prayed that it wasn't an omen of things to come.

In the end I missed all of training camp. In fact, the deal was inked five days before the start of our first regular season game. Now my entire team had a four-week head start on me, and I had less than a week to learn the defenses and find my spot on the team. I was on a plane to Charlotte immediately, and I stopped to drop my shit off at the new apartment before I was to head down to the stadium for my crash course in the Panthers defensive strategy. Pulling up in a cab, I realized immediately that something was wrong.

The cars. The cars had been stolen.

When I had left Charlotte they had both been sitting out in front of my apartment. Now there was an empty driveway. I cursed, threw my bag to the ground, and started frantically calling people. My agent picked up.

"Jason, is there a problem?"

"Yeah! Somebody took the cars! The fucking Suburban and the Tahoe are gone, man! I think I've been robbed!"

"Look, just relax for a moment. Let me make some calls."

So I went into the apartment and dropped my shit off. I was trying not to let the events of the past month get to me, but there was the niggling feeling that this move to Charlotte was ill fated. My phone buzzed into life.

"Yeah?"

"Well, good news and bad news. The good news is that the cars weren't stolen."

"Great, well where are they? I wanted to drive over to the stadium, you know?"

"Well, that's the bad news. They're at the dealership."

"What? Why? Can I pick them up?"

"Well, not exactly. They decided . . . you know, with all of the negative press that you were getting because of the contract thing . . . well, that they didn't want to give you the cars anymore. I guess they feel that your image is a little . . . tarnished at the moment."

I lost it. I kicked over the furniture screaming *"Those motherfuckers!"* as my agent tried desperately to calm me down.

"Look Jason, this will pass," he was assuring me frantically. "This is just a blip. Give it a month and this will all be forgotten about. This is just some temporary bullshit, OK?"

"But this is fucked up! I didn't do anything wrong!"

"Yes, I hear you Jason, but you have to look at it from their point of view! The whole thing was because they wanted to have your name associated with their dealership. At the moment—and this is just *at the moment*—your name has some . . . negative connotations because of the contract dispute. They just have to wait for that to blow over. As soon as you get out there and start playing, you will be a hero again and you can have whatever fucking car you want, OK? You know, they aren't being dicks about it. The press, they were being dicks. This . . . well . . . it's just . . ."

"Don't fucking say it," I warned him, cutting him off. "Just don't fucking say it."

The first team meeting that I was in, the defensive coordinator stood up and made a point of telling everybody that they needed to chip in to ensure that I was up to speed in time for Sunday's game. Everybody nodded in silent agreement.

"And for Christ's sake," he added. "We don't have time for any hazing shit. We need Jason up to speed, and not worrying about getting tied to the goalpost naked or some shit!"

For the next five days I practically lived at the stadium. Trying to cram all four-and-a-half weeks' worth of practice that I missed into five days was grueling work. The coaches stayed with me, going over defense after defense, quizzing me on what I was supposed to do if a tight end motioned, or if a running back flared or if whatever . . . scenario after scenario. I truly felt lost; there was just so much shit to learn and so little time. The guys on the team were very helpful. They were supportive, and determined to help me get up to speed.

By Sunday, I was ready to play in my first NFL game, against the Atlanta Falcons. Although this was a huge moment for me, the chaos leading up to the game had not allowed me time to focus on the immense nature of what was about to happen. I had made it! I was living the dream! Despite all of the fuckups and disappointments along the way, I was about to step out onto the field as a professional football player for the first time. This was a huge moment.

I wasn't starting, but I was prepared to play. I watched the game unfold, breathlessly, from the sidelines. About a quarter of the way into the game, Ted Gill, the defensive line coach, called over to me.

This was it.

This was my moment.

I stood up and stretched my muscles. I was instantly aware of the NFL logo on my helmet, on the field. I had the fleeting sensation that this was the culmination of my life until this point: I was about to step out onto the field as a pro in the NFL. My life would never be the same again. I drank it all in—eighty thousand braying fans in the stands, and I, Jason Peter, number 97, about to make his debut. I stepped out—

And it all came crashing down around my ears.

As I stepped on the field, I was suddenly, painfully aware. The air in the stadium became hostile, poisonous.

Booooooooooooooooooooooooo!!!!!!!!!!!

I realized immediately that the focus of the crowd anger was me. It seemed conceivable that I was the most hated man in Charlotte. That is when the reality struck me: It wasn't just me that was reading those half-truths and distortions in the press. This was bigger than a Chevy dealership wanting to protect the bottom line by refusing to deal with me. It seemed that every person who had read those stories in the papers was in the stands today, and wanted to vocally show their disapproval of my perceived wrongs. It was so unexpected, so brutal, that momentarily it threw me off. This was my first introduction to the power of the media.

After I got over my initial shock, it served to make me even more pissed off, more determined than ever.

For my first snap as an NFL player, I was as nervous as all hell. I hunkered down in my stance, lined up slightly outside of the offensive tackle, and as soon as the ball was snapped I put an inside move on the fat fuck. I ran at him, imagining the booing crowd, the sniveling sportswriters all in my crosshairs. And fuck, did I hit hard that time! *Crunch!* I had the running back in my arms three yards behind the line of scrimmage.

The crowd, the same crowd that seconds earlier had been booing me, almost screaming for my blood, was now going *crazy*. People were on their feet, hollering and cheering, and I knew that for my first play I made an immediate impact. For now, for the moment at least, I had everybody back on my side.

More than the fickle nature of the crowd, and the hostile press from virtually day one, something about the whole fucking experience in the NFL just felt *lacking*. I think a lot of that feeling stemmed from my sense of isolation down in Charlotte.

I didn't have too many friends on the team. For the most part I was a loner. I've never been someone who has surrounded themselves with people, and in Charlotte it was no different. I had two best friends in high school, and they are still my best friends today. I didn't really let anybody else into my life, except in the most casual of ways, and this has been a habit I have carried with me throughout my adult life. I guess I would rather have a handful of good friends than be surrounded by a big group of people without knowing if I can trust them.

The truth is that while having someone you can share your innermost thoughts with and talk to about anything is a great thing, the flip side is that if one of those people is not available to visit with you, then you'll probably end up spending a lot of time by yourself. That's what happened to me. I spent a lot of time alone with my thoughts, especially when I was in Carolina.

There were two guys on the team that I got close to. One was Eric Davis, the Panthers cornerback, who lived across the street from me. The other was a player I'll call Greg Volpe, a fellow defensive lineman who was originally from Boston.

Eric was a veteran who had been in the league for about nine or ten years when I first met him. He was a former All-Pro who played with the San Francisco 49ers prior to coming to the Panthers. Despite the difference in age and experience, Eric and I immediately clicked. Besides being my neighbor, Eric was the guy I sat next to on the plane trips when we played away from Charlotte. That's really how we got to know each other. It was the first away game, I had just boarded the plane and was looking for a place to sit. Being a rookie, you do what you're told, talk when spoken to, and you respect the veterans. The team plane has an odd similarity to the hierarchy of the old grade school bus; the veterans take all of the seats in the back, where they make the most noise. The new kids sit in the front and behave themselves. However, when I was looking for a place to sit, Eric waved at me, motioning for me to sit next to him. I did as he said. I was a little shocked that I was allowed to sit back there, but I wasn't going to complain. Even though I was twice his size he did still make me sit against the window while he stretched out in the aisle. It was a strange feeling, sitting back there with guys that I had watched on TV for a long time.

Eric took me under his wing during my early days in Charlotte. We talked about all kinds of shit, from football to family to everyday kinds of things. Eric had a career that I wanted, he had played in the league for ten years, he had been selected to Pro Bowls, he had won championships, he had made a ton of money, and he was a great guy. Eric was married and had a few kids, so looking at it from the outside you wouldn't think that we would have had so much in common, but we ended up being good friends. I wanted what he had, and I looked up to him as a model of what I aspired to be in ten years.

Eric was popular among all the guys who played for the Panthers, a major presence in the locker room, and definitely one of the team leaders. He was a real laid-back guy who was always cracking jokes or playing pranks. I looked to him for a lot of advice when it came to making a career in the NFL. He would tell me to be cool: "You're a great player, and you're going to be playing this game for a long time. You have years ahead of you to worry about this shit. Right now, just enjoy the experience."

My other best friend on the team was Greg Volpe. He was my wingman. We would go out at night together, we'd grab dinner, we would do a lot of things that single guys do, like hitting the titty bars and nightclubs. If we had the day off we would go to the movie theater during the afternoon and see a couple of movies. He's the guy I would get into trouble with when we'd take weekend trips to Miami or the Carolina coast. We'd misbehave together; we were definitely bad for each other, and I'm sure people on the outside would say that we shouldn't have spent so much time together. But that kind of crazy friendship and fierce loyalty is something that I valued. We had a lot in common being from the East Coast, since I was from Jersey and Greg from Boston.

Those weekend trips were a time when we would completely let loose, which I did a little more than Greg. He liked to party hard, but there was always a destructive element to my personality that would propel me to take it farther. Greg would shake his head in horror sometimes when I would really get messed up on these trips away, but he always saw me safely thought my worst jags, and he was never patronizing enough to give me the *"Hey, Jason, I think you need to slow down"* speech, which cemented my respect for him. Not even the night that he found me passed out naked outside of the wrong room of the W Hotel in New York during one particularly memorable round of debauchery.

I liked Greg. He had an intense work ethic and was a blue-collar type of guy. I really respected him and the way he had survived in the league. He had played at a private high school in New Jersey that my high school, Middletown South, played against. He wasn't drafted by anyone coming out of college. He was a free agent and had to work hard to get where he was. He originally signed with Seattle and after spending a few years there he signed with Carolina.

He owned a house about ten minutes from mine, so we usually were at one place or the other. If there was someone I was going to grab a bite to eat with after practice it was Greg. It was so different in the NFL than it was in college. In college when you leave the stadium you'd go home where you have two, three, or even four roommates. You don't have time to get lonely; there's always someone to talk to, to joke with. In the NFL, when you leave the stadium, most guys go home to their families. That left me with a lot of time to get bored, to brood over the team's losses, and to medicate against this sense of isolation with the limitless supply of pills I had access to.

On most teams there will be only a few young single guys to hang out with, and a lot of veterans that have a wife and children. Even if there are a bunch of young single guys, getting along with them is a whole other story. There were a few guys on the Panthers that I liked but not enough that I would want to go hang out with them. My relationship with Eric was completely different than my relationship with Greg. They both were friends of mine, but neither one got to know the Jason Peter that the other did. When I wanted to act like a mature adult I would hang out with Eric and his family. When I wanted to act out, I hung out with Greg.

Like most rookies, I came into the NFL expecting everything to be a step up from college football: the players, the facilities, and the coaches. Maybe I had unfairly high expectations of the coaches after my experience in Nebraska, but Ted Gill, the man who coached

Carolina's D-line my rookie year, certainly didn't compare to Charlie McBride, my college line coach. To be frank, I felt that I had better coaches at the high school level, but I was still shocked by the way a lot of the guys on the D-line disrespected Coach Gill. When he would try to coach during the practice, guys just wouldn't listen, some of them talking right over him, holding their own little conversations among themselves. That's the thing in the NFL: If you have some really high-priced guys who have bad attitudes, or at least think they know better than the coach, they will not listen to him. I knew he wasn't the greatest coach, but I was smart enough to understand that I was still a rookie, so when he spoke I listened.

When I was an NFL rookie, I used to call Charlie McBride on the phone back in Lincoln when I needed an answer to something. The relationship between coach and player is a special kind of chemistry. Some players never find a coach who can push them to their true potential. I did find that in Charlie, but unfortunately nothing close to that while I was playing in the NFL. I thought that Dom Capers, our head coach, was a good coach. In 1996 he took the Panthers to the NFC championship game. This was only the Panthers second season in existence. He has a great defensive mind and has had a lot of success as a defensive coordinator. After the Panthers fired him, he took the head-coaching job with the Houston Texans, also an expansion team, but he didn't fare well there either.

It took me a while to be able to admit it to myself, but I missed playing at Nebraska. I missed the camaraderie. I missed the fact that we busted our asses three days out of the week in preparation for the big game. I missed the coaches who got up in our faces and screamed at us and pushed us to new extremes. Playing in the NFL was totally different; everybody was a *professional* and nobody wanted to do shit unless they talked it over with their goddamned agent or their manager.

Rather than focusing on football or our next opponent, a lot of the Carolina players would start complaining about bullshit, or less than bullshit, like how they felt disrespected because some coach didn't ask them how their kids were doing. I'd sit there in the locker room, listening to them bitching and complaining, and I'd think, *"You're being paid millions to play this game! Now shut the fuck up and PLAY!"*

Back at my place, when I couldn't stand it anymore, I'd call Grant and ask him how he was doing. Something about hearing my friend's voice calmed me, took me back to a happier, more secure place in my life.

"Wistrom, man, what up?"

"Jason! Goddamn! How's life in Charlotte?"

"It's OK. What about St. Louis?"

We'd shoot the shit about our respective teams, but it would always come back to either Grant or me admitting, "You know something . . . it's just not the *same.*" And we'd get into reminiscing about Nebraska and talking about what our old friends and team-mates were up to, but by the time I'd hang up, I would feel that sense of belonging draining from me again. It wasn't just the team that was to blame for my frame of mind, it was the increasing amount of pain and discomfort I was in. Something was happening to my body, and it weighed upon me heavily.

From the moment I made it to Charlotte I was playing at half capacity, and it ate at me. I was having problems with my shoulders the whole summer I was working out before coming down to Carolina. I hoped blindly that it would right itself. I took more painkillers to dull the edge and played through it. By the end of my rookie year I was playing with both my shoulders in harnesses.

Playing in the NFL is tough when you're healthy. When you're injured it's almost impossible. So my first concern was to prove to the team that their faith in me was not misplaced. It was always my mentality that I would play through my injuries. I took painkillers, and I hustled my ass. I got out on the field and I played pissed-off. Sometimes this was because of the pain. Sometimes it was because I had been snorting coke the night before and I was hungover. I had tried cocaine for the first time after returning to New Jersey from

Nebraska after the Panthers drafted me. I was celebrating the fact that I had just become a millionaire, and I enjoyed it enough to find a regular source for it. Since leaving the intensive life of Nebraska football, a part of me had decided that this was my chance to cut loose and party. I was living away from home for the first time, and my college years—for most people the years of debauchery, experimentation, and nonstop partying—had been anything but. They had been ones of hard fucking work, and endless pressure. Now, away from home, wearing an NFL uniform, and with what felt like unlimited money in the bank, I figured it was time for *me* to have some fun. Why not?

I stopped doing drugs when I first came down to Charlotte, but during my rookie year I started partying a little again. There was little else to do. To combat the boredom of the time that I wasn't playing football, I started getting fucked up again.

After my shoulders it was my neck. The body is like that: Strap the shoulders up, and like a domino effect, the pain pops out somewhere else. That was the beginning of my first round of surgeries.

In December of 1998, I had the first. The pain in my shoulders was becoming unbearable, and it was decided that I should undergo surgery to correct the damage. I had tears through the labrium and part of the rotator cuff. This meant that they had to cut me open, about three inches on the right shoulder.

When I woke up in the hospital, the pain was intense. It felt like someone had shoved a blade into my shoulder and was violently twisting it. Coming out of the sedation, I was disoriented and nauseous, and all I could feel was this incredible, intense pain. I started screaming for a nurse, and within seconds the room was buzzing with activity, and they were pumping morphine into my arm. The relief was immediate, and for the whole time I was in the hospital I was given morphine every three to four hours. When I was well enough to leave, I was given a bottle of Vicodin. The pain lasted for a long while, and the Vicodin was the only thing that kept me from losing it.

It seemed that almost as soon as I could finally wipe my own ass again, I was back for more surgery, this time on the left shoulder, in February of 1999. The left really needed the same kind of intensive surgery as the right, but with so little time left before the start of football season, the surgeon, the team, and I came to the decision that the left shoulder would be fixed arthroscopically. This meant that they would stitch my labrium back together, and scrape out some of the damaged tissue and cartilage. I had the surgery done on a Monday morning, and was on a plane by Tuesday night. For the next few months I did my rehab on both shoulders. It wasn't until almost the end of April that I was able to start lifting weights and working out in preparation for the upcoming season.

Most guys start their training for the season a couple of weeks after the previous season finishes. I wasn't able to start training at full throttle until May, giving me just three months to get my ass in shape and ready to play for the Panthers. But the press didn't seem to give a fuck about any of that.

The bad press continued. It seemed that down in Charlotte, if they didn't have a negative story, then they just didn't have a story, period. I'll take the rap for some of those stories. When I did stupid shit off the field, like the time I got busted driving my car drunk, well, I hold my hand up. That stuff was my own goddamned stupid fault, and they were perfectly within their rights to spread it all over the sports section. Although when they called into question my dedication to the game, my dedication to the team—that shit was completely unforgivable.

There was one little bastard in particular, a beat writer who wrote about the Panthers practically daily. He was a short, dumpy man who hung around the Panthers stadium like a bad smell. He'd always give me this greasy, insinuating smile whenever he saw me and I would burn holes through him with my eyes and fantasize about picking him up and snapping his spine like a twig. This guy— I mean, he wasn't exactly what you'd call the athletic type. I doubt he had ever played football, even just for fun. He also seemed to take a particular delight in rubbishing the team, and I was a particular bone of contention for him. I tried to take my father's prescient advice: "Don't read the papers, because you're never as good as they say . . . and you're never as bad as they say." I knew it made perfect sense, and the coaches down in Charlotte said the same thing, but when you'd show up for practice and there'd be twenty copies of the local paper lying around in the cafeteria, it was pretty hard not to sneak a look.

My neck problems started at the end of my rookie year, prompted I'm sure because I was overcompensating for my shoulder injuries. Not only did I have to take the pills before and after I practiced or played, but also at night so that I would have enough relief to go to sleep. And I can't bullshit myself on this one. I liked the way those pills made me feel.

When I had enough of those pills inside of me, the house didn't seem as lonely. Not only did the pain in my back, my neck, and my shoulders recede enough that I could function again, the chattering in my head would cease. The homesickness was forgotten. The crippling loneliness and isolated nature of my life in Charlotte stopped bothering me. When I was on the phone with my mother and father I could tell them that everything was just *great*, and for a moment I could believe it myself, while the painkillers carried me through the day on a cushion of angel farts. When I had enough pills inside me, maybe a glass of wine or a few beers, I felt immortal again, I felt like the Jason Peter who had made a pact with his best friend, Grant Wistrom, to win the championship and had succeeded. I felt like I could keep my unspoken promise to my younger brother to go on and play professional football on his behalf, to carry the Peter name forward. I was Jason fucking Peter, master of all I surveyed. I was untouchable.

When I was a child, I rarely got sick. The worst that ever happened were occasional bruises or sprains when a game of soccer would get out of control. When this happened you saw a doctor, and our family physician was Dr. Maktel. He was an old Indian guy, who'd peer at me over a pair of gold-rimmed glasses. My mother respected the family doctor, as did my father. As a career choice it was beyond reproach. A child that grows up to be a doctor is as great a source of pride for a family that a child who went into the priesthood a few generations ago might have been. There was something priestly about them: You go into their hushed rooms, confess what ails you, and then they heal you. I remember as we'd drive to the doctor's office I would play the game of trying to guess which of the cars parked outside belonged to Dr. Maktel. I had it narrowed down to the BMW or the Mercedes. I knew that doctors were men of influence, men of power. I also knew that I would get a lollipop when I was done, and that made me like him even more.

Now, though, my perfect ideal of the profession was tainted by experience. I no longer thought of doctors in this childlike, idealistic way.

A doctor who was a regular of mine back in NYC, who I'll call Dr. Mitchell, was typical. I'd met him at a party, a pretty dull shirt-and-tie event I'd been dragged along to. My host was a football superfan. His whole reason for inviting me was to hook me up with this doctor friend of his. Mitchell was absently talking with someone, holding a champagne glass, when he noticed me lurking by the buffet and feeling uncomfortable. He smiled and made his way over.

"Jason Peter! It's a pleasure to meet you! Evan Mitchell!"

"Hi, Evan."

We talked a little about the team's lackluster performance that season, although Mitchell was careful not to characterize it that way. He asked me about the surgeries I had been undergoing. As I talked to him I felt his eyes burning into me. When I made eye contact with him, he quickly averted his eyes and looked nervously at his feet or around the room. As always, I played down the extent of my surgeries, and kept hammering home the line that I was eager to get back on the field and kick some ass for the Panthers.

"But still," Mitchell conceded, "the surgery you have undergone is quite a serious one! As a doctor I know that the recovery can be quite painful."

When he said he was a doctor, my ears pricked up. My gaze stopped wandering around the room, and stayed on Dr. Mitchell. Doctors were good people to know. I gave him my standard line for testing the waters.

"Well, I am in a lot of pain right now. You're right, the recovery is pretty painful."

"What pain control are you receiving?"

"Vicodin."

"Hmm. That seems . . . hmmm."

I knew that I had him then.

"What were you going to say?" I prodded, gently.

"Well, for the kind of surgery you have had, I would have gone with something long-acting like Oxycontin or Dilaudid. Vicodin has a lot of acetaminophen in it, and if you take extra for any breakthrough pain, it can do some liver damage in the long term."

"Well, the doctor I currently have doesn't like to give out Oxys. You know the whole deal with the DEA."

Mitchell hissed derisively.

"We laugh at the Europeans because they have free health care, and cry out that it is government interference to hand out false teeth, prosthetic legs, and insulin to those that need it free of charge. But if you want to talk about government interference, how about doctors who are too scared to prescribe essential medication to someone such as yourself? That's an altogether more insidious form of interference if you ask me!"

He reached into his suit, and produced a card.

"Feel free to pay me a visit, any time. It would be my pleasure to be of assistance."

"I'll do that. Great to meet you, Doctor."

That week I was in his office with my standard bribe: a signed jersey. Mitchell got all googly-eyed when he saw that. On his wall I noticed other sports memorabilia, all football related, all signed by grateful players. I flattered Mitchell by asking about the family picture on the wall, told him that the fans were the reason I played football in the first place, and spun some war stories of life in the NFL. I walked out of there with prescriptions for Dilaudid, Oxycontin, and Xanax. It was that simple.

There were several doctors I had solicited in this manner. Most of them were so starstuck that they would write for anything I asked for. I rotated doctors in Charlotte regularly. There was always a doctor or a dentist willing to write a prescription for sixty or eighty Vicodin. But it was back in New York where the candy store was really open. It got so I could walk into one particular pharmacy without even a prescription and I'd leave with a bunch of pills. My painkiller habit was becoming extensive, but as far as the team doctors knew, I was not taking any more than was absolutely necessary.

My use of painkillers steadily increased as the seasons wore on. This was out of physical need: I was in some kind of pain almost constantly because of my repeated surgeries and the physical rigors of life in the NFL. It also was because of my abuse of the pills. I was occasionally using cocaine and other drugs during my weekends away from the Panthers.

Often I had to be at the stadium first thing in the morning, practicing through a vicious hangover. I can only speak for myself, but I would be shocked if this was an unusual story. Drug testing in the NFL, at least drug testing for street drugs, is pretty lax. The tests, for every player, take place between May 1 and training camp. So, to a certain extent, you know when the test is coming. If you can manage to pass that test, you are golden for another year.

Some people can use street drugs their whole lives and never have a problem with it, and if it isn't affecting their performance, I say why interfere? Especially when opiates are a way of life in the NFL. How can we condemn one man for smoking weed or snorting cocaine in a profession where the use of high-strength opiate painkillers is not just a reality but often a necessity? That is a question for society at large to answer, whether we are talking about the illegality of something like marijuana and the legality of killer drugs like tobacco and alcohol. If society can have things as backward as this, why should we expect the NFL to be any different?

So my use of drugs in the NFL carried on at a pretty steady pace, unaffected by the annual drug test from the team. It may have carried on like this indefinitely, if I had not received a DUI in March of 1999.

Now, getting a DUI was my own fault. I knew that there was a chance that I was over the limit, even though I didn't feel drunk. The more pills that I was taking, the less alcohol I drank. There was simply no need to get drunk anymore. I was out with a couple of guys from the team, feeling pleasantly woozy on the Vicodin I was taking, and nursing a couple of drinks, more out of habit than anything else. When it was time to leave the club I knew that I was capable of driving safely. What I didn't count on was the likelihood that someone driving a tricked-out Mercedes Benz at three in the morning—in the eyes of the police—would be suspected of being either a drug dealer or a professional athlete. Also, busting either of those looks great on a police officer's record.

When the cops flashed the lights, I knew that I was in trouble. I hadn't been driving erratically, but the cop made some excuse that I hadn't signaled properly a couple of turns ago. I handed over my license and waited. Sure enough he returned, with a Breathalyzer. I blew into it, prayed that somehow I was just under the limit, and cursed silently when the machine flashed red.

I had little idea of just what a big deal the DUI would turn out to be. I was fined, my name was splashed all over the papers, and, even worse, I was placed on the NFL's drug-testing program. This meant that my use of drugs other than opiates had to pretty much stop. So I upped my recreational use of painkillers because they were easy to get, and they didn't show up on my urine test. After all, the team doctors were prescribing painkillers to me. How could they tell me that it was wrong to take them? In the months following that initial arrest, I figured out that two drugs that weren't tested for in the NFL were the animal tranquilizer Ketamine, known in the media as special K, and the sedative GHB. I soon had connections for both, and routinely knocked myself out on them after practice. I guess the NFL thought that no professional athlete would be crazy enough to start abusing Special K. Well, they were wrong.

Another immediate impact from my DUI was that I was brought to the attention of the Panthers owner, Jerry Richardson. Up until that point I knew who Jerry was, I'd see him driving around on his little golf cart while we were practicing, and he was famous for never missing a Panthers home game. Jerry was smart enough to let people do their jobs, a good delegator, so my relationship with him was pretty slight. A week or so after the bust I received a call from Jerry's secretary, saying that he wanted to meet with me in the Palm Restaurant, in Charlotte. I immediately felt my stomach drop to the floor. I hadn't had what you would call a stellar season so far, and the thought crossed my mind that I was being called in so he could can me.

The Palm Restaurant wasn't Jerry's place, but it might as well have been. Jerry's face was all over the wall. Jerry had been a thirteenth pick in the NFL draft of 1959, going to the Baltimore Colts, although his career lasted only two years. He took his money and used it to create Spartan Foods, which soon became the biggest franchisee of the Hardee's restaurant chain. Spartan Foods later created Quincy's Steakhouses and Dooley's Seafood Emporium, and he later made it as the CEO of Flagstar Cos., Inc., the company responsible for bringing Denny's and El Pollo Loco to the Carolinas. He used his money to fund his dream of purchasing an NFL franchise. In 1993, he became the first player to own a team since George Halas of the Chicago Bears, when NFL owners unanimously selected Charlotte as the next site. It is pretty safe to say that faced with a man of this stature, walking into the restaurant, I was right about to shit a brick.

Jerry was a big guy, with gray hair and a face that looked like it could have been carved from stone. I frequently saw him smiling in the past, but on this occasion he was not betraying his emotions one little bit.

"Mr. Richardson," I said, shaking him by the hand and sitting when he motioned for me to do so.

He looked me over in silence for a while. He opened his mouth to speak.

"Jason," he said, in his thick southern accent, "do you want to be a Carolina Panther?"

"Well, yes, sir, I do. I'm very proud to wear this uniform."

"Well, lookee here. One thing I won't tolerate is my players' messing up with the law. If you don't feel that you can keep your nose clean, you should tell me now and we can start the process of trading you. Or you can tell me that this won't happen again and we can move on from this. Maybe I can tell you a little of some of the plans I have for you as a player . . ."

I nodded my head silently, before spluttering, "You have my word, Mr. Richardson. No more trouble with the law."

As soon as I said it, that stoic face of his cracked a grin, and the atmosphere at the table changed. He laughed, slapped me on the shoulder, and began to talk animatedly about the team and his dreams of success for us. I felt relief flood my body. The crazy thing was, it seemed like the DUI incident brought Mr. Richardson and me closer. Over the next year we had a few good laughs over it, and I eventually told him how scared I was that he was going to cut me that night. He found that pretty comical. He told me that night that we were going to have a much closer relationship, and that I should expect to be getting together more often. So we did: I would meet him for lunch or sometimes we would leave the stadium together. The latter made me uncomfortable. When your teammates see you drive off with the owner it kind of gives the impression that you're in their hip pocket. But what the owner says goes, so I never argued with it. In the end I couldn't really give a fuck what anybody else thought. He was a good man, and in this day and age there are a lot of owners who probably don't know the names of all the players that are on their team. Most of them only give a shit about the win-loss column. Jerry Richardson is one of the few that actually cares about his players.

The second year, playing in a game in San Francisco, I took a particularly bad hit. I knew immediately that something was terribly, terribly wrong. On the sidelines the trainers and doctors anxiously looked me over. I fought my way to my feet, but I couldn't feel my arms anymore. After I got up, the adrenaline still pumping though my body, I grabbed my helmet and pushed my way past the team doctors to get back onto the field. The team doctor looked mortified. He grabbed me, just before I made it to the field and screamed: "Where the hell are you going?"

"I'm going to do my job!" I yelled back.

"You need to stay here, Jason! I need to make sure that you're OK!"

"I'm fine! Let me go!"

"Wait!"

He motioned for me to stand still with his hands, so that he could test something. I sighed, and relented. He stood in front of me, made a fist, and knocked me solidly on the top of my helmet. As he did that, my knees buckled and I almost came crashing down to the ground. I fought my way to my feet, but the look on the doctor's face said it all. Something was badly wrong. By October of 1999 I was back in surgery again.

This time it was for a decompression. Following the San Francisco game I could literally feel nothing in both my arms. A bone in my spine was irritating a nerve in my neck, and the nerve had gotten so bad that I would sit there, running a fork down my arms as hard as I could, and feel nothing of it. This was the first time that an injury seemed so serious those awful thoughts of what it was going to do to my career as an athlete began to surface.

Fuck that, I'd try to tell myself, you're gonna be fine. Then I'd think of Damian. He dived into a pool wrong and, bam! his career was over, just like that. I was putting my body through car wreck after car wreck, and bit by bit it was giving out.

Fuck that, Jason. If you think like that, you will get hurt. You have to keep slugging, all out.

That's what we used to say in Nebraska. *You only get hurt when you half-ass it.*

The procedure involved them shaving some of the bone from my spine, so it wouldn't affect the nerve anymore. The surgeon's name was Tim Adamson, and he was a part of the Panthers organization. He was a confident, middle-aged guy, and I felt better immediately after I met him for the first time.

"You're going to be fine, Jason," he told me. "This is standard stuff. You'll be back to full capacity in no time."

And it was true. Almost as soon as I woke up after the surgery I could feel the improvement. It took eight weeks of physical therapy before I was able to play again. Stepping out for my first game after the surgery, I could feel the doubt starting in my gut. That first impact after a surgery is the one that makes you think. Whether you want it to or not, the thought crosses your mind: *Look at that big motherfucker. He must weigh at least 300 pounds. How do you know that when you crash into him, that patch job on your neck isn't going to pop right out? You could be in a wheelchair by tonight.*

There was nothing to do but banish such thoughts and run at that bastard as hard as I could. My feet pounded the dirt and I kept my eyes on him, his face twisted up in an endless, soundless scream that was drowned out by the pounding of my own heart, my face stony and determined, scanning his eyes for the sign, the sign that meant that I was going to be alright, and I careered toward him, thirty feet away, each second stretching out to infinity, my ragged breaths the sound track of the entire universe, twenty feet away, altering my trajectory slightly so that I would meet him head-on in an earth-shattering crash, the flash of his teeth, mouth twisted up in feral, primal hate, ten feet away, the blood pumping though my veins like lava, the burning, raging, spewing, roaring, nuclear eruption of adrenaline inside of me as I see *it,* for the tiniest fraction of a second, the flicker in his eyes: The Fear.

The Fear lets me know that I will take him down.

That I will walk away from this impact unscathed.

That I will break him into a thousand tiny pieces.

That he will shatter like china.

That *thhhuuuuuddddddd!*

The momentum I have lifts him clean off the ground for an instant, and the breath is knocked out of our bodies in unison, in a brutal grunt, as I take that motherfucker down, take us both down like a kamikaze pilot, and then bodies rain down upon us. Thud! Thud! Thud! *Thudthudthud!*

When I stand, the roar of the crowd is indistinguishable from the roar of the blood in my ears, the ringing in my skull and I know that I am OK again, that the next one and the next one will be easier. The fear is banished, conquered, defeated. I taste blood—and vindication.

Afterward I would sit at home, the painkillers making it so that I could walk to the fridge if I had to, without my body screaming in protest. Some evenings I would knock myself out on GHB, if I had a drug test coming up. Anything to elevate myself out of my prison of flesh and bone for a few hours. Anything to feel normal for a while.

When the season was over the disappointment of losing was doubled with the growing realization that my shoulders were still not right. The slight improvement after the initial round of surgeries had started to fade, and now they were worse than ever. Whenever I'd slow up on the painkillers, the full extent of my body's fragile condition would reveal itself. Rather than endure it for too long, and the inevitable brooding over my career and my health that feeling pain would entail, I would simply up my dosage and try to pretend that everything was fine. My body was my career. Without that, I was finished.

I flew out to California for the surgery. When the doctor examined me, he realized that I had damaged tissue and cartilage floating about in my left shoulder.

"We are going to need to open you up again," he told me, stony-faced, and I balked. I knew that if they did that again, there was no way I would be ready for the next season. Getting into shape and getting on the field was becoming more and more of an uphill struggle with my body hurting the way it did. Every extra month of recovery was making it harder and harder for me to remain the best on the field. The Panthers freaked when they heard the doctor's initial assessment. Their $7.5 million investment couldn't possibly go under the knife again. I asked for a second opinion.

"Well," the surgeon eventually agreed, "we could do a less serious procedure, which would involve scoping the left shoulder in the same way we did the right, last time."

"Great."

"But . . . in the long term . . ." The doctor removed his glasses and rubbed his eyes. It was obvious he had been here before. He knew that the long term was of little concern to me.

"Well, Mr. Peter, you do know the risks."

"Yeah, I do."

Within hours they were prepping for the procedure.

While I was laid up in the hospital, some asshole in the press described me as a malingerer. I was recovering from my shoulder surgery at the time that I read it. More than any of the negative press I had received in my time in Charlotte, that one stung the most. Malingerer!

My rookie year, when I had gotten into an argument with one of my teammates during practice and punched him so hard that I broke my fist, I didn't miss one game. Not even one practice. They set the hand in a cast and I was back to work the next day. When I tore my biceps during the game against New Orleans that same year, I argued with the coaches and the doctors for twenty minutes in my determination to get back into the game. When I eventually realized that they were not going to back down, I reluctantly capitulated. In this day and age, when some of the players out there will miss a game because they have a motherfucking hangnail, insinuating that I was crying wolf about my injuries was about the worst thing anyone could have said to me.

After each surgery, after each long, painful recovery, the hope would return. The hope that maybe this was it, I was fully recovered, I could get back to the business of playing and winning games. The hope would last as long as it took for another collision, another crunch of bone, another agonized realization that something was horribly wrong with my body. Then came the sad look on the face of the team doctor as he examined me: "Jason, it looks like you're going to have to get this fixed."

In the end it got so that it wasn't the despair I couldn't stand. It was the *hope*.

7 BUSTED

EVERYTHING CHANGED FOR ME ONCE MY DUI arrest forced me into the team's drug program. I had the feeling that they knew it was bunch of bullshit as much as I did. I'd get called in for these pointless, airless meetings with the doctors and therapists, they'd ask how I was doing, we'd shoot the shit, and I'd be sent on my way. Also, a rep from the NFL would test my piss six times a month, so for a period I had to lay off of the cocaine and ecstasy. But I have to tell you, I didn't mind that too much. There are ways and means to get around a urine test, and of course my main drug of choice—opiates—were still being prescribed to me by my team doctors (although the vast majority of the pills still came from those starstruck nonteam doctors, willing to write a prescription in exchange for a signed jersey or whatever). Until this thing blew over, I was happy to rely on my stockpile of Vicodin, Percocet, and whatever else to get by.

Don't get me wrong: Those pills were a necessity for me and many others on the team. The sheer fucking brutality of life as a defensive player in the NFL means that heavy painkillers are always going to be needed to keep you on your feet. I don't know how many others on my team, if anyone, were using the pills to get high. It wasn't something we discussed. Indeed, the addictive nature of the pills was not something that even the team doctors discussed with us. But we were big boys and I know that I would still have been eating those pills like candy if I was warned about their dangers. Well, shit, when something feels that good, wouldn't you?

I had my own sources for painkillers away from the team doctors, and they would arrive by the boxful. This way I made sure that I was never in danger of running out, and questions were never raised about how many pills I was taking. Sometimes in the locker room, guys would ask each other for pills because they were running low and in pain, but I tried not to get involved with all of that shit. The last thing I needed was someone mooching pills from me, when in all likelihood I would never get them back. I needed those things to get me through the day.

I had settled down into a routine during this period: Life in the NFL forced me to keep my drug use under control. After we played a game, a lot of the guys would like to go out and party, but unless we had one of our rare wins I wouldn't be in the mood. I couldn't understand how players could come away from losing a game and still be in the mood to cut loose. Every defeat we suffered on the Panthers was a personal affront to me. I would go straight home, take some pills, and have a few drinks, ruminating on what went wrong. It took a year of this before I was able to adapt somewhat and find myself able to go out with teammates despite the Panthers' regular defeats and setbacks.

I was still messing around with Ketamine on occasion. Ketamine is a cat tranquilizer that had started finding a market in the club scene. I used it on occasion because it wouldn't show up on my urine test. Ketamine is a mild hallucinogenic and a sedative, and when I was high enough on it I could barely move a muscle. There was nothing to do but try and hold on to your sanity and enjoy the trip. Another drug I really started to get into while I was in the drug program was GHB. GHB became one of my regular indulgences because it didn't show up on a urine test. In this period it had just been scheduled in the United States, so I was getting it mostly through black market sources. My connection for it would sell it to me in an old Evian or Sprite bottle. However, in some of the more hard-core health food stores it was legally sold as a product called "Blue Nitro." Blue Nitro was either pure GHB, or so close that it was practically indistinguishable. So I would buy that stuff by the caseload.

The kick from GHB was very similar to an opiate kind of high. After you took your dose a warm feeling would start to grow in the pit of your stomach, radiating outward until it felt as if your whole body was enveloped in a warm bath. It also gave a pleasant, woozy kind of drunken high. The problem with GHB was that if you misjudged the amount, it would knock you clean out, especially if you made the mistake of mixing it with booze.

It happened after a game up in Washington, D.C., against the Redskins. We had got our asses beat, and so I was in a foul mood. We flew back to Charlotte that night, sober and quiet in the aftermath of defeat, and early the next morning I was back at the stadium for a round of team meetings where the defeat was picked apart and analyzed. Then I knuckled down to some running and lifting. The harder I ran, the more I lifted, I still could not get the taste of defeat out of my mouth. Maybe the losing streak at the Panthers was part of the reason I wanted to get high so often. Until coming to Carolina, defeat was a rare thing for me. Now it was becoming the norm, and I hated that more than I had ever hated anything. The next day, a buddy of mine and I decided to hang at his place and get high.

My buddy liked to get fucked up as much as I did, and we regularly got stoned on GHB together. He was a big guy, too, and had a high tolerance for the stuff.

We were in the living room and had just dosed ourselves. GHB comes on pretty fast. Once you swallow it, you have about twenty minutes before you are really out of it. Once it hits your stomach, kind of like when you smoke weed, you start to feel a terrific hunger.

"Shit, man," I said to my buddy, walking over to the fridge, "You got nothin' in here. I'm getting hungry."

"Me, too. You wanna go out and pick something up?"

I knew I had taken a pretty sizable dose. There was no way I cold safely operate a vehicle. I shook my head and said, "I'm already feeling too fucked up to drive."

"Fuck it, I'll drive!" my friend said.

"Are you sure?"

"I'm cool! Come on, before this shit really kicks in."

There was a fast-food place not far from his apartment. We figured we could be there and back within twenty minutes. As we got in the four-by-four my friend stopped, checked his reflection in the mirror, and shook his head. He seemed momentarily unsteady, and then he caught himself.

"You sure you're OK?" I asked him.

"Oh yeah, man. I'm great."

He started the truck, and as we took off I realized that I was getting real messed up, real quick. The midafternoon sunlight shining through the windshield had a kind of translucent glow around it. I was looking at everything from under water. The music coming from the radio seemed to be floating up to me in waves. I looked over at my friend, but his eyes were fixed on the road, his expression stoic. I remember thinking that the music sounded as if it was coming from a bunch of different directions at once, and I found myself getting lost in it. Then I remember nothing.

Thump.

Nothing, that is, until the top of my head smashed into the roof of the car. Something had jolted me straight out of my seat and up into the upholstery. My eyes opened, but I could not comprehend what I was seeing through the windscreen. Everything seemed surreally out of place.

We weren't on the same stretch of street anymore. We were on a small, two-lane highway near the house.

Only we weren't *on* the highway at all.

We were riding up the embankment in what seemed like some kind of half-assed attempt to make a turnoff. The car was tilted at a forty-degree angle and I could hear the undercarriage scraping the tarmac underneath us.

Oh Jesus Christ!

I jolted awake and turned to my friend, but my muscles felt like they were made of treacle, and my head weighed five hundred pounds. It took all of my strength to turn around.

"Are you all right?" I heard myself demanding, but the words sounded wrong. It sounded like I was yelling through a mouthful of food.

Arr woo awwite?

My buddy just looked back and stared at me. I could see his face in flashes. He was grinning at me with a big, stoned vacant smile. I don't think he could even hear me; it was like all of the lights had gone out in his face.

And then it all went black again.

Something

in the black

was

Bangbangbangbang

calling me

bang

bangbangbang.

I did not know where I was or how much time had passed. As I started to come out of it I became aware of my chin pressed down onto my chest, and a long trail of drool hanging from my lip. My eyes blinked open.

No blood.

I was alive.

I raised my head in time to hear it again, louder and more demanding.

Bangbangbangbang.

I looked to the left. My buddy was still at the wheel, passed out. I looked to the right. A leather glove was banging on the glass. Oh shit. It was the fucking cops. A cop was yelling through the glass: "Wake up! Wake up!"

With a cold start of terror I was fully conscious. I grabbed my friend by the arm and shook him, hard.

"Wake the fuck up, man! It's the fucking cops! *Wake up!*"

"What!?" he yelled, jolting into consciousness. "What!?"

He looked at me and saw the cop pounding on the window.

"Oh shit!" he yelled.

"Get the fuck out of the vehicle!" the cop was screaming. I straightened myself up.

Looking up, I realized that we were still on the road; at a stoplight that I knew was way across town, in an area dotted with lonely-looking strip malls, car dealerships, and chain restaurants. I unlocked and opened the door. The cop stepped back as I swung the door open, and with a clatter an umbrella rolled out and hit the road. I leaned down to pick it up, still dazed from the GHB, and as I did the cop pulled his gun and screamed: "*Do not move a muscle, asshole! Keep your hands where I can see them!*"

I stepped out slowly, the cop's gun still in his hand, ready for sudden movement on my part.

"Turn around."

As I did, I realized just how messed up everything was.

We were the first car at the stoplight. Four cop cars surrounded our vehicle, all with lights flashing. I counted two ambulances as well. But even over the sounds of the sirens and the cop radios, and the screams of the other cop who was dragging my buddy from the vehicle, the loudest noise of all was the honking of horns. From our vehicle traffic stretched back as far as the eye could see. It was an incredible sight. A sea of fucking chrome. . . . People had gotten out of their cars and were watching the spectacle of us getting busted, calling their friends and families on cell phones, cursing, or just sitting there blasting their horns endlessly. The entire street was in total fucking pandemonium.

I was watching all of this with my hands on the hood as the

cops patted me down, yelling questions at me. I was trying to piece it all together in my head. Somehow we must have made it over here in a blackout, and my buddy managed to stop the car at the red light before passing out completely.

To add to the surrealism, in the other lane heading back in the opposite direction, people were slowing their vehicles to rubberneck at us, and guys were leaning out of their windows yelling at me:

"Go Panthers!"

"Keep going, Jason! You guys will turn the corner!"

"Tough break at Washington! Next time, baby! Next time!"

What the fuck could I do? I just looked sheepish and yelled back, "Thanks!"

The cops spun me around, and the one who had been pounding on my window cuffed me and led me away. We were taken to separate cars to be questioned. The cops managed to tow our vehicle to the side of the road to the cheers of people stuck behind us, and the traffic started to disperse.

As they were leading me to the car, the questions started.

"Jason," they demanded, "you want to tell us exactly what the fuck is going on?"

I just told them everything, apart from the fact that I had taken GHB. That I'd had a game in Washington the night before and got home late. That I was up early in the morning for practice. I said that I'd been having trouble sleeping and took some Ambien, and that we had just popped out to get something to eat.

There was no way in hell that the cops believed us, but I didn't smell of booze and I was acting perfectly lucid.

"Yeah," the lead cop said finally. "You guys had a tough break there in Washington." I gave him my best *aw shucks* smile and said, "Well, I appreciate that, sir."

My buddy told the cops a similar story. The kicker came when the cops asked me: "Jason, do you know how long you guys were stopped at that light?"

"Well, no, sir, I have no idea."

He looked at his watch.

"Forty-five minutes! You guys have been stopped there for forty-five minutes."

They gave us a break. They could have taken us downtown to be tested for drugs, but the test would have shown up negative anyway. The whole thing obviously puzzled them, but they felt they had no choice but to let it go. A teammate happened to be passing by when all of this was happening. He pulled over to see what was going on and ended up giving us a ride home.

"You motherfuckers are crazy" was all he kept repeating the whole ride over.

It wasn't until later that night that I started to think about how close I had come to dying. For a moment, my life had been completely out of my hands. If my buddy had blacked out a little sooner, we would have both been dead. We could have killed other people. It was terrifying to think about. I momentarily resolved to stop using GHB, and then settled on never getting into a vehicle while under the influence of GHB. That seemed like a more realistic idea.

The police notified the team a few days later. No charges were ever brought. Of course I was pulled aside and asked about the whole thing, but I stuck to my Ambien story and that was the last I ever heard about it.

Still, it gives me the chills to think about how else that night could have played out. Some of us are just born lucky, I guess.

IT WAS NOVEMBER 2000, AND I FOUND MY-
self back in my parents' house in New Jersey. I was on the recliner,
half nodded out on pills in front of the television. I didn't know
what I was watching anymore. The faces blurred into one long indistinguishable monstrous thing. One minute they were trying to
sell me jewelry, the next they were talking to me about bombs and
elections, the next they were holding the hand of a sobbing woman
whose husband was cheating on her. I was not even aware of my
hand on the remote control. Time had become fluid, elastic.

I could not move a muscle.

They had cut me open again. Throughout the whole season
my neck was fucked up. The pills could not make it feel OK anymore. I was getting used to the doctor's fretful expressions whenever they examined me. I cursed my own motherfucking body for
letting me down. I started to get paranoid that the GHB and the
Ketamine were weakening my bones somehow, eating away at me
from the inside. The more painkillers I took, the worse the pain
seemed to get. I was sensitive all over. If I stubbed my toe, it felt as
if the bone had snapped. More pills. Then out on to the field for
practice. *Crunch.*

And again: "Jason, I'm sorry, but we're going to have to operate."

This time, they did a fusion. They cut my neck open to fuse two of my vertebrae together. They sliced open my hip to remove a suitable bone to put between the two vertebrae for the fusion. While you wait for the bones to fuse, you cannot move an inch. When I woke up, I was immobilized inside of a hard neck brace, and in a weird switch of fortunes, it was Damian—Damian, whom I had nursed through his own paralysis a long time ago—who flew to Charlotte to look after me. He drove me up to New Jersey, and I was placed on the recliner, where I was to remain for what seemed like a lifetime.

My mom would make sure I had everything I needed before she would go out to work. I didn't need much. The pills sapped my appetite, and my entire schedule revolved around making sure I had enough pills inside of me. Mom was working in the restaurant alongside my father at this point. I could see the worry in her face every time she looked at me. I'm sure the image of me in that neck brace was a little too close to another image she had burned in her brain—that of Damian in his halo. Although Mom would never come right out and say, "You need to quit playing football," she, in her own gentle way, tried to suggest alternatives.

"There's always broadcasting. You'd be good at that. You know a lot about the game."

"Oh yeah," I said and winced, "it'd be great until I dropped my first F-bomb on live television."

I started to chuckle at the thought, but it hurt, and so I quit it.

"Or you could go back to school. You're an intelligent boy, Jason."

"Ma! I'm going to get better! I'll be able to play again!"

"I know! I know!"

We fell silent for a moment. I told her: "This is just a test, is all. God's just testing me."

Even as I said it, I winced. That little comment was more for mom's benefit than my own. I kinda thought that's how she'd like me to think about it. But the comment had gone over her head. She was still sitting there, lost in fretful thought.

"Or swimming! You were such a good swimmer. I bet with a little practice you could try out for the Olympics!"

I said nothing. I knew that she was just trying to help. I hadn't been in a swimming pool in a long time. Although Mom knew that my entire life was football, even she could see that my professional career had been something of a disaster. My body had let me down. It was shitty luck, but there it was. She knew I'd get mad if she came out and said, "Jason, I don't think you should play anymore," but the thought that I would recover from this surgery and then go out and basically run headfirst at a charging 300-pound lineman was obviously scaring the shit out of her.

Well, it was scaring the shit out of me, too. I was imagining myself with a broken neck, or worse. I knew that some kind of crazy miracle had prevented Damian from being stuck in a wheelchair for the rest of his life. The way my luck had been going lately, I wasn't so sure that lightning would strike twice in the Peter household.

I was alone with myself, and alone with my mind. I learned things about myself, with nothing to do but be still and think. I learned that the human mind can be a poisonous thing, can be an agent of destruction to itself. Without the ability to numb myself with illegal drugs, I found myself swallowing painkillers like candy.

This was when I graduated, I guess. I moved from being a fucked-up polydrug abuser to an actual, grown-up opiate addict. A junkie. A dope fiend. All of that cartoon shit that I thought I would never, in one million years, turn into.

Sometimes I would be awake all night, the eerie glow from the television my only company. I would watch for hours, uninterrupted, the god-awful infomercials that the TV set would vomit out for the 3:00 A.M. crazies and the insomniacs. I watched commercials for slicers, dicers, cleaners, exercise machines, thirty-minute abs, ten-minute abs, five-minute abs (I think I even saw one that promised ten-second abs), and I got to know all of these strange, nocturnal flimflam artists whose job it was to hawk bullshit products to the bored, the crazy, and the gullible. I took more pills. I had all the time in the world.

And in those quiet hours my mind would start its assault:

Funny how things change, huh, Jason?

Remember when you were eighteen?

When Damian had his accident?

How you thought that if this ever happened to you, you would want someone to kill you? To save you from a life trapped inside of a prison of immobile flesh?

Well, it seems as if fate has finally gotten around to it!

Shutupshutupshutup.

I'm recovering.

I'm gonna be OK. The doctors said so.

They said that to you before, didn't they?

They don't give a shit about you!

They care about their investment!

You think they would care if you landed in a fucking wheelchair?

Fuckyou!

Fuck

You!

They care about me. Jerry Richardson cares about me! My teammates care about me!

You know what you are?

You're an eight million dollar liability.

Eight million dollars, and you couldn't even wipe your own ass right now!

What are you gonna do when they finally cut your ass loose?

There was nothing else to do but take more pills. It was the only way I could stop thinking. I knew that the truth rested somewhere in between the two extremes my mind was screaming about, but I knew that once I recovered enough I would be back out on the field and doing it all over again. The hits were coming faster and faster now.

I saw myself as a bull in the ring, with two swords shoved deep into its back, staggering, dazed, still dangerous, though—still willing to risk all to gore that murderous bastard torero—but weakened, targeted.

Already a new bull was ready to take my place. Already the crowd had sensed that the final move had been made. Only a miracle could save this bull, and who the fuck believes in miracles anymore?

With enough pills inside of me I could sleep, and I would have vivid, sensory dreams. Sometimes, half in sleep and half out, I could conduct them like a movie director. I replayed games in my head, allowed myself to move quicker, anticipate the quarterback, and inflict more damage than I had done in disappointing reality. Sometimes the dreams would mesh with the television. I would be out on the field, about to play a snap, and someone would walk over to me and try to sell me a mop with a lifetime guarantee for nineteen dollars and ninety-nine cents.

It was at least six months before I was once again able to participate in team practices. When I returned to Charlotte I had a Vicodin habit that was out of control. On a good day, I could take sixty. There were two minicamps that year. I missed the first one completely, and was only allowed to take part in the second one under the stipulation that I did not take part in any contact drills. It was decided that I would have to wait until training camp to test out my neck. The months leading up to training camp I practically lived in the weight room and the physical therapy room. I knew that this was going to be my last shot: I swore to myself that I would leave no stone unturned. I did everything possible to be ready to play. Whatever was asked of me by the trainers or the strength coaches, I did without complaint.

Throughout this training, I managed to get my consumption of pills back under control. I cut down, little by little. With the renewed structure of the workouts and the practices, I started feeling better. Slowly, that elusive sense of hopefulness started to return. By the time that I made it to training camp, I was feeling pretty good. The coaches threw me right in, and I was going great! I got through all of training camp without any major incidents.

"*Goddamnit, you lucky bastard!*" I thought to myself. "*You fucking pulled this out!*" On our second week of regular practice, we started to do some work without pads on. We were practicing in helmets only. While we were working on offense versus defense, a young offensive lineman who didn't really know the tempo and was pretty new to practicing without pads on came off the ball and *smacked* me on the side of the helmet.

Holyfuckinshit.

For a moment I thought I had been shot.

Immediately I lost all feeling:

Arms.

Legs.

I fell to the ground with a groan of agony. I knew that it was fucked up. Something was badly wrong.

The feeling started to come back in my legs, but as it did, the pain was unbearable. I just lay there thinking: "*This is it. It's over. Your career is over. It's over.*" The surgery hadn't worked. It had all been for nothing. Oh Jesus fucking Christ, what was I going to do now?

After I managed to get it together enough to walk off the field, the trainers were quick to try to reassure me that this was just a minor setback and that everything was going to be OK. But I just didn't buy it anymore. I knew that my days were numbered. I couldn't fool myself any longer.

I limped through the rest of the season. I'd play a game, take two games off. Each time I stepped onto the field, I did it with the fear gnawing at me that this would be the last time I would ever play professionally. Shit, this could be the last time I even walked out anywhere. My every living moment was consumed with fear for what would happen to me in the event of another bad collision. My days of playing full-force, without fear, without forethought, were gone forever. The team doctors told me after one of the games, *"Jason, if you continue to have these setbacks, there are going to be some major problems,"* as if I hadn't figured that shit out already.

After I had taken a couple of weeks off, I was due to play in the game against the New Orleans Saints. I had worked hard to try and strengthen my neck in the vain hope that somehow I could miraculously recover. The game started, and I didn't play in a lot of snaps, but I managed to hold up in the plays that I did. Slowly, I was starting to get my confidence back.

Maybe I was right, when I was trying to make my mom feel better. Maybe that little platitude was close to the truth. Maybe this was all some kind of test from God. I mean, imagine how much sweeter the victory would be if I could come back from this horrible experience and actually achieve the kind of success I had dreamed of?

New Orleans had just scored, and they were kicking off. The coaches put me on the kickoff return team. As they did, I felt a twinge of anticipation. This was a risky move. This meant that my job was to block a guy who had a thirty-yard head start running down the field. There was no way I was getting out of this snap without one high-impact incident.

Somewhere in the back of my mind I started to fear that the coaches *wanted* me injured, that this was their way of getting rid of dead weight.

No, fuck that, Jason!

They're asking you to make this play because they know you can do it.

Now focus.

Focus.

They kicked the ball.

I watched it arc through the air, and heard my heart pounding over the roars of the crowd.

I saw my guy.

The bastard I had to block.

I was part of the wedge, a group of three or four guys who come together to form a wall for the kickoff return man.

As soon as we were close enough, I broke away,

Heading straight for him,

To take him *out*.

Crrruuuunnnnnnnccccchhhhhhhh.

OHJESUSFUCKINGCHRISTINHEAVEN.

MOTHERFUCKINGSHITFUCKPISS.

As soon as the impact happened, I knew my career was over.

Just like that, my entire life drained away from me.

Everything went numb. Everything.

I collapsed to the ground, and the rest, as they say, is history.

Afterward, showered and changed, I was lying down with an ice pack on my neck. I was thinking about all of the hard work I had put myself through, all of the training, all of the sacrifices. Everything, every moment leading up to this impact, had been rendered completely and totally worthless. I have never felt anything approximating that kind of despair before. I don't know if there is a word in the English language that can adequately describe the sense of utter and total devastation I felt at that moment.

When I went to the doctor's office after that game to go through the usual round of tests that one goes through after sustaining an injury, there was no talk of my career being over. They did what they had to do, grimly joking with me as I remained stoic and silent. They sent me on my way with a whole bunch of Vicodin, but I wasn't holding out any hope anymore. I went straight home, dosed myself with a cocktail of Vicodin and booze, and collapsed into a dark, dreamless sleep.

The next day I was called out of the training room and into the office by the head coach, George Seifert, and the general manager, Marty Herney.

"Jason? Could we talk to you in private for a moment?"

I knew what this was. This was the Death Blow. I approached the office slowly and silently. I felt like a man stepping up to the gas chamber. I closed the door behind me and was ushered into a chair. Everyone sat in silence. I took in the office, the polished mahogany desk, the pictures of the trainer's family. As dull and ordinary as it all was, today every little detail had doom-ridden overtones. George and John looked at me awkwardly for a moment. Also present was the head trainer, John Kasik. They were men who knew and loved sports. They knew that what they were about to say to me was one of the cruelest things you could say to an athlete. I had the sudden, confusing urge to laugh, or to get up and run out of the office, pretend that this wasn't happening. But, crushed by circumstance, I just sat there and did my best to smile.

Coach Seifert asked, "So how are you doing, Jason?" and we made chitchat for a few awkward moments, before he cleared his throat and came right to the point.

"You know . . . I've coached men who have damaged themselves so badly playing this game . . . that they can't even hold their own children, anymore. They pushed it too far, and once your body reaches a certain point . . . well, there's just no coming back. Do you understand what I'm telling you, Jason?"

"Yes, sir."

"Jason, you can't keep doing this. I'm worried that you're going to keep trying to come back and one day . . . well, you're just not going to get up again. And I don't want to see that happen."

"Yes, sir."

"Look, the bottom line is this: We can't clear you to play anymore. The doctor has told us that you're at risk for a major injury. I'm really, terribly sorry."

"Yes, sir."

I was unable to look anybody in the eye. I was finally living the moment that every professional athlete fears above anything else. I didn't have some brilliant, eloquent argument to convince them to give me another chance. The thing is, I knew what they were saying was perfectly true. I could feel it, deep inside of myself. I was one good hit away from being a cripple, and that scared the living shit out of me. This little talk in the office was just the final confirmation of something I had known for a long time.

It was game over. I was finished.

SUICIDE SQUAD

THE DRIVE FROM MY APARTMENT IN NEW YORK City to my parents' house in New Jersey is one that I had taken on many, many occasions, but this time everything had a sense of special significance. This time the journey had the air of finality about it. I tried to take in everything, every familiar scene and noise. The sky was bright and clear, in contrast to the thunderstorm that was raging in my skull. The traffic was steady, and as I left behind the honking taxicabs and lunatic right turns of Manhattan I speeded up.

Coming onto the Jersey Turnpike I was immediately tossed into a chaotic swarm of automobiles. Even with the windows up and the air-conditioning on full blast I could not escape the toxic smog vomited out by all of those spewing exhausts. There was a mass of cars, all trying to get into the correct lanes to go through the tollbooths. The worst traffic was in the pay lanes.

I imagined what it would be like to be one of the poor bastards whose job it is to sit in these tiny prisons, taking dollars from the thousands of grim commuters who do this disgusting ritual every goddamned day.

I found myself looking for a way to cut in front of a taxicab to make the E-ZPass lane, when I stopped and thought: *What the fuck am I doing?*

It was laughable, really. I was in no rush. I had all of the time in the world. After all, by tomorrow morning, I would be dead.

My mind was in pieces. The tears would not even come anymore. The skies, the sun, the air, nothing could make me feel alive. Every honking horn, every sudden movement by other drivers made me jump. My nerves felt exposed, raw. I was a full-body wound, weeping and infected.

Since the end of my professional football career, my life had been in free fall. When the shit hit the fan in November of 2001 and I was let go from the Panthers, I got the fuck out of Dodge. Charlotte was just a painful reminder of how everything had gone wrong for me. It seemed that my life had started falling apart almost as soon as the Panthers had signed me, and an air of sadness and failure clung to every place I went there. I didn't want to see my teammates anymore. I certainly didn't want to see the coaches or Jerry Richardson. This was not some kind of residual anger at being let go, it was something worse than that. Shame. The unlivable, unbearable shame of letting the Panthers—and myself—down. I honestly felt that I had signed for all of this money, come to Charlotte with all of this promise, and then had systematically let everybody down. With Jerry Richardson it was particularly painful. He had been so good to me, even after my DUI bust. He wrote the checks, and he never stopped believing in me. And this was how I repaid him!

Of course, I knew that the injuries were beyond my control, but shit! The mind-set that you need to be the best—the blind focus, the dogged self-belief, the adherence to the team and The Life at all costs—is something that came back to haunt me when I could not play anymore. I had made football my life; everything else came a distant second or third. With football gone, I was left with a gulf, an endless black void, deep inside of me.

I fled to New Jersey without even saying goodbye to my old teammates. I went back to my parents' house to nurse my wounds. I sat around there, depressed and aimless for a couple of months, before renting an apartment in New York City. All of my friends were in the city, and I felt that the quiet and the isolation of being out in New Jersey was not good for my state of mind. I had too much time to think about the wreckage my career had become. Goddammit, I needed to have fun. I deserved it!

With an excess of time and an excess of money, I started doing more and more cocaine. Without the fear that I would have to be up at 6:00 A.M. to practice, I allowed myself to truly gorge on drugs. I didn't want to just be high; I wanted to be the highest person in the room! I took that same pit-bull attitude that I had toward playing football and applied it directly to doing cocaine. No half measures! Cocaine would arrive daily, and I found myself moving in social circles where constant cocaine use was the norm.

At first I reconnected with old friends, but come Monday morning they would have to go to work, and I would be on my own, bored and antsy. So the scene in my apartment changed. I started hanging out with the hard-core partiers, those who had no concept of a workweek, or any kind of structure outside of partying, sleeping it off, and starting all over again. On coke, I was the life and soul of the party. I hung out at all of the hottest nightspots, and my biggest responsibility became to choose between the daytime soap actress who wanted me to come over to her place so we could snort coke and screw, or the model who was trying to drag me into the bathroom of the Pangaea Club for a drug-fueled blowjob. Every night of the week I would have someone different to hang out and party with. When they couldn't take it anymore, I would replace them. I laughed at their weakness! But what could you expect? They were only amateurs. I was a professional!

In the mornings, when I would wake up hungover and achy, I would simply down a handful of painkillers and start all over again. As my cocaine use increased, so did my use of pills. They would balance me out, make me feel somewhat normal the next day. Damian was living in New Jersey at the time, and so once a week I would meet him for dinner. I would dose myself up on pain pills so I wouldn't seem so frazzled, so manic. On weekends, I would go home to New Jersey to stay with my parents. It was good to have at least two days away from the cocaine and the clubs. I would be so loaded on painkillers that I would barely move from the couch. All I wanted was to be left alone so I could enjoy the serene hum of the opiates in peace. My mother only tried to broach the subject of my drug use once.

"Jason? Jason?"

I was nodding out in front of the TV. I tried to focus my eyes and said, "Yeah, Ma, what is it?"

"Honey . . ." She sat down next to me, and took one of my hands in her tiny fingers. "I've noticed that you're still taking a lot of those pain pills."

"Uh-huh."

"Well, are you sure you still need to take quite so many? I mean, now that you're not playing?"

I immediately lost my shit with her. You see, in my head I was taking the pain pills for my injuries. The fact that they felt good was just a pleasant side effect. However, I did know that when I stopped taking them, I started to get sick. I had never felt full-blown withdrawal, just a feeling of depression that would settle in, short-temperedness, and what would feel like the beginnings of a cold. In other words, the perfect excuse for more pills. I had an abstract notion in my head that these things were addictive, but I figured that this couldn't be more serious than the myriad dangers I faced playing in the NFL.

Still, when she said that, I got real defensive, real quick.

"I need these pills! I'm in agony most of the time! I need to keep taking them until I have surgery to fix all of the damage inside of me!"

"I know! Look," Mom repositioned herself and tried a different tack. "I just think that maybe you should try cutting down on them a little. I don't think that they're doing you any good. You seem so . . . quiet. So tired all of the time. Like the life has gone out of you."

"I'm just exhausted. I've been busy."

"Doing what?"

"I dunno! Stuff! I had a meeting . . . about a job . . ." I started desperately struggling to find a suitable lie. "Something in broadcasting . . . I don't want to jinx it by saying too much, but it could be a big deal for me."

She smiled, either relieved or faking it.

"Oh, that's wonderful. You need to do something like that! You'd be so good at it."

Of course, there was no interview. I did briefly take acting classes, but the first and only time I showed up I was high as hell, and just watching all those people being enthusiastic about acting made me want to vomit. Everybody seemed so . . . happy and . . . eager. Fuck that shit. I went out to take a piss halfway through the class and never came back. Although that conversation with my mother made me consider some uncomfortable truths. So I did the best thing I could under the circumstances. I ignored it, took more pills, and started coming back to New Jersey on a less regular basis.

All I had now were the pills. Gradually, there was no pretence anymore that their primary use was pain control. They were just another way to stop me from feeling. I was taking up to eighty Vicodin ES a day. When I could get my hands on Oxycontin, I would do them. I would swallow them by the handful, or grind them up to snort. Nothing could ever get me where I wanted to go.

Total oblivion was my ultimate goal.

Even in the fleeting moments when I achieved a kind of death-like peace, I was not truly happy. No amount of drugs could give me my career back. Without a team, without a career, I was nothing. I was a 250-pound drug addict, forty-five pounds already eaten away from my NFL playing weight of 295, living in a penthouse apartment, all alone. Sometimes I'd get paranoid when I'd watch the news, and some stupid kid would steal their parents' Oxy and overdose. When that happened, the people in charge would start making noise about cracking down on doctors, outlawing the pills altogether. I was very fastidious about stockpiling my medication. I would have literally hundreds of pills of various types and strengths hidden around the apartment. But it was never enough to make me feel secure.

Sometimes I would have these crazy fantasies of what would happen in the case of a war or a natural disaster. What if a rogue state nuked the United States? What would happen to me? Where would I get my tablets from then?

Yeah, my main concern in the event of a nuclear attack was "Will I still be able to get drugs?"

You should try it sometime.

If you think that sounds funny, or weird, you just try it.

The first time you ever run low on those motherfucking tablets, the blood turns to ice water in your veins, then the cramps and the hives and the shitting, and finally your brain turns into a lump of white hot shrapnel. Fuck. A nuclear warhead couldn't scare me. I knew what *real* fear was.

This was the pattern of my life for the next eighteen months. I had prescriptions from doctors all over New York City. Shit, I had one mom-and-pop pharmacy that was so good to me that I could walk in there without even a prescription and they would hand the pills over, two hundred at a time, with at least two or three refills. Nevertheless, as my pill usage grew, it became a problem—even for me—to source enough pills. I had connections on the black market, but they could not be relied upon to source enough pills at a time. I started running low, and turning up to the pharmacy a few days early, only to be told that they wouldn't refill my prescription. At the point that I was averaging between fifty and eighty pills a day, I knew that I was in real trouble. Making sure that I would have enough pills in case I ended up going on a wild two- or three-day cocaine bender was becoming a hassle. All you heard on the news was that the DEA was cracking down on doctors prescribing painkillers. You could hear Control all around you, closing down a doctor here or there, busting a dealer, making the pharmacists nervous. Goddammit, why couldn't they leave me alone?

Once, over at my parents' house, I started feeling antsy. I had burned through my pills too quickly, and something unpleasant was happening. My parents were out, and I had suddenly remembered that my father had been prescribed Vicodin after having some surgery on his teeth. My stomach flipped. Maybe there were some left over! For the next two hours, I systematically turned their house upside down trying to locate the phantom drugs. Then I returned to the couch, and silently hung my head in despair.

My NFL physique was already withering away. I didn't go to the gym anymore. I barely left the apartment. I was just a shell, barely eating, barely surviving. The muscle started to wither away on me, and I noticed that my face, too, was hollowing out. The dimensions of my face were changing. Along with the painkillers, I was snorting cocaine at epic levels. That was the only thing that got me out of the house and into the nightclubs so I could try to drink and fuck the misery out of myself. The next morning, when I'd wake up in a ménage of coke-smeared mirrors and nude, snoring strippers, I would truly know the meaning of the word "misery."

I had no friends. I had people who liked to party with me because I was an ex-NFL player. I won't give you the old cliché of "money can't buy you happiness" because I'd even make myself groan to say that. Money did buy me drugs, and money bought me company. But drugs or company could not bring me anything approaching happiness.

Sometimes I'd stand naked in front of the mirror and look at my body. I'd think, "Why did you do this to me? Why did you let me down like this?"

This wasn't how it was meant to happen. I was meant to be playing right now. My mind would drift to Grant, in the midst of a highly successful career with St. Louis. He was playing in Super Bowls. Why? Why did our paths diverge so suddenly, so unfairly?

I'd always thought we'd both have long careers. We'd get married to all-American girls, and go on cruises together. Our kids would play together. We'd make enough that our grandchildren wouldn't have to worry about money, never mind our kids! I had worked so hard, and the payoff was this? An empty apartment? A painkiller addiction? A body so ruined by the rigors of life as a professional athlete that I was tossed away, discarded like an imperfect piece of meat at the grand old age of twenty-seven?

I was a has-been.

A once-was.

My older brother, Christian, was still in the game. If I had to look around at all of the people I knew from college, and imagine who would be no longer playing football by their midtwenties, never, not in my darkest imaginings, would I have chosen myself as a candidate.

I had been promised the world.

I had been promised a long career.

When you have been promised something for your whole life, when you have worked toward something all the way through your childhood, your teenage years, your college years . . . when you have no plan B . . . when you have no self-image outside of being the greatest athlete you can be . . . to have it snatched away from you is more than you can take.

I got to thinking that maybe I would be better off dead.

And the thought stayed with me.

It ate away at me, because I knew that at the moment I was nothing more that an unemployed drug addict, and the *shame* of that was unbearable. Nobody had a clue of how bad my addiction to painkillers was. If they had—oh Christ, it would have killed my mother, I'm sure. Her son, once so full of promise, now hiding away in an apartment in New York, washed up, his only comfort a five-hundred-strong collection of painkillers.

Better for her to have a dead son, one she could idealize and eulogize, than one whose very existence would be a constant source of disgrace to her. Better that I end it all now.

It was that thinking that led me to make the drive from New York to New Jersey. My parents were away and I wanted to be somewhere familiar. I didn't want someone breaking down my apartment door and finding a rotten, bloated mess on the bathroom floor. I at least wanted the dignity of leaving behind a good-looking corpse.

I made the long, solitary drive back to my parents' house to end it all. After pulling into the driveway and letting myself in, I watched TV for a while, barely able to concentrate. All I could do was turn the last year over and over in my head. Then, suddenly determined, I sat down and wrote a suicide note in a burst of inspiration. I had already taken thirty Vicodin and was halfway down on a bottle of Grey Goose. I was not scared. Taking one last look at the place, the home I grew up in, the home I had spent many glorious, carefree summers in, I emptied out the bottle of painkillers and shoved them, five at a time, into my mouth, knocking them back with great gulps from the bottle of vodka. I figured that an additional thirty Vicodin and the twenty Ambien I had on me should do the trick. When I had swallowed everything, I took another good solid hit from the booze, killing it. My guts gurgled and rumbled, ominously.

I didn't feel sad, or scared, or any of that.

I felt curiously blank.

It struck me just what a dull little scene suicide really was.

Then I went to my bedroom, lay down, closed my eyes, and waited to die.

10 GETTING CLEAN

THERE WAS A WHITE CHRISTMAS THAT YEAR IN New York, or so they said on the radio. But I was a long way from home, a long way from my family. I was a long way from anywhere.

I was writhing on a paper-thin hospital mattress, in the grip of violent opiate withdrawal. I would gladly have paid ten thousand dollars if it meant that I would get even an hour of sleep, but sleep was as unlikely an event in this place as finding some pills would be. There was no way to sneak any shit in. They checked everywhere, under the tongue of my sneakers, under my tongue, in my asshole. I hadn't slept in days, and my mind was driving me crazy, pushing me to the edge. I was soaking wet. The sweat smelled metallic, chemical.

As I groaned in despair the seventy-year-old guy who was rooming with me was loudly filling the communal toilet bowl with shit. So much for a white Christmas.

. Last week, when I had attempted to take my own life, I was saved—or so the doctors told me later—by my own body mass, and the incredible tolerance to prescription drugs I had built up over the last year. After I had drifted into the deepest, darkest sleep I have ever known, I did not expect to see the sunlight again. When its unwelcome rays started to drag me from the dark place I had put myself into, I did not feel relief. The coming consciousness I was experiencing was truly unwelcome. I opened my eyes, realized I was still alive, still in my childhood home, and just lay there groaning, wondering what it would take to end my misery. I had expected an easy end, and what I got instead was the most vicious hangover of my entire life. I got up, and vomited toxic-smelling goo from the pit of my stomach. The house was quiet. Nobody had even noticed my attempt on my own life. I picked up the suicide note, barely remembering what I had written. I started to read, and then slowly, methodically, tore the paper into dozens of tiny pieces.

I started to cry.

It hit home that I had indeed tried to kill myself. The worst part of it was, not only had I tried to kill myself but I had failed: My problems were all still here, and now I had the guilt of having to consider the heartbreak I almost inflicted upon my family. I wondered if I should try it again. In Charlotte, I had once tried to snort heroin. After I did it, I got sick, and spent the rest of the night throwing up violently before passing out around 3:00 A.M. I knew that one of my coke connections also sold heroin. If I bought enough from him, I could surely overdose, and this time not even my own body could cushion the drug's blow. In a daze, I washed my face and walked downstairs.

My sister-in-law, Monica, was in the kitchen. She said, "Would you like me to cook you some breakfast?"

"No, thank you, Monica. I have to go."

I left the house, and started the drive back to New York. I was crying most of the way over. I wanted to die, but the fact that I had survived my overdose made me wonder if this was not all part of some greater plan for me. Maybe my death would break up our family. Maybe my life was about to turn around. I just did not know if I had the will to stick around and find out. Distraught, I called Christian, and when he picked up, I started bawling like a child.

By the time I had made it to my apartment, Damian was already there. He obviously knew everything, that less than twenty-four hours ago his older brother had tried to take his own life. He hugged me, and it felt good. We just stood there, secure in each other's arms, and my body shook as I cried and cried.

I remembered an ex-girlfriend, long ago, telling me that her life was saved by a treatment center in Arizona called Sierra Tucson. Damian made the calls, and by that evening we were on a plane to Arizona. Driving to the airport I was speaking to the administrators over there, and they recommended that I keep taking my pills right up until I arrived in Arizona. I had already left them back at the apartment. It was too late to go back, and so I drank like a condemned man for the whole flight over. In the tiny, shuddering airplane toilet I vomited and shat viciously. Every time I thought I could get up, my guts would contract, and more toxic goo would explode from my body. I was drenched in sticky, vile-smelling perspiration. I threw down vodka after vodka in the hopes of getting drunk enough that I could ignore the screaming in my skull. My body burned, and then chilled to the bone at irregular intervals. Damian held my hand, and looked scared. A stewardess asked, "Is he all right?" and my brother said "Yes, he just gets panic attacks. You know, with flying." The stewardess smiled sympathetically, and said, "Don't worry. We have a very experienced pilot, and no turbulence. It's going to be fine." I nodded weakly, knowing that nothing would ever be fine again.

At the check-in I panicked. I knew that soon Damian would return to New Jersey and I would be alone. I did not know what to expect. I knew that it was going to be painful. I had not yet spoken to my parents, and knew that I would not be able to admit to them that I had tried to kill myself. I answered questions, filled out forms, and then gave my brother a long, terrified hug. It was late December, and the sterile offices were decked out with cheerful bunting, with a lone Christmas tree propped up in one corner.

Christmas 2002 was shaping up to be a pretty lousy experience all around. They told me that Sierra Tucson was one of the best facilities in the world for treating addiction. I suppose I was naïve. I went in there not knowing what to expect. I mean, even in my most guileless fantasies I didn't expect withdrawal from the amount of pain pills I had been doing to be anything close to painless, but after being put in a room with Stan, the aforementioned seventy-year-old detoxing from a lifetime of alcohol abuse, and another pale, sweating guy called Enrique, with nothing more than Librium, clonidine, an antidepressant, and some Advil for my troubles, I realized that this was going to be a tough time.

Enrique was rolling about on his bed, his hands clasping his guts, moaning in Spanish and asking for his mother. He had been delirious for the past fifteen hours, and he was driving me crazy. If I'd had the energy to get off of my bed, I would have gone over there and shoved a goddamned pillow over his face. Instead, I just lay there, mute and resigned in my misery, waiting for the sickness to pass.

Of course, when we talk about my roommates, we have to mention Mike.

Mike wasn't a junkie. Mike was technically medical staff, although whether he had a PhD or a GED, I don't know. Mike looked like the world's most pissed-off bouncer. He was paid to sit in a chair in the corner of the room to make sure that nobody died. Every so often, if Stan, Enrique, or I fell silent for too long, he'd yell over, "You still with me, boys?"

After my failed attempt on my own life, they had me pegged for a suicide risk. I suppose that they figured that Stan, the septuagenarian juicer, was about ready to pop off anytime now. As for Enrique, I don't know what his deal was, but he didn't sound too happy as he vomited and sweated and shat the dope out of his system. We were truly the sorriest-looking trio you could imagine.

I almost felt sorry for Mike. He didn't look like a man who was in love with his job. I started to wonder what path in life you take that would result in you being this guy. I wondered, was he a former drug addict himself, involved in some extreme form of aversion therapy? I mean, the air in that room was toxic. Toxic! I changed my clothes every few hours because they had soaked through. Nobody talked; everybody was resigned in his complete and utter misery.

Suddenly, I kicked the blankets clean off me. I was having extreme, involuntary muscle spasms pretty regularly now. Afterward my calves would ache like hell. Aw, Jesus, every part of my body was screaming out for drugs. After three days the symptoms seemed to peak, and it was only the fact that I was too ill to move that stopped me getting the fuck out of there. I started having crazy fantasies of somehow trying to get to Phoenix and making a connection for Oxycontin, but I knew that this was nothing more than fantasy. I wasn't a street-smart drug addict like the other guys here. Before he got too sick to talk, Enrique had boasted that he could walk into any city and score within the hour.

"You just gotta know what to look for. The right kinda neighborhoods. Make eye contact. You know when you see another fiend, man. It's all in the eyes. An' they spot you, like you're part of some big secret society or some shit like that. Like the fuckin' Masons!"

I knew Enrique was a heroin addict because of the needle marks on his arms. When I saw those needle marks I thought, "Well, shit, at least I'm not a heroin addict." However, once the withdrawals really started to kick in, the differences between Enrique and me were invisible.

In Sierra Tucson, I was assigned my own shrink. I didn't have an opinion either way on them before I started talking to them in this facility. After two weeks in the detox room, I was moved into the general population, and I more than made up for my previous lack of experience with psychiatrists. I saw more motherfucking headshrinkers during my stay there than is healthy for any sane human being.

I knew going into the place that I had problems.

I was addicted to painkillers.

I snorted way too much coke.

I had physical problems, and most of all I was as depressed as hell following my being let go by the Panthers. So, yeah, I had some stuff to deal with. A week after starting my therapy I started to suspect that maybe I'd been a genuine, foaming-at-the-mouth, certifiable nut job all along, and I just hadn't realized it up until now.

I mean those bastards had me diagnosed with *everything*.

When one doctor asked my about my physique, and started asking—I thought—pretty innocent questions about how I kept in shape, and I told him about some of the bingeing and bulking up that I would do in the NFL, he ticked a box and suddenly I was the proud owner of a brand spanking new eating disorder. I mean, me! A fucking eating disorder. Me and every other professional athlete in America, I guess. But I didn't want to be a cynic, and I didn't want to be a prick. I was here to get better. I was here to follow instruction and get my life back. So I nodded my head, and took what they said at face value. I had an eating disorder.

It wasn't so bad. Now I didn't have to line up in the cafeteria anymore. Also, nobody bitched at me when I went up for second helpings of lunch. I took pleasure in the meals there since there was little else to keep me entertained. Even with my plate piled high, sometimes a doctor would pass by and practically insist that I pile more bread on my plate. I guess they didn't want me wasting away.

Another surprising diagnosis had even odder consequences for me. Talking with one counselor about what I'd do when I was snorting coke (my answer basically amounted to "bang models and strippers"), I accidentally talked myself into being diagnosed with another condition: sex addiction. Yes, folks, I was not only was a junkie and a fuckup, now I was an anorexic nymphomaniac, too.

Again, this had some plusses. I got to skip out on some of the boring, regular AA meetings and attend a group just for the sex addicts. At first I may have doubtfully accepted what the doctors said, but after I sat through my first sex addicts meeting I knew that for a fact I was in the wrong place. Not to make light of other people's problems, but I was sitting there listening to a small, balding guy talk about how he found it impossible to get through a day at his office without sneaking off into the bathroom to masturbate at least six or seven times a day. Everybody was extremely serious, nodding in sympathy. I did my best not to smirk, and to hide my shock, but all I could think was: *What the fuck am I doing here?*

The final straw came when I was being drilled about my

childhood. This one doctor just could not accept that I had a great childhood. He kept bringing the question back to my upbringing and my parents. Though hearing that I had a mom and dad who always supported me, who loved me and made me feel loved at all times, well, it just didn't work with his particular diagnosis. His questions got more and more pointed, until he at last came out and asked me if I could ever remember a time that my father had beat me. Exasperated, I said, "Sure."

"Aha. Could you tell me about that, please? I mean, if it's not too . . . difficult for you."

"It's not difficult at all. I was ten years old and I wanted to stay over at a buddy's house."

"Uh-huh." He was taking furious notes.

"And my pop, he didn't want me to go."

"And how did that make you feel?"

"Well, it made me feel pissed off, Doctor."

The doctor was scribbling like a madman.

"So what happened next?"

"Well, I got a little pissed off and I started yelling and what not—and I . . ."

"Yes?"

"Well, I called my father a fucking asshole."

"OK. And then?"

I shrugged. "My father smacked the shit out of me. And quite rightly so."

The doctor was not listening anymore. He was scribbling, ticking boxes, and doing a bunch of other shit. I had given him all of the information he needed. Now he could go and make the diagnosis he had wanted to make from the moment I walked in.

Looking up, removing his glasses, and rubbing the bridge of his nose thoughtfully, the doctor asked: "Jason, have you ever been diagnosed with post-traumatic stress disorder?"

I laughed. "Isn't that something that veterans get? Like people who've lived through war and shit like that?"

"Well, yes, but it can be triggered by any traumatic event."

"You mean Pop hitting me? That event wasn't traumatic. I mean, I haven't thought about it in years."

"You probably internalized the trauma. It's quite common."

"But . . . I mean, I think he was kind of in the right. If I had a kid and he called me a fucking asshole I might do the same thing."

"Well, the abused becoming an abuser is often a part of the cycle."

"But—I mean—it wasn't abuse! I do not consider that abuse! And if I don't consider it abuse . . . How am I traumatized by it?"

The doctor smiled and said, "Jason, the mind is an incredibly complex . . . and mysterious thing."

"I guess it is."

It didn't take me long to figure out what the whole deal of these places is. They take a cookie-cutter view of addiction. Basically, we are all the same. The cokehead businessman, the painkiller-addicted professional athlete, the crack-smoking gang kid, and the shoplifting heroin addict. Basically, we are all the same. The reasons we use are the same, and the treatment is the same.

Which is all very nice, except for one major flaw: The whole concept is pretty much bullshit.

I knew what the twelve steps were. They have become so much a part of American culture that I knew there was such a thing as the twelve steps. But as for what the steps actually entailed, and how they were phrased, that came as something of a shock. Suddenly, a lot of people were talking to me about God. A "God of my understanding." They also were telling me that I needed to ask God to take my failings away.

The first time somebody dropped that bombshell on me, I took a while to process it.

"So what you're telling me is that I need to give my life over to God, and ask God to take away my addiction to painkillers?"

"A God of your understanding, yes."

"So this is like a religion? Like I have to convert?"

"No! Not at all! This is nothing like a religion! This is a treatment program."

"But the God thing—"

"Don't worry about God! You need to worry about your recovery."

Then I heard the standard line for anyone in a twelve-step program who asks too many questions, or questions the legitimacy of such an approach.

"This sounds an awful lot like a religion. I mean I can't believe I'm paying thirty thousand dollars to come here, and the best advice you can give me is to start praying."

"Jason, that's your disease talking."

I heard that same conversation stopper maybe a hundred times in the sixty days that I was in Sierra Tucson. I learned a whole bunch of other helpful catchphrases, all designed to help me through my recovery. I learned that *"one drink* (pill, line, whatever) *is too many, and a thousand is never enough"* (quite true, although a thousand pills would keep me happy for a month at least). I learned that *"Denial is not a river in Egypt"* (which was almost funny the first time I heard it, but rapidly lost its appeal as convert after convert, eyes wet with the zeal of the newly saved, repeated it as if it was their own, startlingly original thought). I learned that my ego was *"easing God out"* and I was urged to *"let go and let God," "keep it simple,"* and—of course— take it *"one day at a time."*

Sometimes I wanted to smash my head against the wall, rather than hear another one of those motherfucking catchphrases.

I learned that patients were like numbers in a place like Sierra Tucson. The first ten days I was in the dorms, I had a roommate called Patrick. He was a cool enough kid, around my age, who was in because he was an alcoholic and a drug addict. He seemed to be doing pretty good, was enthusiastic about the place and the work he was doing there. One morning he checked out, never said good-bye, and I had a new roommate by lunchtime.

I heard stories around the place that it could be incredibly hard to find a bed in a center like this, that treatment services are overextended in this country. Although I never had a problem finding a bed. Over the years I learned that doctors *like* to treat professional athletes. They like to probe us and find out what makes us tick. They want to find out about "the zone," the place that we get to mentally when we play professional sports. Since less than 1 percent of the U.S. population ever gets to play professional sports, I guess they relish the opportunity to pick our brains a little bit.

I was also ready to check out myself at this point. I knew that what the powers that be expected of me in this place—that I would check out and never take drugs again or drink again—was just not happening. I promised myself that I would not let myself get into the same mess that I had done with the pills before, but I knew that I would need them for basic pain control. I was not ready to give up booze or cocaine. Despite the fact that everyone—including my ex-roommate Patrick—would be at great pains to point out to me that I was an alcoholic whether I believed it or not, I disagreed. I still disagree, and this assertion is one that I will take with me to the grave.

I have never found that I could not get through the day without a drink of alcohol. I have never awakened craving alcohol. Once I was inside of Sierra Tucson, I was not freaking out that I couldn't get a cocktail. Sure, I wanted to take painkillers while I was sick, and I certainly was craving some cocaine, but my being cut off from booze was no worry at all. I had always had a pretty casual relationship with alcohol. It was always—and is still—a social thing for me. To deny myself a cocktail at the end of the day on principle seemed pretty self-defeating.

No, I decided, now that I had a little bit of time to clean up, get my strength back, and calm the fuck down, I would go back to a sensible level of recreational drug use, and that would be that. There seemed little point in staying at Sierra Tucson if I wasn't planning to stick to their program. So I started telling the staff that I was ready to leave.

Strangely enough, they didn't see it my way. I had to listen to them, because my insurance was paying for this. They told me that if I left before thirty days they would be obligated to say that I had left against medical advice and that would play havoc with my insurance program.

"That's blackmail!" I spat out.

"It's the way we do things. We want to give you the best possible chance with your recovery!"

"But I'm fine. I'm drug free."

"Your problem," they told me, "lies between your ears. The drugs are just a symptom."

At the center's—and my family's—insistence I reluctantly decided to stay the full thirty days.

My next roommate was a comedian from Los Angeles. He was wiry and hyper, and I knew that he must have been a cokehead before he ever opened his mouth to tell me. Joey would regale me with the greatest hits from his stand-up routines after lights out, and I would often be literally in tears of laughter. Joey told me that coke was a huge problem among comedians; it's like the comedians' drug. I guess that's not a big secret. I suppose coke is to comedians what painkillers are to athletes, weed is to college students, or heroin is to rock musicians.

After Joey moved in with me, at least I was having a good time when I was in my dorm room, but the rest of the time there was miserable. The problem with AA meetings, besides all of the God talk, is all of the drug talk. I mean, that's all that anybody talks about in those meetings. Getting high. Even though they're talking about it therapeutically, when you're trying to abstain from coke, the last thing you need to hear is some guy reminiscing about all of the 100 percent uncut Colombian blow he was snorting last month. I mean, it's like have a bunch of starving guys all sit in a circle talking about how delicious the last steak they ate was. It's fucking *cruel*.

Another guy I met in Sierra Tucson was David Rosenberg, a wealthy young cokehead who came from a family that was pretty much Hollywood royalty. We got on well, we had a lot in common—we were both successful young men, with access to money that allowed us to *really* fuck ourselves up on drugs, and we both shared the feeling that we didn't *belong* in this place. Whatever free time we had, we'd sneak off and talk. He was a football fanatic and was dying to get the inside scoop on what life was like in the NFL. I 'd seen a bunch of TV shows that he had produced and loved getting an insider's view of the television industry. I heard stories about many well-known celebrities that almost defied belief, and David would have me doubled over in laughter as he dished the dirt on them all.

"You know," he would say to me, "you should come to Hollywood."

"Nah, fuck that. I'm a sports guy. What the fuck would I do?"

"Shit, they'd eat you up. You're good-looking! You're a tough guy! TV would love you."

It was flattering to hear, but the idea seemed pretty far-fetched. I figured it would be one of those things that died a quick death, and that David and I would probably never speak again after we checked out. However, David would turn out to be someone I kept in touch with over the upcoming years, and someone that I would most definitely see again.

After thirty days, Sierra Tucson pulled the same shit on me again, and told me again that if I discharged myself that I would be leaving against medical advice. They told me that this was because I had spent so long in detox that I still hadn't completed a full pass of the program. That really soured my relationship with them. For the next thirty days, I had already checked out mentally. I was counting the days until I could sign myself out and get back to New York. As soon as the sixty-day mark came, my bags were packed and I left Arizona pissed off, but in better health than I had been in a long time.

I was ready to prove them wrong. When I got into JFK, I ordered a limo to take me to the apartment downtown. As I drove back into the sprawling chaos of the city, I felt all of the anger draining from me, and that familiar excitement building in my guts. I had learned my lesson: Never again would I treat opiates like they are a joke. No more pills than strictly necessary. Even as I thought that, I realized that I had quite a few of them stashed around my apartment. Now that I hadn't had any for almost three months, they would feel pretty damn good. And Jesus, my back was kinda achy after that flight.

Well, one night of behaving badly wouldn't be the end of the world, I figured. And then by the morning, I would be back to living it—what was it they said in Sierra Tucson?—*one day at a time.*

Yeah, I liked the sound of that.

THE DAY IT ALL FELL APART

11

OVER THE NEXT YEAR, MY LIFE SLID BACK INTO the same old patterns. In fact, after my first stint in rehab, my cocaine use got steadily worse. In the past my drug of choice had been the serene hum of opiate painkillers. After my stay in Sierra Tucson, and especially after the painful detoxification, I tried my best to keep my painkiller use under control. This marked the beginning of my first sustained obsession with cocaine use. My apartment in New York saw a nonstop parade of rich cokeheads, wannabe actresses, models, and drug dealers. My routine was that I would stay awake snorting coke for two or three nights straight, before my body would start to give out, my eyelids would feel like steel shutters, my sinuses ached like I had been shoving broken glass up my nostrils, and I would finally give up and sleep.

The next morning, I'd wake up with aching nostrils and a coke hangover. If I needed to give my nose a break, I would switch for a little while to painkillers. Mostly, for the whole time that I was awake, until the next time that I collapsed into bed unconscious, I would be snorting cocaine nonstop.

I knew that this could not continue forever. My family, an hour's drive away in New Jersey, had not seen me in months. For the most part I avoided even their phone calls. There was always a reason, the most common one being that I was too high to talk to them. If it wasn't that I was too high, it was that I was not high enough. First thing in the morning was no good, because before I had the energy boost of my first line of coke, I was depressed and anxious. In my fractured state of mind, I felt that talking to my brothers or my parents in that state would only cause them undue worry. Of course, within a few hours I would be literally vibrating with artificial energy, and on the odd occasions that I had picked up the phone in this state, I was increasingly aware that I had little or no control over what was coming out of my mouth, and frequently I would catch myself midsentence with no idea of what the fuck I was talking about, or indeed how long it had been since I last drew breath. The only people that seemed to be able to make sense of me when I was in this state were other cokeheads, all of us talking frantically at once about anything at all, a psychological compulsion to talk like machine guns, each of us sitting there, fidgeting, waiting for the others to shut the fuck up so we could continue to pummel them under an avalanche of garbled dialogue. Soon, I avoided picking up the phone when I was in this state as well. There would be a grace period early in the day, when I was just high enough to feel normal, where I would answer the phone if it rang, and assure my worried mother, father, brothers, and sister that I was fine and they had nothing whatsoever to worry about.

The day it all fell apart started like any other.

I saw the sun rise, as I often did, while snorting outrageously long and fat rails of cocaine in the apartment of a drug buddy over on the Upper West Side. The party had burned out some hours earlier, and by the early afternoon the place was in total disarray, and the only one left was Jason Peter, the king of purgatory, surrounded by all of his adornments: my razor, my mirror, and a pile of cocaine that probably represented a sizable chunk of the Colombian economy, and would have made Tony Montana green with envy. Even my host was now catatonic on the floor, with white powder caked to his nostrils and an empty champagne flute in his hand. On the TV, a music channel silently played an Eminem video, and outside the honking of traffic and wailing of sirens provided the only sound track.

I left at around three that afternoon and hailed a taxi, heading over to my place. I shoved a twenty into the driver's hand and stumbled out, the sunlight burning my eyes. I had already gone over in my mind whether to go to sleep or carry on: I had left a couple of eight-balls of cocaine stashed around the apartment, so I knew that sleep was probably not in the cards. I didn't even see them standing there, as I walked over to my door and slid the key in the lock.

"Jason?"

I jumped. My nerves were on edge from the cocaine and the lack of sleep. I turned, and to my horror I was presented with the unwelcome sight of Christian, Damian, and a childhood friend called Bruno. I knew immediately what this was. A goddamned intervention. This was terrible! A nightmare! I was coked out of my brain, I stank of booze and cigarettes, and all I could think of was getting up to the sanctuary of my apartment and hiding away from my family's judgmental eyes. Fuck!

"Oh, hey, guys," I said, my mind furiously calculating exit strategies. I said it as if I saw my brothers all of the time. In actuality I cannot remember the last time we had spoken face to face. I opened the door and walked in, and they followed in silence. I walked as slowly as possible, my brain turning furiously.

My apartment was on the second floor. I could think of no way to get rid of them. Then I thought about what they were about to see when I opened my door: the mirror on the coffee table, covered in coke residue, with the telltale razor blade sitting right out on top. The baggies, some empty, some still full of powder, lying all over the work surfaces. The pill bottles and the total disarray of a life in free fall. My heart began to pound, and gripped by panic, I ran. I bolted up the stairs ahead of them, shoved my key into the lock and barreled into my apartment, desperately trying to clean the place up in the thirty or so seconds before they made it to my door.

I knew that I must have looked like a madman, and that they knew that I was high as a fucking kite, but it didn't matter. If I could only conceal the physical evidence of my drug use, then they couldn't accuse me of shit! I grabbed that big old coke-covered mirror and tossed it into the sink, and started frantically grabbing at baggies of cocaine, shoving them into my pockets, breathless and hysterical. Then, trying to figure out a way of getting them all the fuck out of my place, I grabbed my cordless phone and tried to look nonchalant as they walked up to my door with quizzical expressions on their faces. I could feel toxic cocaine sweat dripping from my brow, soaking through my clothes, and stinging my eyes.

"Yes, yes," I said to the mute phone as they walked in, ushering them toward the couch with my best attempt at a genial expression. "This *is* Jason Peter. Uh-huh . . . yes . . . excuse me, could you just hold on for one second? Thank you!"

I nodded to the couch and covering the mouthpiece with one hand said, "Why don't you guys have a seat? I have to take this call. I'll be right back!" before I scuttled off to the bathroom where I had stored the eight-ball of coke I had been coming home to.

I locked the door and sat down on the toilet, terrified and defeated. My brothers hadn't said as much as two words to me so far, but I felt more accused and more betrayed than I ever had in my life! *What right had they to do this?* my mind demanded. I am a grown man! Who the fuck just shows up without so much as a phone call?

I shoveled some more coke onto my keys, and sucked it up into my protesting nostrils, masking the wheezing rattling *snoooorrrrttttttt!* by flushing the toilet at the same time.

I decided that there was only one way I could retain my dignity. I silently placed the phone on the bathroom floor, crept over to the door, and after slipping the drugs into my pockets I wrenched the door open and literally ran out of the room, straight past the three of them, and away from the apartment as fast as I could, leaving them sitting there with expressions on their faces pitched somewhere between incredulity and horror. I bounded down the stairs two at a time and fled headlong into the New York City streets.

I am not sure how long I wandered around for. Hours. I walked through the streets of the Lower East Side, cutting into bars and restaurants to use their bathrooms and shovel more and more cocaine into myself, in a desperate attempt to shut my mind off even for a second, but the peace I so desperately wanted wouldn't come.

It hurt! The thought that my brothers had come out to my apartment and had dragged Bruno here to use as emotional leverage. My kid brother, Damian! A guy whose ass I had wiped when he was too helpless to do it for himself! When he was truly destroyed by fate, crushed by circumstance! Back when it was I who was on the brink of a career, of a future. How that had turned around again? Now I was washed up, a football player who could no longer play football, a fucking has-been, not yet in his late twenties.

A drug addict.

I wasn't a drug addict! I just liked to get high. I wasn't like the assholes I saw in Narcotics Anonymous meetings, with missing teeth, and fucked-up veins, and legs removed from deep vein thrombosis. I wasn't a wreck reduced to living in his car, or on the streets, or begging for change to buy a bottle of Night Train! I was a millionaire! I liked to get high! So fucking what?

The night before, I got my prick sucked by a model I had seen on the cover of a glossy fashion magazine only three weeks ago. How in God's name could I be considered an addict? I was a success story. Who wouldn't give his right hand to swap places with me? I was living the American dream!

Now I was wandering the streets of the Lower East Side, too ashamed to look my own family in the eye, jumping into public bathrooms to snort more and more coke, hoping against hope that by the time I made it home they would have evaporated.

I couldn't think about it. The more I thought about it, no matter which way I tried to look at it, it always came back to the same thing:

I am hurting my family.

I love my family.

But I cannot stop doing cocaine, not even for my family's sake.

I am a drug addict.

The back and forth in my head lasted as long as the cocaine did. Then, defeated, I started to trudge back to the apartment. I slid my key into the lock and crept up the stairs. I listened outside the door. I couldn't hear anything. Maybe they had got bored and left. Anything was possible. I slid my key into the lock and opened the door.

They were still there.

I smiled sheepishly and entered the room, closing the door behind me. I threw my hands up and looked at the three of them, thinking that maybe I would see anger in their faces, but there was none.

"I'm sorry," I said, "I'm sorry. I'm really fucked up right now."

Christian smiled. "Yeah. We know. It's cool. Listen, Jason, we just want to help you. That's all. We're not here to judge you or any of that shit."

I waved them silent. I didn't want to hear it right now. I said, "Look, bro, I know. Things are fucked right now. I'm worse than I was before I went into the treatment center."

They came over to me and Damian placed an arm around my shoulder. I relaxed a little. There was nothing to do but give up to this. I had no way out, and I knew that what they were trying to do was for the best.

"You need to get out of the city for a while. You need a break."

"Yeah."

"Look, why don't you get some stuff together and come back to Jersey with us?"

I looked at Christian, and Damian and Bruno, and then back to Christian. I had nowhere to go.

"Sure," I said. "Why not?"

The drive back to New Jersey was long and silent. I started nodding out to the gentle hum of the car's engine, days of cocaine abuse catching up with me. I begged Christian not to take me to Mom and Dad's house. I couldn't bear for them to see me in this state. I looked like something from a cheesy zombie movie. Christian decided to take me to his house.

"You know," he told me as we pulled into the driveway, "I've got the number of a really good doctor I think you should talk to."

I woke out of my half sleep, and snorted, "You mean a shrink?"

Christian looked at me witheringly and said, "Yeah. I mean a shrink. He's a good guy."

At Christian's house, Monica came over to me with a concerned look on her face and gave me a long hug. I managed to mutter something to the effect that I was sorry to be such a bother to her. She laughed at me and told me not to be so stupid. I was an emotional wreck. I think we all were. Later, in the spare room, when sleep came, it was fitful, and full of troubled dreams.

The next day we tried to get hold of Christian's shrink, Dr. Deptford, but there were no appointments until the following day. Business must have been good, I thought. There's no shortage of crazy people in New Jersey. Christian dragged me along to an AA meeting to stop me moping around the house. I was out of cocaine, and I felt tired and anxious. Still, the painkillers helped a little. We drove over to a meeting in the basement of a Presbyterian church ten minutes or so from the house. Meetings vary from place to place. Depending on the neighborhood, you can have a bunch of ex-crackhead gang kids sharing stories of running around the city with guns, robbing people for drug money. On another side of town, it will be all elderly matron types sharing about hiding empty bottles of gin under the kitchen sink. This one was something in-between: a bunch of comfortable looking ex-boozers and druggies, now with big homes and families, and gleaming smiles, thanking God and the twelve steps for their newfound happiness.

Sitting at the back of the room, I wanted to spit on people.

I wanted to stand up and yell that this was bullshit.

That they're all just as dependent on AA as they once were on booze.

Fuck the world. Fuck all of 'em.

Then I'd look over to my brother, sitting through this ass-numbingly boring meeting, and I realized that he would sit through a thousand of these meetings for me, if he believed it would help me. And I knew that my brother loved me. So I kept my ass on the chair, my mouth clammed shut, and when the time came I stood in a circle with all of the other drunks and fuckups and recited that god-damned stupid prayer they were all so fond of: *Lord, grant me the serenity . . .*

The next day, at 11:00 A.M., I sat in Dr. Deptford's office, listening to his verdict.

"Jason," he told me, sitting back in his chair and removing his reading glasses, slipping them into a shirt pocket, "may I be frank with you?"

"Sure, go ahead."

"I think it's obvious that you need to go back to rehab. But I think your problems aren't going to be addressed in the kind of place you attended last time. Frankly, there are two kinds of rehabs, the country clubs, and the places where they make you work for your sobriety. Now you're a tough guy. You're an NFL football player! I think that you thrive on challenge, am I correct?"

"Sure. That's my job."

"Well, I think that your attending another rehab where they will mollycoddle you is frankly going to be counterproductive. You do want to get clean, correct?"

I cleared my throat, and looked over to Christian, who was sitting next to me. He had an expectant look on his face, so I answered, "Yes, of course."

"Well, in that case, I have just the place for you. How do you feel about Pennsylvania?"

12

TRY, TRY, AGAIN

HOW DID I FEEL ABOUT PENNSYLVANIA?

Not so fucking good.

I made arrangements to be picked up from my apartment early the next morning to make the drive. I wanted to straighten the apartment out, pick out enough clothes for a thirty-day stay, and get as high as I could in the meantime. The thing is, when I was crashing from coke and feeling vulnerable I may have been able to come around to my family's point of view that I was out of control and in need of help, but once I had a few nights sleep, food in my belly, and a bit of breathing space, well shit, I'd think, what's the problem? Over the past twelve months I had seen my very identity stripped from me. I was no longer a football player, could no longer be a football player. After I agreed to get help for my cocaine use, and was left alone with the aftermath of this decision, the fear began. If I submitted to treatment, indulged the doctors and the psychologists, started "working the steps" as everybody seemed so keen for me to do, would there be anything left of me at the end of it all? No football. No drugs. A life that would now revolve around AA meetings and sobriety. A vision of the perfect Jason, thrashed out between my family and the treatment center. A nice Jason, one who didn't misbehave or cause people undue worry. The idea terrified me, and I knew in my heart that I was not ready to get clean.

My dealer paid a visit and I prepared for my stint in rehab by snorting an eight-ball of cocaine and popping a bunch of pills. The more cocaine I put into myself, the more of the "real" Jason I was trying to cement within myself. I couldn't articulate it properly at the time, but the idea of submitting to treatment was sparking an identity crisis that would make it impossible for me to accept treatment. I made sure to stash an extra couple of eight-balls in the apartment for my return. I figured if I came out of rehab a changed man, full of the joys of fucking spring, I could always flush the coke. Otherwise I would probably be fiending for some so bad that I wouldn't want the delay of having to wait for my connection to drive the shit out to me.

After the shit, vomit, and sweat-stained nightmare that was the detox unit in Arizona, I decided to take some medication along with me. Although out of fear of another brutal detoxification I hadn't been taking as many pills as I had prior to my first trip into rehab, I was sure that I would have some kind of withdrawal symptoms, and I wasn't intending to do it cold turkey. Under the tongue of my left shoe I taped twenty Vicodin, and under the tongue of my right I taped ten Ambien. I wasn't about to be caught out again.

So the next morning an old guy who introduced himself as Dave arrived to take me to Marworth Treatment Center. I had been snorting so much coke that my sinuses were giving me real trouble. On the drive to Pennsylvania I think I freaked Dave out a little, who seemed to be a nice, well-meaning sort of a guy. It was virtually impossible to get any air through my swollen, painful nostrils, and I huffed and snorted in annoyance the whole ride over. Dave looked over uneasily to me as the snorts and the sniffles took on various frenzied pitches and tonalities, and every so often I would hiss "Mother*fucker!*" in exasperation. Dave, unsurprisingly, didn't say much in return.

As we approached Marworth, I got the impression that the place was not going to be so bad. With Dr. Deptford's warnings that I needed to experience a tougher rehab ringing in my ears, I expected the worst. Driving up the hill to this leafy, countryside retreat, I thought that maybe I had gotten this place all wrong. The building itself was an old-fashioned sandblasted stone exterior, that looked a little like a country mansion. There was something quaint about it, down to the white wooden door, and the medieval turret that sat at one corner of the building.

However, as soon as I walked inside Marworth, the atmosphere was different. Even though the outside of the building had a charming, woodsy feel to it, the inside was Spartan and institutional. The air smelled of bleach, not quite masking the faint odor of vomit and boiled potatoes. The furnishings put me in mind of an old people's home, with seats covered in garish flower prints, and an ugly oil painting of a stern-looking man in a doctor's robe hanging on one wall. The patients looked different, too: These weren't the pampered sons and daughters of the elite or rotund businessmen here to take a break from their insane work schedules as much as to clean up from drugs or alcohol. The men and women here were mostly lost souls whose faces had been hardened by years of tough living. Their bodies were eaten away by years of poverty and drug abuse. There were a number of teenage girls milling about the place with fucked-up teeth and skin raw and picked away by methamphetamine use.

I had to do the typical treatment center check-in, where the counselor ran down a list of drugs and I had to answer "never," "occasionally," "regularly," or "daily." It started off with fairly benign, ludicrous shit like "cough syrup"—I mean, who gets high from cough syrup anymore?—to the old favorites like cocaine, meth, and heroin (and, funny to think of it in retrospect, I fairly bristled with indignation when he said heroin, as if to say, "Do I, sir, look like a *heroin addict* to you?") and then stuff that I thought went out with bell-bottoms and disco, like PCP and Quaaludes.

The deal was that I was to remain in the medical wing until my detox was completed, before I could be moved over to the general living quarters. The first thing that struck me about the place was how many petty rules it had. The first one, and one that a few other staff members were at great pains to point out to me, was: "No consorting with the opposite sex."

At first, I figured that consorting was some kind of euphemism for fucking. Like, "Please do not have sex with other patients." No, they meant no talking, no contact, period. I asked the guy who checked me in, "So if I hold a door open for a female and she says, 'Thank you,' does that constitute a violation of the rules?"

"Absolutely."

"And she could get into trouble?"

"Technically she could be asked to leave the facility. Frankly, Jason, if she's been able to support a dope habit without no man to help her all this time, she don't need you opening no doors for her now. I'd keep my mind off of chivalry, and keep it on recovery."

Aside from rules regarding the patients communicating, there were also many others. The dress code seemed particularly moronic, banning "music-related T-shirts" and "sandals without a strap in the back."

Despite the warnings that this rehab didn't take any bullshit, when my bag and my person were searched, the pills in my shoes were not discovered. Sneaking the pills in was a no-brainer. You get a free pass in a place like this, especially one that follows the "addiction as disease" model. It's almost like they expect you to do sneaky shit when you're coming in off of the streets. They are so quick to blame everything that has gone wrong in your life on this mysterious "disease," so why not take advantage of their gullibility? If I got busted with the pills, my defense would have been to simply throw up my hands and tell them that the *disease* made me do it.

After I was assigned a room in the medical center, I was given my medication—a pill to regulate my blood pressure and an antianxiety tablet. They served as nothing more than tokens. There are no drugs that ease opiate withdrawal to any significant degree, apart from—of course—more opiates. I would be dosed again in the evening with something to help me sleep. I slipped four Vicodin from my shoe and swallowed them as well. Then I was escorted to the dining room.

There was anger in the air. The entire population of the facility was standing in line, pissed and testy, checking their watches and clearing their throats. Looking down the line I could see the canteen staff stood in position, but nobody was moving. After a few minutes of this I tapped the shoulder of the guy in front of me.

"Hey," I asked, "what's going on?"

"Nothin'. We're just waiting for someone."

"Who?"

"Someone ain't in line. So we're waiting."

I fell back into silence for a moment. More time passed. The mood in the line was starting to get ugly. My mood was starting to get ugly. It wasn't so much that I was hungry, but I didn't like being made to stand around like a dick for no good reason. I tapped the guy on the shoulder again.

"Why do we have to wait for this person to get in line?"

"That's the rule."

"What's the rule?"

The guy sighed, finally realizing that he was dealing with a newbie. Then, in a tone of voice that suggested that he had to go through this—and explain this to some unsuspecting new person—on a regular basis, he said, "Nobody eats until everybody is in line. That's the rule."

As he explained this, the straggler, a bewildered guy with gray hair and prison tattoos, ran to join the line, yelling, "Sorry! Sorry!" and a few people yelled, "Asshole!" or jeered at him. The guy raised his palms and screamed "I was taking a *shit,* goddamn it! I can't even take a shit in this fuckin' place?" eliciting giggles from the line as it finally lurched into action. We shuffled forward, and when it was my turn, a sweaty man wearing a hairnet shoveled some unappetizing goop onto my plate.

"Yuh want dessert?" he asked, nodding toward a vile blob of what I supposed might have once been apple pie.

"No, thanks."

I was sitting eating lunch when it started. A few guys approached me, and I knew instantly from the way they introduced themselves and sat down that they were football fans. "Hey, aren't you Jason Peter?" I was happy to sit down and talk to them, even sign a few autographs, but I started to get the uncomfortable feeling that my privacy in this place could be compromised. The very idea of it sent a chill down my spine.

I suppose there was some part of my mind that hadn't given up the hope that one day I would wake up miraculously healed, that somehow everything that was wrong with my spine, my neck, my shoulders, would right itself and I would be able to call the Panthers and they would welcome me back with open arms. I knew that this was a remote possibility, but I had to cling to this fantasy to keep my sanity. Without my career as a football player, the terrifying truth was that I had no real identity any more. The nearest I had was Jason Peter, party animal, defiler of pretty women, and cocaine king of New York, but as gung ho as I felt about this persona at three in the morning while I was high out of my mind, it didn't sit well with me in my rare, quiet, reflective moments. Then the thought was so un-comfortable that I couldn't allow myself to dwell on it. There's nothing worse than some sad fuck in his twilight years snorting blow and chasing skirt as if he is in his mid-twenties. I knew that the Jason Peter who was in charge right now couldn't last forever, but with no idea of who would replace him, I felt I had no other option than to snort more drugs and think about it at some unspecified fu-ture date. Instead of worrying about that here, I focused on the fact that my cover could be blown in this place, scuppering any chances of my glorious return to professional football. I smiled, signed the autographs, and told a few anecdotes, the whole time plotting my es-cape.

I stayed for five days in all. The entire time I was there, I was in the medical wing undergoing my "detox." As I didn't have much of an opiate habit at this point, the detox was all about my cocaine use. But a cocaine detox is really nothing. There is no physical depend-ence when you use cocaine, like there is with alcohol or opiates. All that most coke users need to do is catch up on the sleep that they lost while they were getting high. Of course, there are psychological cravings, but once you are removed from sources of cocaine they become abstract and hopeless, as if you are craving a holiday in Jamaica but you do not have the means to get it. I looked upon the detox as nothing more than a chance to sleep, and get stoned on pain-killers.

I would have stayed zoned out on pills and sleep except for a bit of gossip on the junkie grapevine that I overheard one lunchtime. The junkies and drunks in there acted like a bunch of gossipy old women when they got together, and the first rumor I heard was that Heidi Klum had checked in the day before me. I knew that they had to be wrong about that: I mean, why would Heidi Klum check into a place like this unless she was a masochist, or she had done so at the insistence of a sadist doctor who thought that she needed to try a "tough" rehab? I started asking around and this rumor was indeed false, but there was a beautiful European model in the building, also sequestered in the medical wing to undergo a detoxification. I discovered that her name was Katrina, and her presence immediately became my sole point of interest in the place. I'd see her ghosting around the halls; she had a classically beautiful face, was willowy and blond, with pale blue eyes and full lips. She had a face and a body that seemed to have come straight from the cover of *Vogue* or *Harper's Bazaar*. Her presence was as weird as seeing an original Van Gogh hanging in a Denny's. I really didn't give a fuck whether the staff approved of my consorting with female patients, but out of respect for her, I didn't brazenly walk up to her to introduce myself. However, over the next few days we established something of a non-verbal relationship as we prowled around each other in the medical wing.

We made lingering eye contact a few times. She would glance over at me, and her lips would betray the slightest traces of a smile. She caught me staring at her once as I waited for my medication, and when she looked up, I glanced away quickly. I looked back a moment later and met her gaze. Her eyes widened and I nodded. I knew that I really needed to speak with this beautiful woman. I knew that by tomorrow or the next day I would be out of the medical wing and in the regular part of the center, being forced to attend daily AA meetings and therapy. I had no intention of staying that long. Soon my only reason for lingering at Marworth was so that I would have the chance to talk to this drop-dead gorgeous blonde who was looking my way with obvious interest. On one of the rare days that the prying eyes of the staff were not on us, we ran into each other in the hallway and I managed to whisper, "Hey, I'm Jason."

"Hi, Jason. I'm Katrina."

She held out her hand and I took it, for the briefest of moments. Her skin was soft and it took all of my self-control not to linger too long on it.

"What do you think of this place?"

Katrina smirked and stuck out her tongue, wrinkling her nose.

I smiled. "No kidding. You from New York?"

"Uh-huh. You?"

"Yeah! Listen . . . I think I have to leave soon. I'm going to check into another place, but—"

A door opened and we jumped apart. I pretended to look at a notice taped to the wall about a patient softball team as a staff member walked past. When I looked around, Katrina was gone. I spent most of that evening in my bed fantasizing about us absconding from Marworth and maybe flying out to Fiji to battle our demons the civilized way: by lying on the perfect white sand, drinking mojitos and watching the sun set over the crystal blue water.

The next day I was shaken out of my fantasies. I went to my first AA meeting, before being moved over into my new room. The meeting was an hour long, but felt at least three times that. It took place in a basement room without any natural light. I sat in a circle with about twenty other drug addicts. The room was cold, the electric-blue carpet threadbare, and the place had the faint whiff of mothballs. The chair of the meeting was an alcoholic who gleefully related the fact that he often drank bottles of mouthwash to clear up his delirium tremens when the liquor store was shut. The blood vessels had ruptured all over his face, and his nose was grotesquely enlarged and misshapen. He looked like a cartoon image of a barfly.

I sat there in silence, listening to women talk about leaving their infants unattended for days while they smoked crystal meth and whored to raise drug money. One guy was all twisted up in a wheelchair because he had nodded out on heroin while sitting on the edge of a garbage dumpster. He fell back into it and snapped his neck when he landed. I sat there on the hard plastic seat, listening to this parade of misery, steadfastly refusing to raise my hand to share. What was I going to say in this situation?

"Hi, my name is Jason Peter and I am an addict. I'm here because I have a ten-thousand-dollar-a-week cocaine habit which has spiraled out of control since my career as a professional footballer ended."

I don't fucking think so. With everybody seemingly determined to outdo themselves with tales of poverty, degradation, and despair I knew that I did not fit in here, and there was no way on God's earth that I was going to stay for another four weeks. Afterward, when I was introduced to my new roommate, my decision was already made. I knew there would be no turning back when my roomie looked over to me and nodded in recognition.

"Howdy!" he grinned, sticking out his hand for me to shake. "I saw you in the meeting earlier!"

Yes, they had decided to shack me up with the guy who drank mouthwash. I gathered my belongings and began the process of checking myself out of Marworth.

It wasn't my intention to drop out of treatment. I figured that I just needed to check into a place that would suit my needs better. I decided that I would go back to New York, hang out for a week or so, and then check myself in somewhere else. Since I was the one who checked myself into Marworth and paid the bill, my family would not be notified when I left. As long as I made it into another facility at the end of the week and called them from there, I knew that everything would be OK. All my mother and father wanted to know was that I was safe and not getting high. If I was going to have to deal with all of this happy-clappy neoreligious recovery shit, I decided that I was at least going to do it in comfort. Having to stand on line to eat crappy hamburgers on top of all of the usual pseudoscience that goes on in treatment centers seemed like one indignity too far.

Before I left I wrote a note for Katrina, and slipped it under her door. I kept it brief, but ended it with my phone number and my address in New York. Praying that she would get it before a snooping cleaner discovered it, I left Marworth and began the journey back to New York. I focused on the two eight-balls I had stashed at the apartment before I left, and the whole way there I felt a giddy excitement in the pit of my stomach at the thought of how great the cocaine was going to feel now that I had been clean for four days. There are a lot of clichés in recovery, but one of them that holds true is the fact that knowing you are about to get high is as big a rush as getting high itself. Maybe more so.

Back in New York, I was at a party with a bunch of my cocaine buddies, when my cell phone rang into life. It had been four days since I checked out of Marworth and I was no closer to checking into another rehab than the day I left. I'd keep thinking to myself "just one more day and I'll check in," and the days passed in a blur of cocaine. I looked at the name and laughed when I saw that it was Randal Davis, a coke-fiend Hollywood real estate mogul I had befriended back in Sierra Tucson. I bent over the table, snorted a huge line of blow, and excused myself from the party to take the call.

"Randal!"

"Jason, you crazy motherfucker! What the fuck's going on?"

I started telling him a fairy story about how things were *great* and I was doing just *fantastic* since getting out of rehab, and how I had a bunch of *wonderful* things going on in my life. Randal interrupted me (with some difficulty, as I was wired and talking a mile a minute) and laughed. "You're high as hell right now, aren't you?"

I considered lying, but I knew that there was no kidding a kidder. Randal was a prodigious cokehead, and for me to try to bullshit my way past him on this would have been insulting to both of us.

"Randal, I'm at a party and I have been doing blow for the past three days straight. I'm a fucking mess. How are you?"

"I'm good, baby!"

"You clean? You're telling me Sierra Tucson actually worked?"

"Yeah," Randal told me sincerely, before pausing dramatically and yelling, "*For six fuckin' hours!* Then I was back at it, baby, worse than ever!"'

"Shit," I laughed, "this stuff is crazy. I dunno if this rehab shit is worth it. So you're using, too?"

"No. I'm clean and serene . . . I'm actually in a place right now. Hey, Jason, hold on."

I heard Randal hold the phone away from him, and he slowly, lasciviously wolf whistled and yelled, "*Yeah, baby! GodDAMN!*" then he was back on the phone whispering to me: "Jason, I'm in Utah. Fucking *Utah!* This place is called Cirque Lodge, and I am telling you they have got these fuckin' Mormon chicks working here, with hot bodies like you wouldn't fuckin' believe! This place is like a fuckin' wet dream!"

Suddenly I was listening.

"Really? They're that hot?"

"White hot! Unbelievably hot! Who knew that Mormons were hot? Why did nobody tell me this before?"

"And how's the place itself? A drag?"

"It's great! It's beautiful here. They have horses! I'm riding fucking horses over here. Can you believe that shit?"

"They make you do meetings? 'Cos I'm telling you, I'm over that fucking mumbo jumbo. It ain't for me."

"Yeah, they got meetings, but only one a day. They don't shove it down your throat here. Jason, this place is great. I was just sitting here, thinking of you, wondering how you were doing. I was thinking about how you'd be getting these Mormon girls worried!"

I looked around by the telephone, and grabbed a pen and paper.

"Shit, Randal, you ain't gonna believe this, but I need to check into a fuckin place pronto before my family figures out I'm not in Pennsylvania no more! What did you say this place is called?"

"Cirque—like circle. It's French, or some shit. C-I-R-Q-U-E lodge. Like those fuckers with the funny hats. Cirque Lodge. I can arrange everything for you, man. All you gotta do is say yes."

That was how, by the following day, I found myself on a plane to Utah. When they called as Randal promised, they seemed eager to have me check in. They told me that the program was based in two buildings, the Lodge and the Studio. The Lodge was your more typical twenty-eight-day type of place. This was where people moved into when they were coming in from an extended period of drug use. Your crash course in recovery, introduction to the AA concept, all of that jazz. The Studio was the extended-care facility where the rules were more relaxed, and the focus was more on helping you to readjust into society than trying to help you have a spiritual awakening. I told them that having just come out of Marworth, and having previously spent an extended period at another treatment center, I really would prefer to be in the Studio. They agreed, and I packed my bags.

To add to the surreal vibes, the Sundance film festival was opening that same weekend, so my plane was packed with movie people. My nose was all fucked up from the cocaine I had been doing, and I was huffing and puffing trying to clear it out practically the whole way there. Spike Lee, who happened to be sitting right in front to me on the flight, was getting pissed off. He kept giving me dirty looks every time I tried to dislodge the caked, bloody mucus I had up there. I was in no mood to be antagonized: I was crashing hard from all of the blow I had been doing over the last few days, and I glared back at him radiating malevolent fuck-you vibes for the whole flight. I prayed he didn't say anything to me, because my psyche was so fractured that I might have attacked him then and there. I grimly chuckled to think of the potential headlines: NFL PLAYER

ATTACKS INTERNATIONALLY RENOWNED MOVIE DIRECTOR ON FLIGHT TO UTAH. EXCESSIVE MUCUS THOUGHT TO BE THE CAUSE OF AFFRAY.

Arriving in Cirque Lodge, Utah, for my second attempt at getting my addiction under control, I was struck by the scale of the place. The building was a huge imposing thing, tucked well away from prying eyes, and guarded by vast wrought iron gates. It was surrounded by acres of green fields, and the air felt so clean, so pure, that it hurt my New York City lungs. The craziest thing about the place, though, was the women. Randal was not exaggerating in that the staff was almost entirely made up of these smoking-hot Mormon girls. It was mindboggling. There they were, manning the reception desk, pushing the food cart around, offering sympathy, empathy, and all kinds of comfort apart from the kind that I really wanted from them.

After the first few days there, I started to toy with the idea that this was the whole hidden agenda of the place. Sure, they hid behind the notion that they were a twelve step–based rehabilitation like so many others in this great, superstitious, and religiously inclined nation, but I began to see the beautiful women as a kind of psychological lure toward sobriety. They seemed to be saying with their sparkling eyes, their full, plump lips, "*Come over to the other side. See what we have to offer. Put down the pipe. Forget about the needle! This is where the action is!*"

I'd imagine them riding the horses that they kept around the place, hot, taut asses firmly encased in clinging jodhpurs, riding crop tapping suggestively against their perfect legs, in soft-focus slow motion, like some perfume ad or soft porn flick from the seventies.

Join us . . .
Join the ranks of the sober . . .
The happy . . .
The liberated . . .

I fantasized that maybe at the end of my stay here, instead of collecting a Certificate of Completion, being confronted with the forced joviality of a "roast" by the staff and inmates, or being sent away with a sobriety chip made of gold that turns green after a few months as is often the tradition in these places, instead I'd be presented with the Mormon girl of my choice, maybe a horse, too, and a little tumbledown farm for us to live out our days with the cry of "One day at a time. Now go forth, and procreate!" ringing in our ears.

My first impressions of the place were so positive, that I immediately paid for a month up front. I would spend fifty days in Cirque Lodge, and they proved to be some of the most pleasant and productive times that I spent in treatment.

Despite Randal's jokes about the place, as well as having gorgeous women working there, I also discovered that they had a very well-thought-out program. The first big difference between Cirque Lodge and Sierra Tuscon was their attitude toward my addiction; they didn't seem to be there to diagnose me with every ailment, hang-up, psychosis, and addictive disorder under the sun. The focus was on keeping me off drugs, and trying to teach me another way to live.

The way they did this was not by keeping me to such a rigid timetable that I didn't have the time to think about getting high, as was the philosophy in my earlier treatment centers, but rather to expose me to and help develop my interests in other activities besides getting high. I think that a huge problem with many treatment centers is that they plan out their client's days down to the last minute. From 6:00 A.M. until 11:00 P.M. you are in meetings, group therapy, cleaning, talking, or whatever. You barely have time to take a shit. It does help in the short term because your entire focus becomes the schedule rather than your nagging urges to go get wasted, but once you leave a place like that, each day looms before you like an unclimbable wall: How the fuck do you fill the hours between waking and sleeping now? You would have to literally go to an AA meeting at 9:00 A.M., and keep attending meetings until midnight to replicate that intense schedule. Frankly, getting high passes the time in a much more enjoyable fashion.

Shortly after arriving in Cirque Lodge I called my parents, and after they got over the shock that I was calling them from Utah instead of Pennsylvania, they relaxed. Especially when I told them how much I liked the facility and the staff. After my relapse following my trip to Arizona, I guess they now had a more guarded view of the benefits of treatment. Now that I was inside they were happy. I'm sure that they would have been overjoyed if I could have stayed inside of drug rehab forever, locked far from temptation.

I checked into the Studio, and Randal gave me a great big bear hug the first time he saw me. He delighted in showing me around the place, which also happened to be where many episodes of *The Osmonds* were filmed.

"And now," he cackled, "it's full of dope fiends and drunks! Funny, right?"

There is a belief in most treatment centers that we are all the same, and the only commonality that we really share is our addiction. I don't agree with that. At Cirque Lodge I felt within my element. The place was filled with young, professional people. It was so pronounced that sometimes when an older person would check in, they would often quickly transfer, realizing that the place wasn't for them. I think that when you are undergoing treatment it helps you to be among your peers. The single AA meeting that we had to attend each day was actually pretty good, because at least I could relate to the stories I heard. As a flip side to the many positive things I heard in the meetings, it was also in these meetings that I heard repeated stories of something called speedballing. When drug users get together, they talk about drugs. It's perfectly natural. Especially when they are away from the drugs that constitute such an important part of their lives.

After meetings, especially when I'd share my story, oftentimes somebody would come up to talk.

"Shit, Jason, that's a crazy story. So you like coke, huh? Me, too. How are you coping in here so far?"

"OK. Good, I guess. This place is better than some of the places I've been in."

"I hear ya. Been in some shitholes, too. You do H?"

"What? Heroin? No. I did it once, threw up."

"Wow, you probably just did too much. There's no feeling in the world better than coke and smack together."

We'd lapse into silence, as I turned the information over in my head.

"I didn't think they'd go so good together. You know, an upper and a downer."

Then the guy I was talking to, he'd get that dreamy look in his eye that addicts get when recollecting a particularly debauched night and his chest would swell with nostalgia and he'd say something like, "I know. It shouldn't work, but somehow it does. First time I speed-balled, man, it was better than *sex!* I'll tell you, I never did coke on its own after that."

We'd walk away from each other, and I'd have that awful fluttery feeling in my stomach that signified the cravings were particularly bad. Despite remembering that night in Charlotte I spent throwing up after snorting a line of heroin, a part of me had to wonder. Many people in here talked about speedballing in the same way one might talk about the great love of your life. It would take all of my self-control to pull my thoughts away from getting high after one of those conversations.

Pain control was a real issue for me, and I knew that I didn't want to get into the same mess that I had slipped into with pain pills after leaving the Panthers. So as part of my recovery, I was introduced to yoga and Pilates. I was a little skeptical at first, it sounded a bit new age for me, but once my teacher explained the science behind it, I gave it my all, and I started to really enjoy it. I threw myself into it, and the other physical activities that were available to me at the center: rock climbing, rope work, and hiking. The natural environment was so beautiful there, although I shied away from pseudoreligious terms such as "spiritual awakenings" that the program espoused, and there were points, high above the ground, looking down from a distant and silent vantage point at the unspoiled beauty below me—the lush green vegetation, the trees stirring in the mountain breeze, and the only sound the caws of distant birds and the serene rhythm of my own breath—when I would start to remember who I was before it all started, before the early adoration of college football, the training camps, the NFL, the injuries, and the drugs. I would feel one with the environment around me, my body would fleetingly produce a kind of natural high, and I would momentarily be able to envision a life without painkillers and cocaine. I started to allow myself to believe that somehow, this time, I was going to be OK.

I would talk to my counselor, Mike, about these feelings. I met with Mike regularly, and enjoyed every conversation I had with him. Mike was an ex-addict himself, and he talked to me with a laconic, knowing voice. When I would tell him that I was feeling good, that I really felt that I could beat my addiction this time, he would smile and nod before striking a note of caution.

"What you are feeling is real. But you have to remember that you may not feel like this tomorrow. Recovery is a long process. Taking it one day at time—as the old cliché goes—is your best bet right now. You don't need to weigh yourself down with thoughts of how you're going to be doing tomorrow or the day after. Now is the time to live in the moment."

Mike had a brother who played professional baseball, and so I think he took a real interest in me. He understood the unique set of challenges and pressures that professional sportsmen face. But more than anything, Mike was a friendly, nonjudgmental face that I could come to and talk about anything that was on my mind.

In one of the most meaningful experiences I had in Cirque Lodge, I participated in "breaking" a wild horse. Each patient could choose a particular horse and that would be the one they worked with for the next three weeks. I picked my horse, a huge brown stallion that at first snorted and stamped and looked antsy whenever I was around him. The process of breaking the horse would be a painstakingly slow one. Three times a week I would get time with the steed (supervised, since those horses could do some serious damage if they kicked you). At first, the horses trusted no one.

In much the same way that I came into treatment wanting to beat the piss out of my addiction, I came into the breaking of the horse wanting to shoot the odds and have the horse under control in record time. Of course, the horse had other ideas. It would not respond to anything I did. The first session was incredibly disheartening. Every time I tried to approach the animal, it bolted. I tried to creep toward it, but no dice. I tried to stand still radiating goodwill toward the horse, but it wasn't interested. I tried to walk toward it fearlessly in the hope of bending it to my will, but the horse would not even acknowledge me. After the first session I walked away asking the trainer if it was possible that I would never break the horse.

"Of course. That is a very real possibility."

"What do I need to do to break it? That fucking animal doesn't want anything to do with me!"

"All you have to do is be patient and follow instruction."

I nodded, waved, and started making my way back to the Studio. The trainer called out after me: "Be patient and follow instruction!"

Over the next few weeks those words became a mantra of sorts. Often it felt as if nothing was happening. I became disheartened. Sometimes, when I was along in my room in the Studio, flicking through the Big Book of Alcoholics Anonymous, I'd find my mind drifting back to that intransigent horse. I had seen people, after weeks of trying, finally being able to mount their horse, or even have the horse eat from their hands. That seemed as unlikely to happen with my horse as the idea that he might tap-dance or burst into song.

The change in the horse happened slowly. The delayed, gradual gratification of watching the horse slowly bend to my will was another world from the instantaneous rush of drugs that constituted my life up until this point. Slowly the horse began to allow me to approach it. Sometimes we'd stand perfectly still, regarding each other. If I broke the deal, and attempted to move even a fraction of an inch closer, the animal would snort and move away from me. I could sympathize with this animal that trusted no one. That was how I came into both Marworth and to an extent Cirque Lodge. I thought that these places had nothing to show me. Seeing that even this wild animal could learn to eventually trust me, I decided to reciprocate and try to trust in the process of recovery.

"Be patient, and follow instruction."

I followed instruction, both out in the field with my horse, and in the twelve-step meeting rooms. I skimmed the Big Book of Alcoholics Anonymous. I suspended my disbelief, tried not to roll my eyes at all the talk of God and spirituality and higher powers. I decided to try to do it their way.

When the time came that I was able to ride the horse, it was an incredible feeling. I felt a bond with that animal that I never imagined was possible. I was even able to lie the horse on its side, and then lie down on top of it. The trainer was close at hand, but there was no need: The animal remained calm and we lay there, silently. I listening to the rhythmic, steady breathing of the horse, perfectly calm, centered, and peaceful.

I completed fifty days at Cirque Lodge and felt totally equipped to battle my addiction. I'd had my car shipped to the Lodge so that I would be able to drive from Utah. I had decided to drive to Los Angeles to visit my old friend from Sierra Tucson, David Rosenberg. Back when I was in Arizona, David had made a big deal of the fact that he thought I should be in the movies. It was not as crazy an idea as it sounded, as David came from a very well-respected moviemaking family in Hollywood and had the connections to make stuff like that happen. We had been in touch throughout my stay at Cirque Lodge, and David had been urging me to pay LA a visit. Since getting clean, he had been getting into a real health kick and was asking for my assistance in helping him train and work out.

"It'll be great!" he insisted. "I'll get you some auditions, introduce you to some people, we can hit the gym, and you can help me get rid of this goddamned gut I've been carrying around!"

After my successes at Cirque Lodge, I felt that a change of scenery would be a good thing for me. I needed somewhere new to put my focus, and maybe David was right—maybe the entertainment industry was the way to go. I waved goodbye to my new friends, and left Cirque Lodge and treatment behind. Randal had completed his treatment a few weeks ago and we had said goodbye then. Now my counselor Mike embraced me warmly.

"It's been great, Mike, thank you so much for everything."

"That's all right, Jason. You just remember—one day at a time. You hear me?"

"I hear you."

"And when you get to LA, run—don't walk—to your first meeting. We have many friends on the West Coast. And if you ever need to talk . . ."

I took his card and slipped it into my pocket. We shook hands; I got into my car and pulled away. I felt stronger, more centered than I ever had. On the passenger seat I had my own copy of the Big Book, which Mike had urged me to keep close to hand. I turned on the radio, and started toward California. I had a long road ahead of me.

Five hours into my journey to California, I started seeing signs for Vegas. I ignored it the first time. But already I'd had the thought: *Wouldn't it be cool to stop off in Vegas?* I looked over to the copy of the Big Book that sat on the seat. It seemed to be looking back at me reproachfully. Chastened, I fixed my eyes on the road and carried on driving.

The next time I saw the sign, I was already considering the possibility of stopping off for a few hours, maybe gambling a little. No drinking, no drugs. Just a little fun. I looked back at the book. I don't think that the book thought it was such a hot idea. I kept driving.

Finally I decided, "Fuck it." I was going to do it. I was going to drive straight past. I had put in too much hard work. I was clean and sober, and I didn't want anything to fuck with that. I felt strong. I was being patient. I was following instruction.

My cell phone rang. It was an old buddy from the NFL. I hadn't spoken to him in months, and the call was completely out of the blue.

"Jason! Where are you?"

"I'm driving to California."

"No shit? I'm in Vegas!"

"No!"

"Yes! There's a charity golf tournament going on. Are you anywhere close to me?"

I saw an approaching sign. It read LAS VEGAS 15 MILES.

"Well, not far I guess."

"Well, if you want to come and hang out, I can get you a free room at The Bellagio if you're interested."

I looked down at the book. It had lost all of its power over me. It knew it was defeated. I did, too.

"I'll call you when I'm in town," I said, shifting lanes and getting ready to make the turnoff.

NEW GAME— NEW RULES

THE SOUND OF A CAR ROARING PAST ME ON THE freeway wakes me up. The desert sun is beaming through the windshield, burning through my eyelids. The engine is still running, and thank Christ the inside of my car is still pretty cool from the air-conditioning, shielding me from the volcanic heat outside. I blink awake. The inside of my mouth feels like I have been eating sand. A dull throbbing radiates behind my eyes. I feel dried out, fossilized. I glance at the clock and realize that I have been sleeping by the side of the road with the engine running for almost three hours. I am quietly amazed that I escaped the notice of passing cops. I reach to the cup holder and grab the bottle of lukewarm Evian there. I take a gulp, and sit up.

I fucked up, big-time.

Snatches of the night come back to me, and under the unrelenting gaze of the midafternoon sun, they seem terrible, unforgivable.

After checking into the hotel I had made a call to a drug buddy back in New York who I knew had connections out in Las Vegas. The decision seemed automatic, as if I had no more power over the hand that dialed his number than I had over the elements. I sat in my room in the Bellagio, not eight hours after checking out of Cirque

Lodge, with two eight-balls of cocaine staring back at me. I remembered the way the dealers had welcomed me with a malevolent calm, as if all that had happened before meant nothing. Confronted with the cold hard reality of all of that cocaine counted out in neat little baggies, the weeks of work I had done in Cirque Lodge melted away like January snow. I knew that, for better or worse, I had found my higher power long before I went to treatment, and it was at this moment showing me who the boss was.

The whole night flew by in a blizzard of cocaine and booze. I did Vegas full-force: I hit the nightclubs, casinos, strip bars . . . blasting lines of coke with peroxided and siliconed dancers in the VIP area of some vast, cavernous nightclub, where the champagne kept arriving by the bucket . . . stuffing twenties into the G-string of a dark-haired dancer while pounding drink after drink . . . throwing chips down on the roulette wheel barely conscious of where the ball was stopping . . . the whole debauched fiasco ending with me barefoot, chasing one of the Bellagio's complimentary limos down the street because I had somehow broken my ATM card and didn't have a dime to spend. The next morning I made it an hour out of Vegas, before my eyelids turned to lead and I started to fear that I would fall asleep at the wheel. I pulled the car over to rest for a few moments.

Now my head hurt. Everything hurt. The sun was way up in the sky, pounding the car with nuclear ferocity.

"That's it!" I told myself. "You fucked up! You need to quit doing this shit! You're back on the straight and narrow from now on. No more fucking around. Once you get to LA, everything will be OK."

So I drove as fast as I could toward the city of lights, hoping to leave my demons stranded at the desert roadside. I tried to think of Cirque Lodge, the horses, the wide-open spaces, but everything had become jumbled in my head. A horse was a horse. I could not fathom how it had somehow made me feel different than I had before. The sensation of being able to stand on my own two feet, unafraid of my addiction, was slipping from my fingers.

A part of me wanted to turn the car around, and get my ass back into treatment. Still, I would not admit my failure to myself, nor allow myself to so perfectly fit the cliché of a man unable to control his drug use. It was bullshit. I had self-control.

"If you don't want to get high, don't get high!" I screamed at myself in the rearview mirror—but my voice sounded shaky and unsure.

Then I thought: I *do* want to get high. And why shouldn't I get what I want?

I drove faster. I needed to get to LA and see David Rosenberg. He had it together. I felt that as soon as I was in LA, with something else to focus on besides my own self-destructive urges, it would all be OK. The auditions! The acting! I had to focus. I had to get my game face on. Shit.

This trip stemmed from something David had told me when I was in Sierra Tucson. When people graduated there, they used to hold a ceremony in a place they called "the pit" which looked like a Roman arena, with everyone sitting around in a circle and the person graduating in the middle. Each person would choose someone to introduce him, and it got so that a lot of people were choosing me to introduce them.

The graduation ceremonies could be a bore. During a bad one, you'd be sitting there with your ass going numb for hours while somebody was getting all teary-eyed thanking God and the twelve steps like you were stuck watching some Oscar acceptance speech in hell. So when I introduced people I tended to turn it into a roast. I'd tell funny stories, do impressions, the whole bit. It just felt nice to prick the atmosphere of sobriety and seriousness a little. The years of standing in front of my team giving captain's speeches and talking to the press had served me well. People would be roaring with laughter, and I suppose that's why more and more people started choosing me to introduce them, not just people that I was really friendly with. After one of my better introductions, David pulled me aside and told me: "Hollywood is waiting . . ."

"Get the fuck outta here."

"I'm serious Jason. Look at you! Hollywood would be all over you. You're a handsome guy, you're fit, and you have smarts! You should come to LA. You'd do good out there."

David 's family was Hollywood royalty. His father was a founder of one of the big Hollywood studios, and had helmed some of the best-known and most-respected motion pictures of his generation. Although David 's achievements were somewhat in the shade of his father's, he had produced a number of well-known movies and TV shows that I had seen before. Even in the circles of wealthy sports people that I moved in, David's family was something else. He was one of the best-connected persons I had ever met. As much money as I had made from pro football, his kind of wealth and privilege was alien even to me. I knew that when David said something like that, there was a grain of truth to it. I knew that if he wanted to make it happen, he more than had the pull to do it. So the thought germinated, and throughout the year following my trip to Sierra Tucson I had kept in touch with David. While I was getting myself together in Cirque Lodge, our conversation started to turn into concrete plans.

David told me that he was clean, but now he hated how out of shape he had become. The idea was that I would help get him into a fitness regimen, and he would help me with the auditions. It seemed like one of those perfect, foolproof plans that just couldn't go wrong. I mean, shit, the whole twelve-step philosophy revolved around addicts helping other addicts. I needed a new career. I felt that if I could only get something going in Hollywood, I would be able to get my drug use under control. I knew that a lot of my self-destructive urges stemmed from the feeling of being used up, obsolete before I was thirty years old. Being out of the game I loved was a bitter pill to swallow, and cocaine made it more bearable. If I were to quit cocaine, I would need something else to fill that hole inside of me left by football. I felt that the only help that would be any use to me was the kind of help that David was offering.

"Refill?"

I had been hanging out with David for a few days. I arrived at his home in Bel Air, and he showed me to my room. The place was beautiful and huge. David had given me the tour, pointing out the impressive view of the canyon that the house overlooked. Things had been going good. We were having cocktails and reminiscing about Sierra Tucson. David was making whiskey sours and puffing on a Cuban cigar.

"Jay, what was the name of that chick counselor you had? Moira?"

"Mary."

"Mary! That's right! I don't think ol' Mary would approve of this!"

He cackled, passing over the glass. I was feeling nicely drunk, and had gotten over the guilt about my relapse in Vegas. Yesterday we had actually hit the gym, David had put his back into it, and that afternoon he had been on the phone with his contacts spreading the word that I was in town, and putting out feelers about possible work. Life was good.

"I think that Mary would think you were an enabler, David."

"I guess so."

Then David got a naughty kid look on his face, a look that I would later come to know very well. He got all coy, and hemmed and hawed for a while before saying: "Jay, you know, I know we're here for work and all, not to party, but . . . well, if you want to get high I have a friend who has some really killer blow."

My ears pricked up. We had been doing a little dance around each other in regard to drugs. We both reiterated our commitment to my stay in LA being about work, not partying, but I figure we both knew that the other wanted to get high.

"That is," David said with a grin, "if you don't mind me enabling your ass."

"Enable away, my friend!" I laughed, and we clanked our glasses together. David pulled out his cell phone. Within the hour we had scored an eight-ball, and were furiously cutting out lines on the glass-topped table. Yeah, LA was working out to be a wonderful place.

Despite our hangovers, we hit the gym the next morning. David was talking up a storm on the treadmill about all of the people he wanted me to meet. His Rolodex was a virtual who's who of Hollywood. I kept on his ass, and pushed him to reach higher, stretch farther. "You're doing great, man!" I yelled at him when it seemed as if he was about to collapse. LA felt like the most exciting place on the planet right then.

Later that night, we were drinking when David told me, "I got a friend you just have to meet. A really great lady. She lives up the road."

"Is she hot?"

"Well, once upon a time, maybe. She used to be married to some crazy rich dude. Anyway, he left her for an actress, the old story, but she still has their place. You want to go meet her?"

It turned out that the woman, Zora, shared David's coke connection. That night we walked over with a bottle of vintage bourbon for her. I noted both the Porsche and the BMW that sat idly in the driveway. Her maid opened the door, and when we told her we were there to see Zora she allowed us in. When Zora came out to the hall to greet us, I was amazed. She had the kind of face native to the West Coast, more specifically to Beverly Hills—smoothed and sculpted by a surgeon's knife, a face that could have been anything between twenty-five and sixty years old. Her skin looked eerily flawless, airbrushed, and she reminded me of the robotic females of the *Stepford Wives*.

"David, darling!" she squealed, air kissing him excitedly. "And you've brought a friend!"

"This is Jason!"

Zora went through the whole two air-kisses on each cheek thing with me. She had a pair of fake breasts that did not move when the rest of her body did. She smelled of vodka and money.

"Let me guess!" she said, staring in my eyes, "A model . . . No, wait! Not with that physique! A sportsman! Am I correct?"

"Yes, ma'am. Football."

"Oh, football! That's wonderful! But Jason?"

"Yes?"

"If you call me 'ma'am' again, I will have to ask you to leave."

Our intention was to stop over, say hello, pick up more coke from Zora's dealer, and split. Three hours later, however, David was getting antsy.

"I don't do that shit," David snorted. "It's a fucking junkie's drug!"

I was sitting with Zora, and she smirked at David. David could put on a good indignant face when he wanted to. The fact was that David had just bought two eight-balls from Zora's connection. He was now acting all disgusted because Zora had offered us a hit on her pipe.

What was going on in Zora's palatial sitting room was something I would see many times during my stay in LA. Often it took place in other vast, impossibly beautiful houses, and it typically looked like the aftermath of some snooty dinner party. Balding guys in Brooks Brothers suits who were uglier than a bucketful of smashed assholes, yet sitting with model-quality wives and girlfriends, laughed and gossiped about the movie industry. Women who looked like professional ex-wives, with faces pulled tight over their skulls and in outfits by Versace, held court with their much-younger boyfriends. Added to this was a smattering of young Hollywood's elite: I'd often recognize a few up-and-coming actors with that eerie, less than human perfection about their faces. There would no doubt be some waiflike models holding champagne flutes and smoking cigarettes, and another guy, who from the conversation seemed to be the head surgeon or in a similar position at one of Hollywood's biggest hospitals. Instead of chomping on fifty-dollar cigars, or drinking forty-year-old brandy, these people would all be sitting around the table watching with avid interest Zora perform something akin to a Chinese tea ceremony. I never got used to the visual disconnect between what I knew was going on, and how respectable the participants of this ritual seemed. I was deeply fascinated by the hunger on the faces of the guests, the air of anticipation in the room, and Zora's steady, precise movements as she worked the ornate glass water bong, the blowtorch, the baking soda.

Despite the fact that this looked like a dull after-dinner party, the fact was that everybody—*everybody*—was smoking crack.

That first night it was just Zora, the coke dealer, David, and I. Zora placed a large piece of off-white cocaine on the gauze, and gently held a flame to it. I actually blurted out, "Is that shit crack?"

It was like one of those scenes in a bad movie when the record stops and the entire bar looks over to the bigmouth in disgust.

Zora looked at me real cool and said, "Jason, this isn't crack. It's freebase cocaine."

Humbled, I asked, "So, what's the difference?"

Zora curled her puffed-up lips in an attempt to defy the collagen and smile at me. "It's the difference between Hollywood and Inglewood, dear boy."

This broke everyone up, and the tension was defused. I looked over at David and saw that his eyes were still firmly fixed on Zora's hands as she lovingly held the glass pipe loaded with cocaine. He noticed me looking, and then started to get indignant.

"Would you like to try some?" Zora asked.

That's when he threw his hands up and made the remark about it being a junkie's drug, but he didn't leave. I looked back to Zora, to David again, then to the pipe and I said, "Sure."

You hear a lot of fantastically hysterical propaganda about

crack, freebase, or whatever the fuck you want to call it. I had always thought of it alongside heroin as a dirty drug, one of the worst drugs you could do. In this setting, however, it exuded no more menace than a glass of red wine. I saw no addicts here, nobody ready to abscond with a handbag to feed their habit, or give hand jobs in exchange for a rock. Just a bunch of seemingly normal, successful men and women. I walked over and sat next to Zora. She went to hold the pipe for me, but I said, "I got it," and took the pipe and the torch—one of those fancy numbers they sell for making crème brûlée and shit like that—and put my mouth to the end. It was an elaborate glass pipe, one of those things that people tend to smoke weed from. It had a long funnel at the end of which you put your mouth. This led down to the bowl, which had some water in it to cool the smoke. Coming out from this was a small stem with gauze on it where you heat the rock. I flicked on the torch, aimed the blue flame at the rock and inhaled. The rock evaporated. I sucked and sucked. When it was over I exhaled and looked around me, confused.

That was it?

That was crack cocaine, the most addictive drug in the world?

That was the shit that everybody gets so hyped up about?

I looked over to Zora, questioningly. She was smiling and shaking her head.

"Jason," she said, "there's an art to doing this. I think you just burned up that rock. Did you feel anything?"

"Well, I snorted a little bit earlier so it's hard to tell."

"Then you didn't feel anything. Allow me."

I soon found out there really is an art to smoking cocaine. Zora took the pipe from me and with practiced hand loaded it, passed it back so I could hold it to my lips, and flicked on the torch. The blue flame danced around the rock, never touching it directly, melting it evenly, and as she did so she breathed instructions: "Inhale, slow and steady . . . not too much . . . just keep it steady . . . Right . . . Right . . ."

Then she flicked off the torch and took the pipe from me. I looked at her and exhaled a billowing cloud of white smoke. The rush hit my system instantaneously and I heard ringing far off in the distance, like the shrieking of a thousand alarm clocks in unison

—and for a moment I was not even in the room anymore. I was blasted out into the stratosphere, and explosions of pure pleasure erupted in my brain

—and my heart pounded in my chest, each beat of it intensifying my pleasure a hundred, a thousand times,

—and I felt the corners of my mouth rising in a kind of automatic grin, as if there was no way to stop it, a great big stupid, stoned grin that just sat there on my face immobile as I felt a rush of pleasure and goodwill flood me

—I felt endorphins flood the neuron transmitters in my brain causing every nerve in my body to burst into life at once

—and I tried to talk but the words flashed across my consciousness and were then jettisoned in favor of ten or twenty better words, more apt words, before they, too, vanished into a sea of possibilities and instead of talking I just settled back into state of pure, mindless bliss.

"Now," Zora's voice was echoing from her lips, "how did that feel?"

I caught my breath. I felt like a new person. A new man. A superman. Every single bit of worry, sadness, anger, and my sense of being adrift, lost in an alien world following the abrupt end of my career in football, was suddenly lifted. This was the experience I had been promised in rehab, the spiritual awakening they had tried to sell me! Here it was! I was fixed, cured! I was all right! I was better than all right! I tried to find the correct words to articulate the intensity and the profound nature of the experience I was at this very moment enjoying, but all that would come out were banalities, "Oh Jesus fucking Christ, that was . . . amazing . . . holy SHIT!"

I was the center of attention for a moment. The room was watching me. David's face was a curious mix of disappointment and hunger. He licked his dry lips and looked troubled. Zora was gazing at me with a big, beatific grin on her face. She looked like a mother whose son had just graduated college. Everyone was staring at me. I couldn't at the time place the look, but in retrospect it was, I think, a kind of envy. They were all remembering their first taste of crack, that first blast on the pipe that affected their body and their brain in that profound, intense way. That first high that no matter how hard you try, you are never really able to recapture.

The pipe was passed around. I sat there as the eyes of the room left me and everything started to calm down a little. My body was still literally vibrating from the effect of the crack. It was like no other drug I had ever experienced. There was something so familiar about that intense rush of endorphins and adrenaline that it felt at once brand-new and yet almost second nature.

It reminded me of something I thought I would never feel again. It reminded me of the dizzying, mind-bending rush of stepping out onto the field, my body in peak condition, my mind focused into a sharp point. That superhuman, transcendental moment of becoming something more than just Jason Peter, the man. I was once again Jason Peter, killing machine.

David cut into my thoughts when he said, "Hey, Zora, you know, thanks, but we gotta head back."

I looked over to David, as if to say, "Since when?"

"Oh, that's too bad!" Zora smiled. "I hope I'll see you boys soon."

"Actually," I interrupted, "I'm not in a rush. David, you don't want to stay some more?"

"No, well, I wanted to hit the gym early tomorrow . . . and . . ."

"We'll still hit the gym, bro. Stay!"

"You stay! It's cool . . . I'm kinda burnt . . ."

I got up to say good-bye, but I didn't get too far from the table where the pipe was being passed around. Something about the idea of straying too far from my place at the table made me anxious.

David was looking all freaked out, but I didn't have the time or the desire to start asking him what the fuck his problem was. After he split, I said to Zora, "I think David was upset that I smoked."

Zora laughed. "Hm! If I'm not mistaken, that boy is going back to the house so he can do the same thing that we are doing."

"I don't think so. Why wouldn't he just stay?"

The pipe had come around to me again. Zora was loading it and preparing to help me to smoke it again.

"Well, Jason, some people just aren't man enough to admit to what they really like. They feel conflicted, and that's what makes people addicts. An addict is someone who scuttles off to get high in secret. An addict lives a life filled with shame and regret. A hedonist is a different proposition altogether. Which are you?"

"I'm not ashamed or regretful of anything."

"That's what I thought."

As she said it, she lit the torch, and I began to inhale again. There was something oddly predatory about Zora's eyes as she heated the rock and breathed, "Inhale . . . slooowly . . . That's it."

I had come to Hollywood to begin a new phase of my life, and for better or worse, a new phase had now begun.

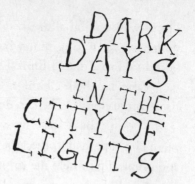

DARK DAYS IN THE CITY OF LIGHTS

I WENT BACK TO THE EAST COAST FOR A WEEK, to assure my family that I was doing OK. I didn't do a good job. Away from LA, I stopped freebasing, but my consumption of coke went through the roof. The whole process with the bicarbonate of soda seemed pretty simple, but I had this fear that if I started freebasing myself, then I would become hopelessly addicted. It felt safer to keep the process mysterious, something that I could only do when I was in LA and in Zora's company. I suppose I could have predicted that pretty soon I would become as dedicated and adept at freebasing cocaine as I was at sports. On one of my first nights there, my sinuses were getting so screwed up from snorting coke I actually got Zora on the phone and tried to get her to instruct me on how to freebase, but I made a mess and ended up wasting about an eight-ball or so of high-grade cocaine.

I think my father was really despairing of me at this point. My mother was sick with worry. When I arrived at their house the expression on her face said it all—a mixture of her mortification at my haggard appearance, and a glimmer of relief that I was still alive. I wanted to reassure them that I was going to get help, even though I didn't want to get sober.

I had called Randal, and told him that I was using again. Randal was back in LA following his stay in Cirque Lodge. Toward the end of my initial stay in LA, David's behavior was getting increasingly cold toward me, and I felt that I had outstayed my welcome. I intended to check into a hotel rather than accept his offer of a place to crash. When I stumbled in, wired on coke, I did not enjoy having to navigate through David's bruised ego. Sometimes he would ignore me. Other times he would try to give the whole "Jason, I think you need to slow down" speech. Mostly he would just harass me until I relented and shared my cocaine with him. The situation was a motherfucking bringdown.

Randal had talked a lot about a doctor he went to, a physiologist called Dr. Dent. Dent was the counsel to a lot of fucked-up rich people in LA, and Randal swore by him. At this point I was very skeptical about what the medical establishment had to offer me. Maybe if they wanted to provide my drugs they could have been of some kind of service, but I was set in my negative opinion of talking cures. These things are great when you are locked up in a hospital and feeling regretful. There everything the doctor says to you makes perfect sense, but out in the streets it's a different matter. Talking doesn't save anybody on the outside.

I told my parents that I was returning to LA to be treated by Randal's doctor who—I assured my parents—was doing "wonders" for him. In actuality, Randal had told me that he was using cocaine again, although "in moderation" these days. I had an appointment to see Dent, but as I had no intention of stopping my use of cocaine, I knew that the meeting would be little more than a charade. I could sense that my parents were getting as jaded about the idea of another miracle cure for my problems as I was, but they had more of a need to believe that something—anything—could help me. I pushed the celebrity angle on them:

"Mom, this guy he treats a lot of movie stars, businesspeople, people who have had incredibly successful careers and have fallen from grace. That was the problem with these other guys who tried to help me—they didn't understand! They had no way of understanding what it is like to walk in my shoes. How could they? They either wanted to talk about football, or they wanted to disregard my situation entirely and start in with all of that 'an addict is an addict and we're all the same' bullshit."

Mom tearfully nodded and gave me her blessing. Inside I felt cold. Lying to your loved ones has to become second nature when you are addicted to drugs. The first few times it feels terrible. You can brood and dwell on the fact that you just crossed a line you never wanted to cross. But pretty soon you learn to subdue that part of yourself and lie with confidence and detachment. You learn how to make yourself feel OK about lying. You learn to become a master manipulator of your loved ones' emotions. When I had this conversation with my mother I was high on painkillers and coke. As much as I wanted to stop hurting my family, I had no faith whatsoever that I had the power to stop myself. I managed to smile and embrace my mother and tell her I loved her without bursting into tears over what I had become. I started hurriedly packing my belongings for an extended stay on the West Coast, the whole time shoveling mountains of cocaine up my protesting nostrils.

A couple of days before I was due to get on the plane, I was shaving when I noticed something odd going on in my nose. At first I thought it was a trick of the light, so I tilted my head back, and pushed my face closer to the mirror. I felt my heart rate quicken, and fear in my belly.

What the fuck was that?

I raised my pinky finger and put it to my nostril. I touched the thing that seemed to be growing out of my right nostril, cautiously. As soon as I felt it, fleshy and firm, I jerked my hand away with a shudder of disgust. This thing was growing out of my nostril like some kind of alien parasite from a bad horror movie.

I snorted more coke, and tried to convince myself that it would go away soon. However, I began obsessively checking my reflection every few hours and I noted with mounting horror that each time I looked, the growth seemed to me poking farther and farther from my nostril. The more coke I snorted the more paranoid I started to get. I would get into these horrible fantasies of this fleshy growth stretching out of my nose, twisting around my head, growing a mouth with rows of razor-sharp teeth that would beg me for co-caine in an inhuman voice.

Jaaaaason! Feeeeeeed me, Jaaaaaason!

After forty-eight hours of this, and the day before I was due to get on the plane, I panicked and called one of my coke buddies, Jenna. I hoped that maybe she would know what the hell was going on. I paced the apartment until she showed up, and then I urgently ushered her inside, double-locking the door.

"Jason, what's the problem?"

"Look! Look at this shit!"

I brought her into the bathroom and put the lights on. Then I cocked my head back and motioned for her to look into my nostril. She peered cautiously and then jumped back screaming "*Jesus!*" Needless to say, her reaction wasn't exactly what I was hoping for.

"What? What the fuck is that thing, Jenna?"

"Sorry! Sorry! Look, I didn't mean to freak you out . . ."

"But what is it?"

"You know, a friend of mine had something like that a while back. Not as big as that one, but that's kind of what it looked like, like there was a snake or something growing out of his fucking nose. It's your blood vessels, they're broken and swollen from the coke!"

"Do I have to see a doctor?"

"No, I don't think so. You need . . . hemorrhoid cream!" she exclaimed. "I remember now! He put hemorrhoid cream on it!"

"Are you sure?"

"Positive. Hemorrhoid cream will fix it! It takes the swelling right out of there."

"And that's it?"

"That's it."

I mulled this information over, relief flooding my system. I needed to make a trip to the drugstore.

"You got any blow?" Jenna asked, and I said, "Sure."

I scurried to the drugstore, high and twitchy, and bought a big tube of Preparation H. Then back at the apartment I smeared it all over the growth and waited, pacing anxiously. Bit by bit, the swelling started to go down. By the time I got on the plane, I looked almost normal again.

The meeting with Randal's doctor was a farce. I hadn't slept in at least four days. I was snorting rails in the bathroom of the plane the whole way over and finally ran out of blow somewhere high above Utah. By the time I was driving over to Dr. Dent's office in Santa Monica I was crashing hard.

I began to get ravenously hungry. I hadn't eaten in a long time because of the effects of the cocaine. Now my stomach rumbled angrily, and I pulled into a McDonald's drive-thru. In the lot, I destroyed my Big Mac meal in a couple of bites. As I gulped down the last of the soda I realized that I was getting extremely tired, and drove away as quickly as possible. I wanted to get this stupid fucking appointment out of the way so I could carry on doing what I wanted to do.

The waiting room was warm and quiet. Filling out the new patient forms and waiting to be called in, I had to fight to keep my eyes open. My body was completely shutting down. I had to fight for every moment of consciousness, and the letters on the page swam in front of my eyes. My hand felt weak, paralyzed almost, and it became a supreme effort to even hold the pen firmly enough to tick the required boxes. By the time the doctor called me in, I had started to drift into the black. When I heard my name, I jerked my head up, realizing that I had been out for a moment.

This set the tone for the whole meeting. It seemed to go on forever, and even Dent's calm, singsong voice seemed to be conspiring to lull me to sleep. I told him that I wanted to stop using drugs, but immediately felt foolish. I realized how I must have looked, and although Dent didn't betray it with his eyes, I am sure he was shocked by my appearance.

I found it impossible to keep my eyes open. I actually drifted asleep on one occasion and woke up with a start. It made the whole pretense that I was here to supposedly ask for help seem even worse. The doctor was looking at me, sadly. I made some excuse that I was jet-lagged, and he just nodded understandingly.

He asked me if I would consider going back into drug treatment. I told him "not now."

Dent looked thoughtful for a moment. "You know, Jason," he told me, leaning back in his chair, "I don't know how good an idea it would be for you and Randal to see each other right now. I know that you were a support network to each other when you were in treatment . . . but now . . . Well, I think it could have a negative impact on the both of you."

I just nodded. I wasn't sure if he was scared that I would make Randal worse, or vice versa.

He wrote me a prescription for some antianxiety medication and told me to come back in a week. He asked how I was getting to where I was staying.

"I'm driving," I told him. "I have the car out front."

"I'm not sure that's a wise idea. Not when you are so . . . *jet-lagged*."

"I'll be fine," I assured him. "It's just been a long day, that's all."

"Jason, would you at least call me as soon as you get home?"

"Sure, I'll call you."

I never went back to Dr. Dent's office. I didn't even call him to tell him that I didn't pass out at the wheel and kill somebody. It was only after Dent had called me a few times, leaving worried voice mail messages, that I eventually picked up to tell him I was still alive and not to worry. I had bigger concerns, already.

That first hit of crack had changed my situation in LA irreversibly. It changed *me* irreversibly. There was no going back once I tried it. Over the weeks following my return, David and I continued to hang out together occasionally while talking absently about movie deals and working out, but more and more I found myself going over to Zora's house to get high with her. The time I was spending with Zora caused a rift with David, and frankly I was getting tired of his goddamned moralizing. Zora had him pegged perfectly—he was a conflicted hedonist. Each hit he took on the pipe seemed to fill him with guilt, and I could sense that instead of turning that hostility inward where it belonged, he was projecting it onto me.

Our trips to the gym became more and more infrequent. The projected meetings and auditions were pushed back, and soon I stopped bringing them up, as I had no more interest in attending them than David had of organizing them. The whole idea started to seem silly to me. A pipe dream, cooked up by two bored guys in rehab. With Zora I had rediscovered my strengths. I was not a wannabe actor. I was not a television personality. That was not what I did. What I did—and did well—was get high.

As I got to spend more time with Zora, I started to realize what an unusual person she was. She was the living proof that you could indeed be a functional crack user. Make no mistake, Zora was not rationing out her cocaine for special occasions. Crack isn't like that. Nobody has enough willpower to be able to put the pipe down for a couple of days so that they can take care of business. As long as you can afford it, you will be smoking it. Occasional crack smokers do not exist. Crack is not just a drug, it is not something you play around with: It is a lifestyle choice. Zora smoked it all day, every day. Yet, somehow, she held it together.

She ran a business from home. She tried to explain it to me once, but the details were lost on me. At the time we were high, so nothing much was sinking in beyond the fact that I wanted to smoke more. It was some kind of Internet-based enterprise that was apparently very profitable. Every so often Zora would run over to her computer and sit there, typing furiously for an hour or so, sucking on the pipe the whole time. Zora ran her house and employed a full-time maid and a security guard. The security guard cracked me up; he was an ex-cop called Bob, who seemed utterly unfazed by the parade of people turning up on Zora's doorstep to get high, or the clouds of crack smoke that would hang in the air of the living room. Sometimes he'd just be sitting there, slightly apart from all of the madness, flicking through a magazine. It was the same thing with the maid. She was a quiet Latin woman, who looked like she was quite conservative, probably a mother. Yet she cleaned and tidied up Zora's drug paraphernalia as if it were dinnerware or cutlery.

Zora's connection for coke was named Christina. She looked like the tabloid image of what a crackhead is. Whereas Zora was in her late forties but had skin as tight and ageless as that of a twenty-year old, Christina looked her age, with interest. She had some broken teeth, and eyes that had obviously seen a lot of bad scenes and brutality. Patches of angry acne covered her cheeks, and the flesh was sucked in against the bones of her face. Christina had been Zora's connection for years. She sold in bulk, and would drive out to Bel Air at the drop of a hat. Christina had been the one who introduced Zora to freebasing a number of years ago.

Smoking crack was unlike any other drug I had ever experienced. Every time I sat down to take my first hit of the day, my heart would pound in anticipation. The kind of habit that it had taken me years to acquire with snorting cocaine appeared within days. When you first start to use cocaine, it is an occasional thing—something you do at parties, a social lubricant just like alcohol. Despite what the government would have you believe, most people never get in trouble with coke. Sure, it makes them talk a whole bunch of shit, but they never become "addicted." Then there is the stage that some of us reach, where doing coke becomes essential before you will go out. You have no interest in clubbing, meeting people, doing the things you always enjoyed doing unless you have an eight-ball in your pocket. That's something that sneaks up on you, and is very easy to justify away to yourself. Most people who get in trouble with coke are people like this. One day a loved one says to them, "You love the coke more than you love me!" and they are shocked into realizing that maybe this is becoming a problem.

The extreme kind of cocaine use that I did, the kind of use that makes you want to stay in alone and snort coke, makes you want to get high seven days a week, where it gets so you don't want to have sex unless you're high: that can take years. You need a lot of time on your hands and a lot of disposable income to reach that stage.

When I smoked crack, it must have taken me less than a week before I was a complete and total fiend for it—but I didn't give a fuck. My rationale was that smoking cocaine was something I would only do in LA. As long as I kept it out of my "real life" I would be OK.

The first hit on the pipe is everything. That is the one that really gets you. That's the one that you wake up looking forward to. Everything after that is just a question of maintaining your buzz and avoiding the crash. As powerful, incredible, and wonderful a rush as smoking crack is, the comedown is just as quick and just as steep. The crash is as terrible as the high is exquisite.

Crack reduces a man to a state of pure need. When the rush begins to wear off, your body goes into full fight-or-flight mode. Every membrane, every cell cries out for more. I could imagine how people who didn't have a lot of money could be driven into desperate acts to score money for rocks, but that was never a concern of mine. My career, as short as it was, had ensured that, for the time being at least, money would not be of any concern to me.

There was another woman who lived with Zora. Julie immediately took my interest. The first time I saw her, she was bouncing around the house in a pair of tight jeans and a little tank top. Julie was very pretty; she had these enormous fake breasts and long auburn hair. She made her living as a photographer, although her past career had been in sales and marketing. She was coming out of a period of heavy drug use, which had taken her marriage and home, and she had lived with Zora ever since they met at a Robert Plant concert. She'd had a little bit of clean time under her belt before moving in with Zora, and she still tried to be the voice of caution despite her renewed drug use. The escalating use of crack in the house obviously made her nervous. She once confided that the appearance of Bob, the security guy, only confirmed her fears that one day soon the house was going to get raided by the cops and the party would be over for good. The house was so big that we could remain entirely separate while we were all there. Zora seemed very protective of me, and although she never tried to make a move on me, it was obvious she enjoyed having a younger man around the house. I learned later from Julie that because of this she had warned Julie to keep her hands off.

Zora also had a daughter, Lillian, who was in her twenties, and she would stop by from time to time. When Lillian came over I would have to go chill out in one of the other rooms in the house. Lillian must have known what was going on. I mean, Zora would be cracked out of her mind, talking a mile a minute, her eyes literally bugging out of her skull from the effects of the coke when she would go to the other room to see her daughter. I guess she didn't care, or she had learned to deal with it. Maybe Lillian had issues of her own. On these occasions, when I was hidden away in another part of the house, Julie would appear and we would have whispered, sexually charged conversations. I took Julie's cell number at one point, and Julie begged, "Don't tell Zora I gave it to you . . . She'd be pissed!" and I promised I wouldn't.

I saw an incredibly varied cross section of society pass through Zora's door to smoke with her. Doctors. Lawyers. Actresses. Writers. Once I found myself smoking with a guy called Mickey, who was an on-duty EMT doctor. He had been at the house smoking with us for an hour when his pager beeped into life and he sprang to his feet.

"Shit! That's me! I gotta go!"

He ran out of the door, barking instructions into his cell phone, on his way to a bloody freeway pileup or some other tragic intrusion of fate.

The party at Zora's house was always ebbing and flowing, and new people would drift in and out of the place constantly. On occasion we would leave the house to visit the homes of other extremely rich, extremely decadent friends of Zora's. It seemed that once you reach this epic echelon of wealth, anything goes. When you are high on crack, your libido kicks in. It is a great drug to have sex on, the best. There was always this crazy sexual subtext between Zora and me. She never made a move on me, and I was definitely not interested in her that way, but sometimes she would say things like, "You haven't had an orgasm until you've had one on crack!"

"Oh yeah?"

"Oh yes! You have so much to discover. I wish I was just starting out like you."

One evening she took me out, into Hollywood. This was an unusual thing. Zora—and I for that matter—really didn't like to get too far from home. Venturing to a place where you couldn't sit around and smoke cocaine felt like wandering into enemy territory. The Club was a secretive affair, nestled away in a backstreet, away from the chaos of Hollywood Boulevard. Feet away was the street that was literally paved with stars, but this was the poorer end of Hollywood, where the likes of Lana Turner and Eddie Murphy's stars were walked over by drug dealers, prostitutes, runaways, and street people. In Hollywood the air was hot, and vibrated with a malevolent energy. Violence of some kind seemed to always be lurking just under the surface. As we drove through all of this, shielded by the tinted windows of Zora's BMW, I began to realize just what a dark place the City of Lights really was. We passed an all-night bookstore, where streetwalkers huddled in groups, approaching the men who flicked through porno magazines, looking for dates. Homeless crackheads, scouring the pavement obsessively, looking for imaginary rocks that they thought they had dropped. There was an insane bum who looked like a sumo wrestler, but when I looked closer was as emaciated as a concentration camp survivor—his outline was inflated by dozens of layers of ripped, filthy clothing— wandering the streets begging for change, his outfit topped off with a space helmet made from what seemed to be broken radios.

We parked in a backstreet and walked to a featureless black door, which opened to greet us. Inside, the space was cavernous and red, like walking into a huge, wet mouth. We entered carrying our crack pipes and drugs, and there was brutal music echoing down the corridor. A steel door in front of us opened and the music vomited out as we walked into the main room.

"What the fuck is this place?"

"It's called the Pit."

"This is some crazy shit, Zora."

"I know!"

The bar was pretty deserted. What was odd about the club was that most of the action was going on in the maze of private rooms that went out from the bar area in all directions. Some of the doors were open, some closed. As Zora and I walked past you could see that most of the rooms had beds, and people were fucking right in there with the doors wide open. At one point I found myself in one of the rooms, this one bare and Spartan, with a young girl. The girl and Zora had a whispered conversation, and Zora closed the door on us and made sure that the blinds were down over the small, prison-like windows. Zora produced a straight shooter—a small cylindrical crack pipe—from her purse and loaded it. As the girl fell to her knees in front of me, Zora placed the pipe in my mouth like she was planting a fifty-dollar cigar between my lips. She started to heat the rock of cocaine in the gauze, and I filled my lungs with smoke.

Zora held the pipe and worked the torch as the girl worked my prick with her mouth. As my lungs filled up with smoke and I exhaled, I felt my vision fragmenting, I saw stars, the music seemed to wash over me in great, titanic waves. Zora's eyes burned through me with the same intensity as the NFL coaches who once examined my body for imperfections, for damage. How were they to know that the damage lay within? What they could never have known, Zora was able to see as clear as day.

I moved into the Mondrian Hotel and started my own business relationship with Christina. Soon she was dropping off cocaine directly to me. I also took the opportunity to get in contact with Julie.

It turned out that she had moved out of Zora's house in an attempt to clean up and get her life back. She asked if it would be OK for her to take some pictures of me. I said "sure." Over time, and with Christina's careful guidance, I perfected the art of freebasing cocaine. Once you get the hang of it, it is quite a simple process. I got so that I could cook it without wasting a fraction of the precious cocaine. My finished product got to be just as good as Zora's.

When I finally had Julie alone in my hotel room that first time she took a few pictures and I tore her clothes off and fucked her right there on the floor. Having Julie was like having the forbidden fruit. I knew that I was putting my friendship with Zora on the line, but that only added to the excitement. I asked her if she wanted to get high with me, and that's when she told me that she had been clean since moving out of Zora's place. Then again, with both of us naked, and faced with a loaded pipe, she seemed pretty unsure.

"Come on," I said to her, grinning. "One little hit on the pipe won't get you into trouble."

After a week or so she was practically living with me in the hotel. Every day she would appear at my door and we would fuck and smoke crack with abandon. On more than one occasion Julie was naked, hiding in the closet, when Christina came to sell me more cocaine. It felt as if time itself was speeding up. The sun rose, the sun set. I sat in Zora's house and smoked with her; I sat in my hotel room and smoked with Julie. The cocaine kept coming. Days and weeks passed: Julie naked facedown on my bed, the tip of the crack pipe glowing in the gloom, wired at 5:00 A.M., seeing in another sickening dawn.

Once, as we sat in front of the TV naked and cooking cocaine, Julie asked me, "What are you going to do now?"

"I am going to cook this coke and get high. What do you think I'm going to do?"

"No, Jason, I mean, what are you going to *do* now?"

I had been in LA for two months. It was true; I had no real reason to stay here. I had finally arrived at a point in my life where I had nothing—*nothing*—to do. As far as my family was concerned I had gone to LA to see a doctor and never returned. I was aware that time was passing, but the idea of hours, days, and weeks was abstract. When you don't go to sleep every night, wake up every morning, as you once did, time itself becomes an elastic concept.

I looked at the cocaine and realized that, beyond cooking up the cocaine and smoking it, I had no idea of what I was going to do next.

"Jason, can I say something to you?"

"Go ahead."

"I like you, Jason. I like you a whole lot. But every time I come over here you have that pipe in your mouth. You're getting as bad as Zora. The pair of you, you're so smart, you could have so much going for you, but . . ."

Julie looked down. She had the pipe in her hand still.

"Look, I know I'm probably not the best person to be giving you a speech and I don't want you to think I'm a hypocrite, but I'm scared that if I don't say this to you, nobody else is going to and you're going to die."

I snorted, derisively. Only it didn't sound as dismissive as I wanted it to. I realized that I couldn't dismiss her words as easily as I could dismiss the words of my parents, my therapists, and my doctors. My standard defense of thinking "What the fuck do you know?" was useless here. Because Julie was right here, and she had been through this, and she knew exactly what she was talking about.

"What are you saying?"

"I'm saying that I want to get clean. I've lived through this fucking scene already. There's nothing new for me to discover here. Jason, I like you, I love being with you, but Jesus, we're so bad for each other. We're poison! I don't like anybody enough to die with them, sweetie, not even you."

I was suddenly gripped by a panicked thought.

What the fuck am I doing here?

Why am I in LA?

What is going to happen if I stay?

I thought about how simple and easy life seemed in Cirque Lodge. How I would stand there at the top of a mountain, breathless from the hike, look to an infinite, azure sky and think: *Life really can be beautiful. I can be OK again.*

There was no beauty here. Julie was beautiful, but this scene was ugly. Dirty.

"Jason, I grew up in California," Julie told me, hesitantly, "and I know this city really well. I've seen what it can do to people. The sun is always shining, and every day seems perfect, and peaceful, and time just sort of . . . stops mattering. There are a lot of professional waiters in this city. They came here because they wanted to act, or write, or play music. But all they are doing is serving food for a living. Time can get away from you here. When you're smoking this"—she held the pipe up, looking derisively at it—"it's even worse. One day you look around and there's nothing left but your pipe and that endless fucking sunshine. And you wonder where your life went."

Julie placed her arm around me. I looked at the pipe in her hand. I looked around the room and tried to remember the last time I left it.

I made plans to flee Los Angeles that night.

15 A STRUNG-OUT LOVE STORY

AFTER A FEW DAYS BACK HOME, MY MOTHER begged me to get treatment for my cocaine problem. I conceded without so much as an argument. I felt physically and mentally drained by my time in LA, and knew that I needed to somehow wrestle back control of my life. My addiction was poison to my family. My brothers didn't know how to deal with me and were keeping their distance. Christian was now running a vending machine delivery business and constantly hinted that maybe I could join him in that line of work, but I knew there was no way I could get it together to hold down an actual *job*. My mother looked about ready to have a nervous breakdown. My father was stoic and controlled in his misery. My family's entire existence now seemed to revolve around my drug addiction.

So I checked back into Cirque Lodge. This time, however, the experience was not as rich as I remembered my last trip being. For a start, my freedom of movement was greatly restricted by my new counselor. I was not allowed to have a car. My schedule was rigid and uncompromising. I still did yoga and Pilates, but only two days a week. Those long hikes through the Utah hills were a distant memory. The work with the horses still kept me interested, but without the joy of discovering the hidden meaning in the exercise, the experience did not have the same resonance.

My counselor this time was a woman called Samantha, and she

seemed to do everything exactly the opposite of my old mentor, Mike. She was an Alcoholics Anonymous purist. I immediately felt that this relationship was not going to work out and I was right. We never butted heads, but I kept my cards far closer to my chest than I had done with Mike. Just the fact that Samantha was a woman made me feel as if I couldn't fully speak my mind to her, nor expect her to instinctively understand some of my problems. Our relationship remained cagey and distant for my whole time inside. I think I had maybe been in there for two weeks when I realized that I would have to start preparing to fight my demons on my own after I returned to the outside world. I felt no better equipped to stay clean now than before entering treatment.

Emerging from Cirque Lodge after forty-five days, I received a phone call from Katrina, the model I'd met in the Pennsylvania rehab facility. Picking up where we left off, we started dating formally. Seeing me fresh out of rehab convinced her that I was finally getting it together. I supposed I must have looked healthy again. Despite my lack of success in rehab, I was still trying to get things under control although—since she was a committed member of Alcoholics Anonymous—I doubt she would have approved of my methods.

My last stay in Cirque Lodge had confirmed my attitude toward the twelve-step recovery method. I knew that it just wasn't for me. Giving my will and my life over to some concept of God was no answer for my problems. Sitting in meetings and talking about my drug use relentlessly made a relapse seem like a self-fulfilling prophecy. I was, in AA-speak, an example of "self-will run riot." But I had to accept myself on those terms and try to live my life on those terms. I felt that if I could only find the balance between my "real life" and my drug use (which I was beginning to realize would always be a part of my life), things would once again return to relative normalcy.

My recovery plan went something like this. I managed to get it down to six easy steps:

STEP ONE

No cocaine before 5:00 P.M., no matter the circumstances.

STEP TWO

No cocaine after midnight.

STEP THREE

Attend the gym regularly. Pay for a personal trainer. If you put the money down for a trainer, you are less likely to forgo a lesson to go get high.

STEP FOUR

No more pain pills. You do not want to have to go through another withdrawal like in Arizona. For god's sake, just stick to cocaine if you have to get high. At least you won't feel like you're dying when you try to stop doing coke.

STEP FIVE

Keep tight with Katrina. Maybe some of her sobriety will rub off on you.

STEP SIX

Keep your parents happy. Tell them you are working. Tell them you are happy. Tell them you bought a new goddamned picture to hang in your apartment. Whatever, just sound happy and productive. Less stress for your parents equals less stress for you and that means less excuses to get high.

There was a real connection between Katrina and me; something that kept me coming back again and again despite the fact that I had to constantly cover up my drug use from her. Sober, she seemed somehow even more beautiful than before. Her skin glowed. She radiated happiness. As my own drug use continued, and began to slowly worsen again, it irritated me when she would use AA clichés. I attended a couple of meetings with her in the beginning, but found them to be dull and meaningless. Katrina was disappointed, I'm sure, but I was such a master at keeping my cocaine use a secret that I suppose she was just happy with the illusion that I was clean, no matter what my thoughts on the twelve steps were.

The first of my six rules that went out of the window was the one about not doing pain pills. The pills were getting a little harder to get hold of, and I only did the pills on the days that I needed to take a break from the coke. Sometimes, my nostrils would be so fucked up it was physically impossible for me to snort anymore. Then I had to switch to pain pills. Going without anything was impossible. Although there is no physical dependence to cocaine, life without the sharp edges taken off became unbearable to me. Without some kind of drug in my system, twenty-four hours could seem like three weeks. On the streets, the people crowding the New York City sidewalks seemed brutish, cruel, and evil. I saw a concealed threat in everything; even the sun seemed unnecessarily harsh and grating. When I took painkillers, everything immediately reverted to the rosy mirage I was used to.

The relationship with Katrina started off as intense and passionate as you can imagine. In the time we had spent apart, desperately keeping in touch through our various attempts at rehab, she had become an object of unobtainable desire to me. When I could finally be with her, it felt as if all of my fantasies of the healing power of this relationship had come true.

For a while at least.

On the other hand, sometimes there would be a reason why I needed my first line of the day at 11:00 A.M. instead of 5:00 P.M. Usually it was because I had broken my rule of no more coke after midnight, and I had not gotten to bed until 3:00 A.M. And then after that fitful, shallow, cocaine-induced semisleep I would be wide awake with the dawn sun, feeling hateful and resentful of the new day. The only thing to fix that would be a quick line to kick my system back into shape. When you wake up at nine in the morning craving cocaine, waiting eight hours seems like an impossibly long time. Hell, thirty minutes seems like an impossibly long time. I started to bargain with myself.

If I can make it to 1:00 P.M., that doesn't seem so bad. It's still the afternoon. I haven't fucked up too badly.

By the time 10:00 A.M. crawled around, and I was looking at the coke, that beautiful, pure white powder that was going to take away the interminable boredom and meaninglessness of my day in one ecstatic swoop, 1:00 P.M. seemed as far off and inaccessible as the most desolate, forgotten continent.

Twelve thirty would be OK. If I can hold off until 12:30 I'll be fine. I have an appointment with Jimmy, my trainer, this morning. If I can just make it out of the door, the decision will be made for me. And then I can really enjoy that first line when I get back.

I would sit there, staring the cocaine down. I was not ready for the gym. I couldn't feel any less like going to the motherfucking gym and staring at Jimmy's healthy, smiling, carefree face this morning. If I missed the appointment, then I would be breaking two of my rules at once, so I compromised.

I will do the line now, and that will give me the energy to go make my appointment. Then I'm still somewhat OK. Two out of three, and all of that . . .

So at 11:00 A.M. I would snort my first line. Now all I had to do was get my ass out of the door and make the gym.

But I've already fucked up, and I won't be able to concentrate. I'll be thinking about my next line the whole time. It doesn't seem fair to Jimmy to come into his class distracted. Maybe I should call and reschedule . . . Hmm, I did this last week, though. I'll have another, and then I'll feel up to calling. I won't feel like so much of an irresponsible asshole then.

I would snort another line, and another. By the time I worked up the nerve to call Jimmy to cancel, it was forty-five minutes past our supposed meeting time. So I just blew it off, figuring I could come up with a brilliant excuse the next time I came in. Locking myself out of my apartment, a gas leak, or some other genius reason for why I kept not showing up to our sessions. After a few more lines I would think: *Fuck Jimmy. I'm still paying him! What the fuck does he care?*

It was then that my plan for not worrying my family began to come unstuck. I remember sitting down to dinner with them at a restaurant in Jersey—my mom, my father, and Christian. I had started up on cocaine earlier in the day, and found myself making an inexcusable number of trips to the bathroom so I could snort more to keep myself going.

I agreed at the table to do some work with my brother the next day, meeting with potential clients and the like. I knew that Christian suspected my jittery demeanor and frequent trips away from the table were cocaine related, and so I agreed quickly just to give the impression that I was OK, and engaged with life. My brother had built his business up from the ground, and was making a great success of it. I suppose that he figured if he could only get me involved, I would realize that I was pissing my life away while he was cultivating a business and a family of his own, and I would therefore be shocked into some kind of moment of clarity. Maybe. Well, though I agreed to go with him the next morning, I stayed up snorting coke the whole night, and when he picked me up and we finally made it to his client's office I sat there in silence as they talked business, crashing hard from the coke, before I was lulled to sleep by the warmth and the gentle tone of their voices. I jerked awake as I sensed Christian standing up to shake the guy's hand, and I stood up too quickly, feeling myself get dizzy. Christian didn't say a word to me on the way home, and never asked me to work with him again.

On the weekends when I wasn't seeing Katrina, I would lock myself in my apartment and furiously freebase all through the day and night. Once I relented and allowed myself that first hit on the pipe, I knew it would be virtually impossible to stop. You surrender yourself, body and soul, to the pipe. I would eventually have to resort to knocking myself out on Xanax and Valium when my heart could take no more. Then I would swear "never again," at least until the next time I had a weekend free and nothing scheduled with Katrina or my family. The thing about crack is that as awful and as dirty and used up as I felt after my last session, the thought of that first hit on the pipe was always enough to take all of my reservations away.

Katrina seemed entirely oblivious to the fact that I was often high when I was around her, and the relationship developed to the point that she even spent Christmas at my family's home with me. Her face was so perfect, so flawless, that waking up next to her in the morning I'd wonder what on earth I had done to deserve this woman. I watched the crystalline sunlight reflecting on her ivory skin as she slept on, unaware of my gaze. In moments like this, the quiet moments before the city came alive again, I could almost want her so much that I would seriously consider giving up my lifestyle for her. But even as I thought this, I knew that the feeling was a counterfeit, that the softness of Katrina's lips, that the warm flutter of her breath against my neck, could never amount to a hundredth, a thousandth, of the joy that my first and truest love brought me. I crept out of bed and into the kitchen to make some coffee to wash down the first pills of the day.

The relationship fell apart over time, in indefinable increments. Apart from the time we spent alone, we had little in common. Her life revolved around her work and her recovery. As time progressed, my life revolved solely around my drug use. The unhappiness inside of me could only be fixed by more cocaine, more pills. No matter how hard Katrina tried to take their place, I knew all along—and she in turn eventually realized—that it was futile. As my drug use began to get heavier, and the scene in my apartment got darker and darker, the relationship fizzled.

It all ended at an AA New Year's Eve party in a church hall in the city. Katrina really wanted to go, and after a couple of lines I figured that it might be funny in a sick kind of way. When I got there it was anything but funny. It was a bunch of extremely sober people, standing around listening to bad music, drinking nonalcoholic punch, and occasionally asking me questions about my clean time, what meetings I attended, or what step I was on. As the night dragged on, Katrina and I began to drift away from each other. She spent more and more time talking recovery with her friends in the program and I spent more and more time locked up in a toilet cubicle snorting great rails of blow just to work up enough nerve to go out there and talk to people.

I received a few looks that told me people were on to me. I was sweating and wild-eyed, and the nasal drip from the coke was causing me to snort and sniff all of the time. The back of my throat was numb, and my mouth was full of cotton, so I was gulping down as much of the punch as I could to try to combat it. I was trying desperately not to act high, but sometimes I would catch myself going on long monologues about nothing, and I would come back to myself midsentence wondering exactly what the fuck I was talking about. My jumpiness and paranoia grew as the night wore on.

This isn't a goddamned meeting of the PTA. This is a room full of ex-drunks, ex-junkies, and ex-coke fiends! You really think that they haven't figured out that you're high as a motherfucker right now? Who are you kidding?

I managed to hustle Katrina out of there before midnight, and we walked the city streets as fireworks erupted in the distance and the beginning of another bullshit year was rung in.

The last thing I said to her was "I'll call you," and I never did. I never broke it off with Katrina; I simply disappeared and ignored her calls throughout the beginning of the New Year. With Katrina no longer around, I felt that I had nothing to lose and I began to freebase in earnest. Then, on a whim, literally days after I last saw Katrina, I called a girl I had met in a strip club.

Diane had danced for me before. She was one of the sexiest women I had ever come across. I mean, this girl was incredible. I called her that night because we had had this long, flirty relationship where we had constantly talked about getting together, but with my unstable lifestyle this had never happened. I would show up at her club, she would dance for me, and we would hang out until closing time flirting and groping each other. The night she finally came around to my apartment, she brought some other girls from the club to party.

After the months of having to hide my drug use from Katrina, it was a welcome relief to have a girl like Diane in my apartment. She not only tolerated my use of drugs, but also joined in. The scene the first night she and the other girls came by was one of pure, crack-fueled decadence. As well as the cocaine, there were pills and meth, which I would later discover is a common drug among dancers. Diane told me that she used it to keep going through long shifts at the club, for a confidence booster before going on stage, and as an aphrodisiac when she was called on for a private dance. As the evening degenerated, I would never have figured that this was the beginning of one of the longest—and craziest—relationships of my life.

Diane, Diane, Diane.

I mean, even with four other white-hot strippers in the room, I still couldn't take my eyes off of her.

Diane.

She had this look in her eyes that hinted at unfathomable depths. When strippers get together and talk, the conversation is usually anything but enthralling. I know nearly every stripper you meet will tell you she's only dancing to pay her way through college, but the myth of the intellectual stripper in my experience is pretty much just that—a myth.

Diane was different. She was smart, and funny. She was a cool girl, one who didn't seem hung up on the nice stuff in my apartment, or the money that I could obviously lavish on the girls, or the labels on the clothes I was wearing. Even when she was dancing around my apartment naked, hoovering up lines of meth, making out with other girls in front of me, I could see that she was something more than just another fuck. When the sun rose over the Manhattan skyline, and the rest of the girls evaporated into the dawn, Diane stayed on. We just talked. About her family, about her ambitions, about her life. There was a free-spiritedness about her that appealed to me. It's funny, in a way. She showed up at my apartment to party, and she simply never left.

That fucking body of hers, it was crazy making. She was the kind of woman who could drive a guy to murder or the creation of great fucking symphonies. After a few days of us hanging out in my apartment, getting high, talking about everything and anything, I thought, "This chick is gonna be the fucking death of me." Honestly, I didn't care.

Looking at that face, that mix of Portuguese, Asian, and at least three other nationalities, those lips, those eyes . . . I mean, how could I? For a girl like this, I could learn to live under death's shadow.

Diane made it easier for me to ignore Katrina's calls. Katrina even came and pounded on my door and frantically rang the buzzer once, while Diane and I stayed up in the apartment ignoring it all, high and lost in that first great wave of infatuation. It was a new year, a new beginning.

There were other beginnings, too.

It was about a week after Diane had moved her belongings into my place. We had been smoking a lot of coke. Diane swept the long, black hair out of her eyes and asked me, "Have you ever smoked heroin?"

"No. I snorted it once. Threw up. Swore never again. You?"

"Uh-huh. Sometimes."

We had been up for maybe twenty-four hours, doing speed and crack. It was getting into that awful in-between stage where the tiredness and the griminess starts to kick in, when the aches in your bones and your lungs start to manifest and you begin to wonder if you shouldn't just dose yourself up with pills and try to sleep the day away.

"It's better to have some around," she continued. "When you're smoking rocks like this. It slows you down a little, and it takes the edge off the comedown."

"Oh yeah?"

I was all ears now. I thought about what people had told me in rehab. *Crack without heroin just doesn't make any sense. It's a goddamned waste!*

"Maybe we should try that sometime," I said, trying to remain noncommittal.

"I have a connection for it. You want me to call him?"

I looked at her. I think that's when I thought, "This woman is gonna be the death of me." Maybe not. Maybe that's just my memories of this period getting all fucked up in light of what came next. Maybe that's too convenient. I can't say.

I remember I smiled at her and said, "Sure, I'll try anything twice." We cracked up as she grabbed the phone and started to make the call. After she placed the order, she hung up and said, "Twenty minutes." Then we fell back into bed like old lovers, and fucked, slowly and gently until the intercom buzzed into life, announcing that a new stage had begun.

Within months, Diane's drug use had spiraled until it had reached a level akin to my own. She stopped dancing. She stopped doing anything except screwing me and taking drugs. When we both lost interest in messy, physical activities like sex, there was nothing left for us to do but get high.

There was something forlorn about her, something sad lurking deep within. We tried to fix each other, to fill the holes in our insides with sex, companionship, drugs . . . fucking, or getting fucked-up . . . any kind of instantaneous pleasure to cover the ruin in our hearts. Over the following twelve months we became two earthbound ghosts, pumping our bones together in some sad, lonely attempt at finding the humanity within ourselves. It was as if she offered her body to me as a receptacle, a depository for all of my anger, my shame, my hurt . . . she took it and she fed off it. Her pain became my pain. My pain became hers. There was nothing but night after night of more coke, more heroin. Soon the apartment was awash in heroin and I would wake up and snort it, leave lines of it laid out for me by the bedside so I would not have to wait for it in the morning. Sometimes I'd have this recurring dream that we were in a vast, dark pool and we were naked, floating on the surface, and she would say to me, "Are you ready, Jason?" and I would say, yes, and judging by the acoustics of our voices, we may have been in some underwater cave, but when we said it, we both held our breath and submerged, deeper, deeper into the inky water, down, down, into what seemed like the very bowels of the earth, and even with my eyes open I could see nothing, my only sense of her was her tiny hand in mine as we swam farther and farther into the murk . . . and slowly, incrementally at first, her hand would become indistinct, losing its form, like melting ice, and I would suddenly realize I was alone in the black, that I was holding hands with the ghost of myself, and I would begin thrashing around desperately, with no idea of where the surface was anymore.

I would awaken, gasping for breath, thrashing about in the bed, and for a moment relief would flood me, until I took in the chaos of the apartment, remembered where I was, and then I would look at Diane's slumbering form, lying next to me.

Diane, lying in bed, the sweat soaking through the sheets, trying to come off of heroin at the beginning of that first summer . . . She lasted three days. She started to cry, and I couldn't take it anymore. I felt so bad for her and told her, "One little line never put anybody back on," and when she did it, and the sickness was gone, I put my arm around her and we were still again, sitting in bed, locked in our private miseries.

Diane, combing through the carpet fibers looking for a rock of crack she might have dropped when we argued, and I told her she needed to lay off the fucking pipe, and I was cutting her off. I watched her obsessively scour the same square foot of carpet for over an hour, and finally relented and gave her some more just so I wouldn't have to watch her do it anymore.

Diane, up on the balcony, threatening suicide and me dashing paranoid through the streets.

"Are you the guy?"

It was the last time I ever saw her.

I don't know what happened to her.

She's gone. Off to another chapter, another life.

I was gone, too.

Gone. Crying. Sobbing. Begging for forgiveness.

Saying to my aunt Lee that yes, yes, I wanted to try again. That I was tired of living this life. I'm tired, Aunt Lee, I'm so tired, and I just don't know what to do anymore.

No matter how fucked up my life had become, no matter the insanity that had led me to the point of actually considering ending it all, cleaning up was the last thing I wanted to do. In some cockeyed way, I felt that if I kept going for long enough, somehow all of my problems would resolve themselves. The process of getting clean again, and starting on the treacherous and painful path to recovery was something I didn't relish. I've yet to meet the heroin addict who thought that kicking smack was anything other than a living nightmare. As long as the drugs keep flowing in, the thought of withdrawal is an abstract notion, something for another day, year, lifetime, but now that I had agreed to clean up again, it was right around the corner. I think Aunt Lee saw the look in my eyes as I pondered this, and she started to ask me if I had ever heard of rapid opiate detox.

"No. What is it?"

"Well, Jason, it's a new procedure. They say that it's painless. What they do is they knock you out with some heavy sedation, and then they put another drug into your system that cleans the heroin right out of you. They speed up the withdrawal so it's over in seventy-two hours. And then they wake you up. Cured!"

I processed this information. Already, somewhere in the back of my mind I could sense the fucking demon that controlled my use of drugs jumping up and down with glee.

Seventy-two hours! You could clean up, get your strength back for a lit-
tle while and then, when you're feeling better, that first blast of dope will feel
AMAZING! And if you get into trouble with it again, well, you can be
clean seventy-two hours later! It's genius!

"That sounds great," I heard myself saying, trying to shut the
little fucker out.

"And then your mom and I found out about a rehabilitation
unit out on the West Coast. They specialize in cases like yours."

"And they're not AA?"

"No."

I thought about it for a few moments.

"I really want to get off this shit, Aunt Lee."

"I know you do. Shall I organize it?"

"Please. Please do it."

That's how I got clean, became a productive member of society
again and . . .

No, wait. That's not the story at all. This is what happened:

There was a little delay in getting the detox and the rehab lined
up. The place was a luxury rehab out in Orange Country called Beau
Monde. They specialized in celebrities, CEOs, sports people: people
who valued their anonymity and had the means to pay for it. They
only accepted three people at a time, so they could devote all of their
time and resources to helping their clients. While Aunt Lee was organizing my stay there, I stayed up in my room. I still had to keep high,
but I at least tried to keep my use as hidden as possible. When the details were complete, I spoke to the director of the program over the
phone. Her name was Heidi. She seemed friendly, and was extremely
enthusiastic about getting me over there and starting treatment.

"Look, Heidi," I told her, cradling the phone between my neck
and shoulder, as I cut out lines of cocaine on the back of a CD case,
"I really need to get off of heroin. But you know, the cocaine . . . I
don't know if I'm ready to quit that for good. I've kind of come to
a point in my life where I have accepted cocaine into my life for
good or for bad."

Snnnnnnnniiiiifffffffff!

To her credit, Heidi seemed utterly unfazed by this.

"Jason. We can talk about all that when you get here. All you need to worry about is getting over here, OK? Do we have a deal?"

"Yeah. We have a deal."

"Cool! I'm looking forward to meeting you, Jason."

"You, too. Bye."

So first I would fly out to the Weissman Institute to go through the rapid opiate detox. Then I would be whisked off to Beau Monde for treatment. I looked at the pictures of the place on the Internet. Jesus, it looked beautiful. A world away from the rehabs I had been at before. The Web site had a series of images scrolling by, inviting you to try the program . . .

A beautiful woman, eyes closed in rapture, receiving a sensuous back rub.

A couple—clients?—frolicking on a golden beach as the sun sets in the background.

What I assumed was a client-doctor meeting. Instead of meeting in a grimy office on metal chairs, these two were relaxing on white leather couches in an expansive open-plan room with stunning full-length windows looking out over the ocean.

I mean, shit, I had booked holidays on the basis of less impressive photographs than these.

Still, the demon nagged at me. He sensed that something was up.

They want to take your drugs away Jason! You're walking right into this one! So they pretty it up with leather couches, beaches, and modern art on the walls, but you know what this is! This isn't a country club—it's re-hab. REHAB. No coke, no smack. Nothing. Just you and your thoughts. And I will drive you CRAZY before I allow you to break us up! Three days from now, you're going to be clean. You have three days to get it all in! Three DAYS!

My aunt came around to the idea of a private plane pretty easily. After all, I was still a recognizable name. I stuck out. There was no way I was going to get on a plane without drugs. Anything could happen.

"Like what?"

"What if the plane gets delayed? I'm going to get sick. What if they have to stop over somewhere? This kind of stuff happens all of the time! I could end up stuck in Detroit or somewhere for twelve hours, no drugs, getting sick. They'll spot it straight away, if I start puking and twitching. I'd just feel better if I knew that it would be private, that nobody is going to be in my business, and I can be sure of getting from A to B with no surprises."

What she wasn't so sure about was the fact that I didn't want her, or my brothers, or anyone coming with me for moral support.

"We want to come and support you, Jason! This is a big step to do all by yourself."

"I know. But it's better this way."

It was better, because I had some steps of my own that had to be completed before I was willing to give myself up to treatment.

Step one was to procure a private plane, so I could take the party with me. After all, if this really was it, if I really was going to try and get clean for good, I was as sure as hell going to go out with a bang.

Step two was the drugs. I would need cocaine and heroin. A lot of cocaine and heroin. Especially as I would not be traveling alone. This would be because of . . .

Step three: Whores. At least two whores. After all, there's nothing lonelier than getting high by yourself. When you're nice and high on coke and dope, as far as in-flight entertainment goes . . . well, watching *Father of the Bride* really doesn't cut it, does it?

Planning for rehab was fairly simple. First, the private plane was organized at a cost of approximately $30,000. I handed Aunt Lee my credit card, and she made the arrangements. It was an eight-seater, and I was due to fly from Teterboro, New Jersey. Then I would be picked up by a representative of the Weissman Institute at John Wayne Airport, in Orange Country. The night before, I had a limo drive me into New York to pick up ten eight-balls of coke and seven bundles of heroin. The girls I procured from my usual source. I had called Magdelina, who ran a high-class escort establishment out of an unassuming Upper West Side apartment building. I requested two girls to make a cross-country trip, via private jet. Magdelina told me that would be no problem. Magdelina herself dealt only with the business side of things. No one could look less like a madam than Magdelina, and her discretion was total. At 6:30 A.M. the morning of the trip, I picked up Lori and Gia, who would be accompanying me to California.

The fact that I would be on a private plane eased my nerves about making the journey. There was a constant gnawing anxiety about making the journey, taking the rapid opiate detox, committing to treatment. And anxiety about other things, too. In the post-9/11 world, it seemed almost inconceivable that I would be able to get on a plane—any plane—without some kind of rigorous security check. I thought of how ironic it would be, to get arrested with cocaine and heroin in my possession while on the way to a detox facility with two escorts.

Gia was a tall, willowy blonde. Lori was a dark-skinned Latin girl. They looked like they had just stepped off the pages of *Italian Vogue,* both dressed in clinging designer dresses, and both hanging on to my every word. I thanked Christ for women like Gia and Lori. There was a bulge in my pants as we waited to board the plane at Teterboro but as beautiful as the girls were, they weren't the source of it. No, the bulge was the thick packages of drugs that I had taped to my pubic area with masking tape. I figured that if there was some kind of security check, maybe the airline would have the decency not to rummage around in my balls looking for contraband.

We were ushered through, onto the runway. No security. Nothing. My luggage was stashed away and we walked up the stairs and into the plane itself. It was small, but functional: two tables, with seats around each of them, and a curtain that led through to the cockpit.

Our pilots introduced themselves.

"Jason, my name is Luke. I'll be your pilot today, and here is my copilot Susan."

"Hi!"

They stood there, in their uniforms. Luke was a taller, older gentleman with graying temples and a well-worn face. Susan smiled, and I shook her hand. She was in her midforties, and had the cheerful, patient demeanor of a schoolteacher.

"Hello!" Gia and Lori chimed, and to her credit Susan's smile never faltered. I swear I saw Luke smirk.

As the plane began to taxi along the runway, the girls and I poured some drinks. The door to the cockpit was wide open, and I could see the pilots making adjustments, pressing buttons, talking to each other through their headsets. I walked over and stuck my head in. "Hey, guys, is it cool for me to shut the door? I kinda wanted some privacy. You know, once we're in the air."

"Of course, sir."

As the plane left the ground, the door closed and suddenly the party was in full swing. There was something strangely satisfying about the look on the girls' faces, the way their eyes got bigger with that "night before Christmas" look when I threw the packages of drugs onto the table. I separated out the cocaine and the heroin. The pile of coke was by far the larger one, as I knew that the heroin would only be for me.

Heroin is not a social drug. Nobody offers you a line of heroin at a party. Heroin is a vocation—you seek it out. It does not find you. If I hadn't walked away from the NFL with an opiate habit encouraged by starstruck doctors and a team that needed me to be able to play no matter how much pain I was in, I can confidently say that I would never have tried heroin, let alone become an addict. I was also not in the business of creating new addicts.

After the plane took off, I decided it was my turn to do the same. Gia sat to my left, Lori across from me.

"Holy shit," Lori breathed, when I cut open a bag of coke and poured a pile of it out on the table.

I smiled. The King of the World. I knew that the coke was top-notch, the absolute best available. The heroin also. My connections only dealt in the best-quality heroin. It was white, and bitter, and had the consistency of powdered sugar.

"This shit here"—"I told them, pointing to the smack—"is mine. We're gonna keep that separate. And this stuff right here is for everybody."

I pulled out a credit card and started chopping out lines. Two generous lines each for the girls. I didn't ask if they dabbled in coke. You show me an escort who doesn't do coke and I'll show you a politician who has never told a lie. I cut out a line of smack and a line of coke, and used the card to push them together into a single, thick line. I had been using minimal, maintenance amounts for the previous two weeks while I had been hiding away at my parents' house. I had made sure I stayed well, but nothing more. Now, as my stomach rumbled in anticipation, it was game on. I pulled out a few bills, and rolled one. I looked at the girls. Their eyes looked like they were about to pop out of their heads.

"Ladies?"

They looked at each other. Gia shook her head and Lori smiled.

"After you, Jason," she said.

So I leaned over and hoovered up the speedball with a flourish.
Holy shit.
Holy fucking shit.
Speedballing is a hard rush to describe. It is probably the most dangerous rush there is, but that's what makes it so fucking enticing. The shit roars into your heart and brain like an out-of-control Mack truck. Your stomach flips like you have been suddenly catapulted a thousand feet into the air. Your brain flashes alive, as if jolted by

electricity, alive in a way that it has never felt before. When you know what it is like to do a speedball, the rest of your life—loves, losses, sex, everything—seems somehow gray and hollow in comparison. Your mind spins in a million different directions. You fight the urge to talk, because you have so many ideas whirling around in equal and opposite directions that if you don't bite your tongue, you might find yourself spouting complete nonsense.

"Oh, *fuck!*" I yelled. "That shit is *good!*"

Gia had already hoovered up a line, and now she reached across the table to hold Lori's hair as she leaned over and snorted a line also. Something about the odd tenderness of this gesture stirred something inside of me. I watched Lori's dark brown skin as she leant over, snorting the coke, and the bronze skin of Gia's arm leaning across me. Her perfume was dizzying.

"The NFL, huh?" Gia is saying to me later. "That explains the physique, I guess." Underneath the table, Lori is running a hand up and down my thigh. I can barely hear Gia's words over the sound of the engine and the thudding of my own heart. I lean in and kiss Gia, and her saliva is so infused with cocaine that I start to feel the inside of my mouth go numb as soon as her tongue snakes into it. Out of the corner of my eye I see Lori snort another line, before she winks at me and slips underneath the table, and starts loosening my belt.

What was it that the AA people used to tell me? *The journey to recovery begins with a first step.* Roaring through the skies in a $30,000 private jet, with $3,000 of cocaine and heroin spread out on the table before me, as Lori and Gia—two beautiful hookers, fashion-model quality, began to blow me enthusiastically . . . well, I had to admit that as far as first steps go, this wasn't too shabby.

Later I was in the tiny bathroom, splashing water on my face. I felt good. I felt better than good. I felt like some kind of junkie superman. That is, I felt like superman until I noticed the plane starting to shudder and shake, suddenly losing altitude. We were hours away from California, but the plane was getting ready to land.

I walked out of the bathroom and saw Gia and Lori looking

panicked and confused. I walked over to the cockpit and peeked my head around the curtain.

"What's going on?"

"We're just getting ready to land in Missouri to refuel," said Luke, cheerfully. "It should take less than an hour. And then we'll be on our way."

"Oh. Thanks."

I walked back to the table, and told the girls. They seemed to buy it—but I didn't.

This is it, fuckhead. You think you can fly around, snorting speedballs, getting blown by hookers, and these guys are just going to let you? They've probably radioed ahead to the cops. You're busted. Dead meat.

Shut up.

Shut the fuck up.

Fucking cocaine. All it takes is for something unexpected like this to happen, and that little paranoiac voice pipes up like impending doom and pisses all over my parade. A part of me wanted to collect all of the drugs and flush them, but another more rational part told me not to be so fucking stupid. Despite myself, I maintained a veneer of implacable calm. The girls, taking their cue from me, seemed pretty unfazed. I needed to keep my mouth shut, and see what developed.

So I found myself in Missouri, standing on the runway with the girls, watching the little jet refuel.

"You don't think they're going to bust us, do you?" Lori asked.

"I don't know," I answered. Everything seemed normal, quiet, but as soon as Lori gave voice to this suspicion, everybody started to think about it.

"There's a lot of fucking coke on that plane," Gia said, quietly.

"Yeah." I smiled.

From where we were standing, about two hundred feet from the plane, I could see Susan through the cockpit window. She had stood up, and was brushing herself off. Then she turned and walked slowly toward the back of the plane.

"Shit," I hissed. "Are you seeing this?"

"Where the fuck is she going?" Gia snapped, her voice rising in panic, tugging on my arm.

"She's going back! Shit, Jason, all of that shit is just lying out there!"

"Fuck, I know. I know."

"We're gonna get popped!" Gia said, pulling her arm away from me. "We're dead. They're gonna call the fuckin' cops!"

"It's cool," I reassured her, halfheartedly. In reality, all I could think about was the horror of getting arrested in fucking Missouri with two escorts and three thousand dollars' worth of hard drugs.

"It's not cool!" Lori said, panic beginning to show in her voice as well. "Look, that's a lot of drugs back there."

"It's *cool!*" I snapped. "The shit is all mine. You guys have nothing to worry about, OK? It's all my shit. Now be cool!"

When it was time to board the plane, we climbed cautiously inside. Some terrible, insistent part of my brain was telling me that we weren't out of the woods yet.

They're containing you, asshole. Any minute now a squad of fucking police cars are gonna be on this runway, lights flashing like some shitty action movie!

As we crept back to our seats, I started to realize that something wasn't quite the same on the plane.

"Holy *shit!*" I yelled, as I saw it. "Would you look at this fucking shit!"

The girls huddled around me, and slowly Lori started to laugh, and then Gia joined in, too. It was one of the most unbelievable things I had ever seen. Susan had come back and tidied up. Off in one neat stack was the heroin, and in another was the cocaine. She had actually come back here and tidied up the messy pile of drugs we had left.

"Well, shit." I smiled. "That's fucking service."

"God bless America!" Lori laughed, and we got back to our seats, and carried on the party all of the way to California.

FUUUUCCCKKKKKK!
FUCK SHIT FUCK SHIT!
HEY.
HEY!
GET THE FUCKING DOCTOR IN HERE! HEY! I NEED
    THE FUCKING DOCTOR
RIGHT NOW OR I'M WALKING, YOU HEAR ME?
GET
THE
FUCKING
DOCTOR
IN
HERE
NOW!

Oh fuck. Oh dear God. How did I get into this fucking mess? Two days ago I stepped off of a plane at John Wayne Airport in Orange Country, and hopped in a limo with the girls, put them up in a hotel until the plane was ready to take them back to Jersey, and left the coke with them. I think I said something like "Merry Christmas, ladies!" as I handed the shit over.

Asshole.

Before that—oh Christ, it hurts to even think about this—since the girls had no use for the heroin, and since I had a limo waiting downstairs to whisk me away for a "painless" seventy-two-hour detox at the Weissman Institute, I snorted a big line of heroin in the toilets of John Wayne Airport before dumping the rest of the shit down the toilet. In the bathroom I had wobbled a little from the effects of the smack and worried that I had maybe taken too much. As the last of my heroin disappeared around the U-bend, I splashed water on my face, composed myself a little, and staggered out to the limo. I dropped the girls off at the hotel, and soon we were off in opposite directions—the girls and the coke back on the plane to the

East Coast, and Jason fucking Peter, flusher of high-grade heroin, off to his nice, clean, painless detox.

NUUUUURRRRSSSSSSEEEE!

I was on a hospital bed with a morphine drip hanging out of my arm that was doing nothing. Upon my arrival, the doctors had whisked me into the Garden Grove Hospital and checked me out rapidly—heart rate, a brief physical, that kind of bullshit—before starting the procedure.

"First," Dr. Benway said, "we need to stabilize you. So we will put you on a morphine drip for four days before we begin the rapid opiate detox therapy. Now tell me, Mr. Peters," he said, mispronouncing my name, "how much heroin do you use a day, exactly?"

So I found myself propped up in bed, with the morphine being fed into my arm. The effects of that last blast of heroin in the airport were dissipating. After being at the center for a few hours I started to feel something happening. Something unexpected, and something worrying: hot flashes.

Now the hot flashes in and of themselves are not the worst thing you will ever experience. They are more disconcerting than anything else. It as if someone is opening and closing a furnace door on you. All of a sudden your temperature shoots up, and beads of sweat are forming all over your body. You thrash around in the bed to try and get comfortable, but it is no use. You feel as if your blood is literally boiling in your veins. Your heart starts to race. And then . . .

Gone. You are back to normal. The sweat starts to cool, and your body temperature starts to drop. So you wrap that hospital sheet around you to try and get warm again, but soon the heat is back.

As I said before, it is unpleasant—but not painful. The worst thing about the hot flashes is the knowledge of what they mean. You are beginning to withdraw. Soon, once the hot flashes start, you can count down exactly to the beginning of the other symptoms. The stomach cramps. Pins and needles. The migraines. The vomiting. The shits. Leg cramps. Twitches. And the intolerable mental anguish that threatens to make you insane.

It was at that point that I called the nurse into my room.

"Yes, Mr. Peters?" she asked, looking at me with a pursed mouth and fucking up my name again.

"Yeah. Listen, something is wrong. I'm not feeling good. I don't think the drip is working properly."

"Hmm." The way she said *hmm* was not encouraging. She obviously thought I was faking for more meds, but she did do me the courtesy of checking the morphine drip.

"This seems to be working just fine."

"Well, I can assure you it's not. I don't feel good."

She smiled, dryly. "You aren't meant to feel *good,* Mr. Peters. You are meant to be comfortable."

"But wait—I don't feel—"

It was too late. She was gone. *Fuck!* I started to wonder about the possibility of ripping the drip out of my arm and getting the fuck out of there. Then I thought of the crushing disappointment that would be on the faces of my mother, my father, my aunt—everyone who had something of themselves invested in this treatment. That's when I started freaking out. I demanded that the doctor see me.

After I had screamed for a while, Benway hustled his ass out of his office and to my bedside. The doctor started coming on with that faux caring, everything-is-fine bullshit that they put on you in these places.

"But, Mr. Peters, there is no reason why you should be feeling like this. The amount of morphine we are giving you should be more than enough to maintain you in comfort."

I looked up at him. Sweat was soaking through my T-shirt. It stood out in beads against my forehead. My pupils were as big as fucking saucers.

"Listen," I said as calmly as I could, "do I look fucking comfortable to you?"

He opened his notes and started reading aloud. When I heard him read, "The patient was using two to three bags of heroin a day—" I cut him off: "What!?"

The doctor looked up and cleared his throat.

"I said, 'The patient was using two to three bags of heroin a day.'"

"Doctor. I told you I was using two to three *bundles* of heroin a day."

A bundle contains ten bags. That's a pretty fucking big difference.

The doctor looked a little taken aback. He looked down at his notes and began to scribble furiously. He looked back at me.

"That does seem like an awfully large amount," he said slowly, "I mean, are you *sure?*"

"Yes," I hissed. "I'm fucking sure. Now can you get this straightened out, please?"

"*Nurse!*"

Within thirty minutes I was fine again, but that should have given me an inkling of what was coming. When the morphine kicked in, I suddenly felt my body returning to normal. My muscles relaxed, and my guts unknotted. Benway and the nurse would look in on me from time to time, seemingly convinced that the amount of morphine they were feeding into me should have proved fatal. When they would cautiously peek over at me, I would shoot them a smile and wave, before closing my eyes and turning my Walkman up.

When the time came that I was deemed ready to detox, they wheeled me into another room. They told me that when I was unconscious I was going to be strapped down to the bed, like a patient at a psych ward.

"Nothing to worry about," the doctor assured me. "Just to stop you hurting yourself. Some clients tend to . . . move about a little, during the procedure."

Benway, the nurse, and another doctor were in the room. They took me off the morphine drip and put something else into my IV feed.

"Now count to ten, Mr. Peters . . . and everything . . . *willlllll bbbbbbeeee ooooovvvvvvv* . . ."

The last thing I remember before the sedative made its way through my bloodstream was seeing their faces looking down at me, and the hard light behind their heads gave the three sets of eyes staring at me a slightly sinister appearance. Then I remember nothing. Just black.

Endless.

Peaceful.

Black.

THE LOST WEEK, PART ONE

FOR A MOMENT WHILE COMING AROUND, I DIDN'T know where I was. I was almost peaceful. For a split second, for all I knew, I could have been waking up on a beautiful Malibu Beach, looking up into the endless, powder-blue skies.

Instead, the sky I was seeing was institutional white. Instead of the sounds of surf, the breeze, and the birds, I was listening to my heart's steady beating on an ECG monitor. Instead of languid and relaxed, I was in the worst agony I had ever experienced.

Shit, I remember seeing some documentary about drugs on the History Channel while stoned, and laughing my ass off when the presenter said that heroin was originally marketed as a cure for morphine addiction. Can you believe that? The cure that is worse than the problem. Snake-oil salesmen have always had an easy time making money selling horseshit cures to junkies desperate to quit their dope habits. Well, after coming round from this latest miracle solution for addiction, I realized that somebody, somewhere, was laughing his ass off at my expense, all the way to the goddamned bank.

Coming out from the sedatives, the world came to me in flashes. With each flash of awakening consciousness came almost unbearable pain and terror. I suppose it makes sense that cramming several days of painful withdrawal into a few hours has to hurt. I suppose in that optimistic, dope-fiending part of my brain I actually willed myself into believing I could simply take a shot, sleep for a few hours, and wake up cured. As the medicated sleep escaped my clutches I found myself in my hospital bed, and the ugliness of my situation hit me.

Honestly, if somebody had told me that an airplane had crashed into the hospital during the procedure, and I was dragged from the wreckage a few hours ago, I probably would have believed them. Every part of my body hurt. Every nerve ending screamed for relief. Not only did I feel as if I had been beaten within an inch of my life, the promised payoff, the cure for the agonies of withdrawal, hadn't even worked. I felt as sick as if I had just stopped cold turkey. My brain was literally screaming for opiates. I began to frantically buzz for help.

Enter a flurry of concerned nurses, and then the good doctor who performed the detoxification. As I frenziedly tried to explain to him how terrible I felt, how obviously something had gone wrong with the procedure and that I was in intense withdrawal, he just smiled and began to talk to me in his infuriatingly calm, measured way.

"Mr. Peters, a period of adjustment is to be expected."

"I need sedatives! I'm in agony! I need to sleep."

"Well, there will be no more sedatives for the time being. But we will monitor your condition and I will personally check back in with you."

"Listen, man, I need sedatives *now*."

"I'm sorry."

With that I was left alone. I writhed about on the bed trying to get comfortable, but it was useless. My wrists and ankles were bruised from my unconscious straining against the restraints. My body burned from the inside, the heat as intense as molten lava, and then suddenly cooled so much that my teeth would begin to chatter. I couldn't hold down food, and barely any liquids. I would get stomach cramps so ferocious that I would have to lie doubled over to find relief. I finally convinced one of the nurses to relent and get my mother on the phone. I lay talking to her in a frenzied whisper, curled up in misery on the soaking bedsheets.

"Ma, I'm telling you—something has gone wrong. The naltrexone didn't work . . . I'm sick, sicker than I've ever been."

"The doctor told me you're adjusting, Jason."

"This asshole doesn't know what he's talking about! I know when I'm dope sick, and I'm telling you that I am severely dope sick *right now.* I ain't asking them for opiates! I just need sleeping pills! Something! If they let me lie here sick like this . . . then, I gotta go. I can't do it like this."

"Jason, *no!* You can't leave."

"I can't stay if this is how it's gonna be."

She knew I wasn't bluffing. I knew that I had acquired a monstrous opiate habit over the years, and the doctor hadn't exactly made me feel secure that he knew what he was dealing with. I knew that unless I was either detoxed again, or at least sedated through the next few days, I was in for total hell.

"OK, OK Jason. I'll call him. I'll call him right now."

"OK. I'm calling you back in ten minutes, Ma. I mean it, ten minutes."

"OK, OK."

The time dragged by until I got my mother on the phone again. I knew instantly from the defeated sound of her voice when she said "Hello?" that things hadn't gone well.

"What did he say?"

"Jason . . . Look, he's really adamant that you are in an adjustment phase right now and that—"

"Did you tell him that I am walking if I don't get proper treatment?"

There was a pause.

"Did you?"

"Yes . . . Yes, Jason I did."

"And what did he say?'

"Well, Jason, he told me that you're an NFL player, and that you should suck it up. He said that you were in no condition to walk, and . . . and that he hadn't lost a patient yet."

Fifteen minutes later I staggered out of my room, with my shirt untucked and buttoned wrong, and my belongings roughly shoved into my holdall. I was determined to be Dr. Benway's first lost patient.

Upon getting to my feet the room began to spin, and I had to support myself on the bedside table to keep from toppling over. My legs felt weak and shaky. I ripped off the ridiculous assless gown they had put me in and started pulling my clothes out of the dresser. I dressed quickly because I had a limited amount of time before my body would give out completely and collapse. I staggered over to the bathroom and flicked on the lights. The sight of the person in the mirror was not comforting. I tried to vomit into the sink, but all that came out was a vile-smelling, burning yellow ooze. I rinsed my mouth out, splashed water over my death-mask face, and tried to make myself look halfway human. I was gonna show that motherfucker who was in no condition to walk! I limped out toward the reception desk, startling the nurses on duty.

"Where's Dr. Benway?"

"H-he's seeing another patient. What are you doing, Mr. Peters?"

"I'm going! Tell the doctor thanks for fucking nothing! Is there a limo service you can call?"

The nurses refused to make the call. I kept at them, and eventually one of them handed over the phone book so I could make the call myself. I picked the first limo service I found, and shakily ordered a car. I concentrated hard on not falling over. I kept repeating to myself *You can do this. You can do it. You can do it!* As I veered toward the door I heard a voice behind me say, "Jason?" and I turned, and found myself looking at an unfamiliar face. Something about her voice sparked a memory, but in my head fog I couldn't place it, and for an insane moment I thought she was going to ask for my autograph. She sensed my confusion and reached out to me, lightly taking my free hand. "I'm Heidi. From Beau Monde."

My mind scrambled to process the information. My brain felt

as if it was full of broken glass. I tried to smile at her, but it came out all wrong, like some hideous drugged leer. I just wanted to be away from her, and away from this place, and in a cave somewhere snorting a fat line of smack, away from all of humanity. My hello came out as a grunt.

"Well," she continued, moving toward me, "I was wondering how you were doing . . . but now I see. Not so good, I take it."

"I'm leaving."

I expected her to pull a face, or for her voice to take on the lecturing tone of a drugs counselor, but she remained amazingly neutral. She just nodded, and asked me why I had decided that.

I tried to explain, but even these few moments on my feet had sapped all of my energy, and the words came out wrong. The best I could manage was to tell her that I was sick, and that the detox was fucked up.

"You could come with me," she persevered. "We have a great staff at Beau Monde, we could detox you all over again."

"No. I have to go. There's a car on its way. I'll call you, Heidi."

I knew that I wasn't far from LA, and in LA I had connections. I had to get well, and nothing was going to get me well better than some heroin. My mind was already full of rationalizations: *The clinic fucked up. I'm not in the state of mind to start another detox. I just need to go and get myself straight—no serious using, just enough that I can feel OK so I can start again somewhere new. One night, one last chance to get high, and then I'll quit.*

So I left the clinic, Dr. Benway, and poor, puzzled Heidi. My last image was of Heidi standing in the reception area as her supposed patient bolted for the door and climbed into a waiting limousine. The guy behind the wheel was a sloppy guy in his late thirties, with a doughy, sad face. His hair had receded to the middle of his skull, and what was left was slicked back tight against his head. He was a big guy, big all over: big face, big hands, and big out-of-shape body that strained against his polyester limo driver's uniform. I recognized something in him immediately. A total inability to fit in properly to the world around him. He looked bleary-eyed, half-shaved, resentful of his tight-fitting outfit and the jaunty little cap they insisted he wear (and which he had tossed onto the passenger seat).

"Where to?" he asked.

"Anywhere," I spat. "Just get me the fuck away from this place!"

He laughed and the car pulled away. I started wracking my brain for alternatives. I thought about how my family would react to the news that I had left. That line of thinking led to an aching hole in my chest, so I crammed it deep down inside of myself, and started thinking instead of how best to cop drugs.

"Listen . . . Hey, what's your name?" I asked the driver.

"Pat."

"Hey, Pat, I'm Jason. Listen, I'm gonna ask you a question, and I don't want you to get offended, it's just a question—I'm not inferring anything—but do you have any idea where I can score some fucking heroin around here?"

Pat whistled and fell silent. I began to wonder if he might ask me to get the fuck out of his car. I mean, Jesus, despite his slovenly appearance this guy could be a religious nut for all I know.

"Shit," he said eventually. "I'm from LA, man, so I gotta be honest with you. I don't know how to score for shit around here."

"Fuck."

We drove on in silence for a while and then Pat piped up: "Hey, Jason? You like to smoke ice?"

"Oh sometimes, yeah."

"'Cos I got some of that up in here if you wanna get high."

It wasn't what my body needed right then, but with nothing else available I said, "Shit, well, pull over, my man."

So Pat the limo driver and I sat in the back of the limo, smoking meth and laughing. The drugs immediately took effect, and I felt human for the first time in days. I looked at my watch. I had walked out of rehab less than fifteen minutes ago.

"You know how it is, man," Pat was saying in his crackly smoker's voice, as he exhaled a white cloud of smoke and passed the pipe on, "When a dope fiend needs dope . . . it's like Batman puttin' on that fucking fruity light-beam thing he has."

"Right, right."

"You could be in fucking Antarctica. If you want it bad enough, somebody's gonna show up with some stuff, man. It's like one of the laws of the universe or something."

By nightfall I was back in my natural habitat, my four-hundred-dollar-a-night crack den in the Mondrian Hotel on Sunset Boulevard. The television played out car chases and freeway pileups, fires, and floods and I was surrounded by the things which made me feel secure—a glass pipe, a cooking ladle, aluminum foil, cocaine, heroin. Every time the thoughts that made my stomach knot returned, I banished them with more drugs. Thoughts of my family. Thoughts of my career. Thoughts of where I would be in a year, two years, five. I stayed in that room, in that frozen moment, for four days and nights, emerging rarely and never allowing the maids to clean my room. The lights were dimmed, and the expansive luxury suite sometimes felt like a cave. The only other human contact I had was with a girl I knew from my days in LA, who I called to tell I was in town. I hadn't seen her in a long time. I had been so full of ideas of where my life was going to go when I met her, as had she, but neither of us had moved on from where we had been the last time we had met. In an odd way it was as if time had stood still. We smoked together, and fucked occasionally, and her presence filled the spaces between the hits on the pipe and the lines of heroin or meth. There was an air of sadness about the whole thing, but it was the only kind of human contact that I could deal with. She left after a while, and I carried on alone.

Sometimes I wondered if I would ever leave this room. I wondered if I even wanted to. I'd marvel at the disingenuousness of my own mind, at the thought processes that kept me here, rooted to the spot. The part of me that still remembered what it felt like to destroy an opponent who was bigger than me, to run without fear headfirst into a 300-pound monster and emerge from the wreckage unscathed, could not understand how a simple chemical reaction in the brain could render me so utterly helpless. I was a slave to my addictions. I could not go anywhere, unless the heroin and the cocaine said that it was OK with them. I knew that, for now, I was essentially unable to reason with myself and walk out of this room. Not while there were still drugs. Not while there was still a sun in the sky.

The room was in chaos, the contents of my bag strewn across the floor, the suite's clean lines and modernist furnishings disrupted by what I had brought here with me. The heavy white curtains were drawn back during the evening so I could see the thousand twinkling lights of Sunset Boulevard below me as flat and as unreal as the stars in a planetarium. Even my own flesh seemed artificial, plastic. Sometimes, when I was high enough, I felt as if I were observing myself from outside of my body: the loneliness of the scene, my naked and hunched-over body perched on the end of the bed, me pacing and cursing, in an invisible cage of my own construction, heating the stem, cooking up cocaine and bicarbonate of soda in grim silence. It chilled my blood. Even the room itself, with its white on white, its clean lines and relentless brightness, started to seem like a morgue.

At some point the phone rang. It was early morning. The sun was starting to create a vomit-yellow haze through the blanket of smog that hovered over the city. I would have to close the curtains soon, as the thought of natural sunlight was offensive to me. I didn't want to see the sun; it reminded me of what I had become, and of everything I found repulsive about the world. I knew who was calling. This would be the fourth or fifth time that my mother had called, sobbing, begging me to check into Beau Monde. I would tell her that I was going to, and not to cry, for chrissake. That I was a grown man. That I loved her and would call her tomorrow. I didn't call. The thought of picking up the phone and dialing her number filled me with almost as much terror as the thought of leaving this room and starting detoxification all over again. I considered letting it ring, but the phone's insistent tone was ruining my hard-earned peace of mind. On TV the Baltimore police were wrestling a young kid to the ground and sticking their fingers in his mouth, forcing him to spit out cellophane-wrapped rocks of crack, which probably amounted to no more than a couple of hundred bucks' worth of shitty street-quality cocaine. The phone kept ringing. Resigned, I picked it up.

"Yeah?"

Silence.

"Hello?"

Silence.

I slammed the phone down. This was the second time this had happened. I cut out some more meth and snorted it; it burned its way into my aching nasal passages like I was snorting shards of glass. I couldn't let go of the two silent phone calls. Was it the police, checking to see that I was in the room before they busted the door down?

Ring-ring.

I dived across the bed and wrestled the phone out of the cradle, yelling "Hello? Hello?" but there was nothing but a dial tone this time. Had I imagined the phone ringing? I had grabbed at it once while my friend was here and she had looked at me like I was crazy. I had tried to play it off like I was playing a joke on her. Had it happened again? Was I hearing things?

The craziness had begun to creep slowly into my psyche. You know that it will come, you are unsure of when, but inevitably the meth and the crack stop getting you there, and you need more and more to even feel anything. Each pull on the pipe left the distinct hint of disappointment in my mouth, I tried to ignore it, but it sat there—like an interrupted orgasm—and suddenly there was a creak, as someone passed by my door and I froze—I literally froze on the end of the bed and stopped breathing—the pipe still dangling from my lips—and I slowly brought my hand up to remove it from my mouth silently—in minute increments—then I leaned over and slid the pipe underneath the mattress before inching onto my feet. The only sound was the sound of my heart, which was pounding so hard that I imagined that whoever was on the other side of the door must have been able to hear it, too, whether it was the hotel security, or the cops, or the Devil himself out there waiting for me.

I knew—somewhere in my mind—that this was the same bull-shit crackhead paranoia that always comes after many hours on the pipe, the same cliché that every crack fiend who tells her story always gets to. In many of the group meetings in treatment centers I was forced to attend, we all sat around and laughed about it: some old reformed cokehead joking about how he believed that the FBI had placed robot birds in the trees outside of his apartment to spy on him, and, shit, we all got a belly laugh out of that one. Here in the hotel room, even armed with this insight and knowledge, that single creak had taken me over the edge, and I could no longer reason with myself because somehow, this time, I *knew* that the threat was real, I knew that *they* were out there, and I didn't know who *they* were, but I knew that they meant me harm and I was maybe facing jail or death if they caught me.

So I threw myself onto the expensive deep-pile carpet, and started to slither across it like a fucking snake, like I was a soldier crawling through the shit and the mud to approach the enemy line, and I shimmied and propelled myself forward, making it to the door silently, and I tried to peek under it but I couldn't see shit, so slooo-wwwlly I got onto my feet and pressed a bulging eye to the peephole.

Nothing.

I slowly lowered my head and then *bam!* I popped right up again.

Still nothing.

These motherfuckers were slick.

I stood there and waited, and tried to count the seconds, but kept losing track: I was counting in time with my heart's thumping and therefore counting two for every second that passed, so I tried to start again and I was not sure if a minute or ten minutes or an hour had passed at this point. I peeked again.

Nothing.

"You're bugging out," I told myself. My voice sounded hoarse and strange. My lips hurt. They were cracked dry, bloody from the coke. I wanted to do some heroin. I wanted to be asleep. I crept back toward my bed, still silently, because any sound at all was freaking me out now, even the creak of my bones as I moved, and I could think of nothing I wanted or needed more right now than to be out of this goddamned room.

It seemed entirely possible that at any minute the door would be kicked in, and the Los Angeles Police Department would storm the room, guns drawn to take me away. The fear grew, grew from the pit of my guts until it consumed all of me. In a moment of panic, I rummaged through my clothes and dug out the piece of paper with Heidi's number on it, and dialed Beau Monde, before I could get distracted and talk myself out of it.

"Heidi, it's Jason. I think I need to see you."

Heidi greeted me warmly and I arranged to check in at 6:00 P.M. that same evening. She assured me that everything was going to be alright. I knew it was just bullshit and pleasantries, but I took her at her word despite myself. All I really wanted to hear at that moment was somebody telling me things were going to be alright.

I left in plenty of time to make the drive down to Orange County. I called the same limo service, and again it was Pat who arrived to drive me down.

"Hey, Jason!" He laughed as he saw me approach the car. "I had this bozo lined up for this afternoon, some fucking guy in oil. Big tipper! But I passed him on to one of the other guys. You're my client, right, pal?"

He took in the crazed look in my eye, recoiled, and we drove most of the way down in silence. Pat was a man who obviously knew the horrors of meth paranoia and wisely decided to leave me the fuck alone. I'm sure that if I had suggested it, he gladly would have pulled the car over and got high with me again. Maybe I was disappointing him, but I didn't give a fuck. I felt numbed out. The coke was stashed away in my bag, talking to me the whole way down.

Jason . . .

Jason!

You're making good time, man. You're gonna be early. What's the rush? This is IT! No more fun! If you're serious about this, this is the last chance you're gonna get.

I concentrated on the asphalt zooming underneath me. I told Pat to turn the stereo up. The local station was playing something pretty heavy, and he cranked it, lifting the crashing drums, bass, and guitars to a brutal level.

You're going to be in that rehab in a few days' time hating yourself for not smoking me.

What are you going to do? Flush me?

Your last bit of cocaine?

You're going to flush me down the fucking john?

Huh?

Jason! I'm talking to you!

So, yeah, I made a pit stop. A hotel in Orange County. I told Pat I needed to spend some time alone, and he just smiled and said, "Whatever you need to do, man," handing me his cell number. He split to go get high, or do whatever else he did in the times he wasn't driving. I flicked through the phone book, called a girl to come over, and then started to freebase the rest of the coke.

When the knock came, I was high as hell, and I opened the door and could see her eyes widen slightly when she walked into the room. Her eyes traveled from the bed, to the crack pipe in my hand, to the aluminum foil with drying cocaine freebase on it on the cabinet, to my bulging eyes and she said: "One thousand."

"What?"

"I want one thousand."

"For what?"

"To stay. I want one thousand dollars to stay here! Take it or leave it."

Pissed, I raised the pipe to my lips and took a long hit, rolling it in my fingers to keep the coke from burning up. I took the pipe from my lips, fixed her in a stare and exhaled a great cloud of white smoke all around her. She stood, rooted to the spot, expressionless.

"Why don't you get the fuck out of here?" I asked her.

After she had split, I started to get paranoid again. It would take one phone call from this pissed-off hooker, and the cops would be all over this scene. I realized that there was no way I could stay here any longer. I had been in this room, smoking cocaine for hours. It was past midnight when I called Pat, and he was at my door in ten minutes chattering like a speed-freak maniac about traffic and the president and Christ knows what else. Maybe it was a sense of kinship that got him there so fast, or maybe it was the wads of cash I was handing over every time I got in or out of his vehicle, but no matter. I hit the road with the yelling in my head subdued for another short while. Pat gunned the engine and we roared toward Beau Monde.

THE LOST WEEK, PART TWO

WAKING UP. IT'S NOT A PLEASANT FEELING.

Why can't I stay asleep forever?

The fear begins the moment I start to surface into consciousness. I am not at home; I am not in my usual surroundings. It's that feeling you get when you wake up as a kid and it's Monday morning and you have a test you spent the whole weekend not studying for. I want to sink into the black again, but something is dragging me up toward the light.

Mwuwu Pwuwuh?

Mwuwu Pwuwuh?

I open my eyes a crack and ascertain that there are figures standing over me. The words are getting clearer, but they still sound as if they are floating to me through a sea of salty magma.

Mistah Peta?

What the fuck is *Mistah Peta?*

"Hello? Mr. Peter?"

Oh shit.

Everything took a turn for the worse when I arrived at Beau Monde. My first impression of the place was that it didn't look like any treatment center that I had ever been in. It was located in a very exclusive residential neighborhood in Newport Beach, and it seemed entirely possible that the neighbors had no idea that this place was meant for dope fiends and drunks. The building looked totally inconspicuous among the mansions of the superrich that dotted the hillside around here. Unfortunately, my pit stop at the hotel had cost me badly, and I showed up at 2:00 A.M., eight hours late for my check-in.

"It's fuckin' late, man!" Pat informed me as we pulled up outside of the address with a crunch of gravel. "Are you sure you don't want me to wait for you?"

"They're expecting me!" I bellowed. "The chick who works here told me to come. I'll be good."

"Maybe I should wait, just in case, buddy."

"Well, shit, it's your time you're wasting."

I swaggered out of the limo, dragging my bag along with me up to the steel gates, and started frantically buzzing the intercom. After the fifth or sixth ring a tired female voice crackled: "Yeah?"

"It's Jason Peter. I'm here to check in."

"Check in? Erm, wait a minute please."

I looked over to the limo. Pat had rolled down the tinted glass and was peering at me. I shrugged my shoulders at him. The intercom clicked back into life.

"You were meant to check in at six o'clock," the woman said. "There's no one here right now. You'll have to come back tomorrow."

I was stunned. Pissed off. Who the fuck did this woman think she was?

"Are you a doctor?" I demanded.

"No. I'm a masseuse. And I'm security. And I can't help you."

"I want to speak to a doctor, then. I was told to come here today!"

"Well, you're late. There's no one else here. I'm it. And I can't check you in."

"Is everything OK?" Pat called over to me, turning off the engine.

"It's cool!" I yelled back at him, then turned to the intercom. "Listen, lady, just let me in. I'll wait inside until someone shows up."

"I can't do that, sir. You'll have to come back."

The rage that had been simmering inside of me since I crawled out of the hospital on Monday started to bubble over. I could feel it starting, my heart rate quickening and my breathing becoming heavier, more deliberate. I put my mouth to the speaker and very slowly, very deliberately enunciated the words:

"Open. This. Mother. Fucking. Gate. Now."

"I'm sorry, sir."

I started to punch the intercom furiously, sending a squeal of feedback out of it, before I screamed: "*You cocksuckers, let me in! Open this motherfucking gate now, or I will kick the fucking thing down! Do you hear me? Open this motherfucking gate!*"

The intercom went quiet. I grabbed the steel gate with both hands and started to wrench it violently back and forth. I continued to scream and yell as loud as I could. Pat started the engine up again, ready to bolt, I supposed. I didn't care. I didn't give a flying fuck. All I knew was that unless I got inside of this gate *tonight* I might never step foot inside of a treatment center again. This was it!

Eventually, the woman returned.

"Jason," she said. "Jason! I have Heidi on the phone."

"Tell her to open the fucking gate, then!"

"I can't, Jason." The woman then conferred with Heidi, muttering, "Uh-huh, right, uh-huh," then came back to me: "Heidi says that because the doctor isn't here, we can't allow you in. He needs to do your admission. Without a medical doctor here to check you out, we can't process you! He'll be here at nine o'clock tomorrow morning. If you'd just come back then, we'll process you and we will have you comfortable within the hour."

"*Fuck this!*" I screamed. "*Fuck this shit!*"

"It's the best we can do, Jason."

"Then fuck you, too!"

"Well, if that's the way you feel, Jason. But I'm telling you that the doctor will be here at 9:00 A.M."

The intercom clicked off. It was hopeless. I could feel the

adrenaline subsiding a little. Shit, with the cocaine it was becoming harder to control that killer rage that had made me so unstoppable on the football field. I suppose I wasn't really screaming at the woman over the intercom, or Heidi, or the stupid fucking gate: I was screaming at myself. I was screaming at the skies and the earth and the ocean. At that time the niceties of it didn't matter, and I didn't have the time or the inclination to ponder it. I picked up my bag and walked over to the car. Pat had been shaken by my outburst, and he looked nervous that the cops were about to show up. This was a nice neighborhood. Shit like this didn't go unnoticed. I wrenched open the door, threw my bag inside, and climbed in. "Take me to the Four Seasons," I said, sinking into my seat.

I handed over my credit card and was shown up to my room, a six hundred dollar a night suite on the fourth floor. My body was crying out for sleep or drugs. I had no intention of sleeping, though, not while there was still coke, heroin, and meth on my person. Sleep could wait.

I called home and got Christian on the phone. He was extremely pissed off when I told him I was at a hotel and not in Beau Monde.

"Jason, you had better be there at 9:00 A.M. tomorrow, bro. I'm fucking serious. Mom is gonna freak if she finds out you didn't make it."

"Shit, I'll make it. Don't tell her anything. I don't want her worrying."

I hung up the phone, knowing that I was a liar. I knew that I would stay in this room for as long as the drugs lasted.

Somehow, it always came back to this. Another hotel room, another breathtaking view that gives me no pleasure, another king-size bed that I will pace around, throw drug paraphernalia all over, nod out and burn holes in, do anything but sleep on. I prepared the cocaine on a marble-topped table, looking out over the beach. The routine was as old as time, but each time I mixed the cocaine and the

bicarbonate of soda in with the water, I did it with the joy of dis-
covery. Every time felt like the first time. Every sensation was alien
and new, yet as familiar as the touch of my own skin.

As the dawn broke, the skies turned a brilliant orange, as if the
sun was going to crash into the earth—an event that I would have
welcomed this morning—then it relented, moving into purple, then
blue, and I pulled the curtains drawn, but it was too late: I was disgusted and defeated already. I cut out a line of heroin and inhaled it,
enjoying the bitter taste of it in my throat, and I opened a bottle and
swallowed some Xanax. I slid my ass onto the bed and flicked on the
TV. I went for the porno channel. I needed something, anything to
focus on until the drugs kicked in. I bought a movie and slid into
blissful, stoned oblivion, the sounds of fucking a kind of lullaby that
eased me over the edge.

"Mr. Peter? Mr. Peter?"

With a start I am awake. I am lying on top of the bed, naked.
The porno is still going, the *uh-uh-uhs* of some girl getting screwed
onscreen adding a strangely perverse element to all of this. Christ
knows how many times it has repeated in its entirety. I am looking
up at three large men in security uniforms. I sit bolt upright, reach
for the blanket. There is no blanket.

"Who the fuck are you?" I manage to gasp.

"Hotel security. You didn't hear us knocking?"

I look over at the door. It has been removed from its fucking
hinges. Apparently I didn't hear a whole lot more than just knocking.

"I guess not," I say somewhat unconvincingly. I glance out of
the corner of my eye at the nightstand. At least I managed to put the
Xanax bottle away before passing out. "I'm a heavy sleeper, I guess."

"Do you need us to call anybody? Are you OK?"

"No, I don't need you to call anybody. What I do need is for
you to tell me why the fuck you are in my room."

I stand up. The drugs have eaten away at some of my footballer's physique, but I still tower over all of these fucking security guards with ease. I can feel rage rising inside of me. I don't give a fuck whether I am naked or not. I stare down at them.

"Well, Mr. Peter," one of them starts. "We received a call from your mother . . . She told us about your condition and expressed worry that she hadn't been able to reach you for a few days."

Mom. Oh Christ, what has she said to the fucking hotel?

"What condition?"

"Well, the epilepsy. She explained about the fits . . . and just wanted us to check that you were OK."

They are starting to back collectively out of the room, but I can already feel my rage dissipating. I need to be alone. I try to be affable as possible, thank them for their concern, reassure then that I am fine, and I get them the fuck out of there. I call my connection and order more drugs. Then I dial my mother's number, furiously.

"Hello?"

"Mom. Are you trying to get me locked up? Is that what you are trying to do?"

"Jason."

"Yes. It's Jason. I just had an interesting wake-up call this morning. I don't remember requesting it though."

"I'm so glad that you're OK, Jason. I've been so worried."

"I'm not OK, Mom, I just had three security guards burst into my room while I was sleeping. They could have seen anything! Anything! Do you think that they would not call the cops because it's the Four Seasons? Is that what you think?"

"I didn't know what to think . . . I thought you might be—"

"What? Dead? Is that it? Well, I'm not dead, Ma, but I am mightily pissed off."

"I'm *sorry!*" she screams, and I am shocked into silence by her sudden outburst. I just sit there, cradling the phone.

"Jason?" she asks eventually.

"Yeah, I'm here."

"I was worried, Jason. So worried."

"Yeah, I know. I know."

"Baby, why didn't you check into the treatment center? Your brother said that you were going to check in."

"I showed up too late. They told me to come back today!"

"No, Jason. They told you to come two days ago."

I looked around the room. The blinking clock on the TV. My watch. I was completely baffled. It wasn't Wednesday still?

"Ma, what day is it?"

"It's Saturday, Jason. It's Saturday. I'd been calling your room all morning before I spoke to security."

My head felt as if it was full of cotton wool. Three days? I supposed it was possible. Without sleep and with the curtains drawn, time had started to become something of an elastic concept. I was operating on dope time. The only time that registered with me was the endless stretches in between hits on the pipe, or between each line of heroin. I had no idea of what I was doing anymore. Suddenly, terrifyingly, the tears started to come. Maybe it would have been better if I had died when I tried to finish it all at my parents' house. Anything would be better than this half-life.

"OK . . . OK, Ma, I'll call Heidi."

"I called her, Jason. She's waiting for you."

"Shit. OK, I'm on my way. I'm calling a car right now."

"Thank you, Jason."

I could tell that she was about to cry. I couldn't stand to hear it anymore. I told her I loved her, and hung up the phone. I meant what I had said, but I knew that before I checked in, there was business to be taken care of. I had more cocaine and heroin en route to my hotel room. I couldn't just bail out before the girl showed. More so than with Beau Monde, or even my own family, the idea of burning bridges with my dope connections was terrifying to me. Maybe if I slept a little now, when she showed up with the stuff I would be sufficiently sober to really enjoy one last blast on the pipe.

The higher I got, the more the order of events became garbled in my head. At one point I was sitting with my old connection,

Christina, the crackhead I knew from my times in LA with Zora. Since the last time I had dealt with her, Christina had shrunken even farther back into her own bones. It was as if something was eating away at her from the inside. She stayed and smoked some coke with me, telling me about the latest comings and goings of the customers of hers who I knew from the first time I stayed in Los Angeles. I asked her about Zora. She just whistled and said, "That's a sad story, man. We don't even have time to get into all of that." Sometimes, when she'd look at me with her wide, terrified eyes it would seem as if some part of her, hidden deep inside, was pleading with me to help her escape from her toxic, wasted body. I offered her a bump of heroin, but she laughed lightly and shook her head.

"I don't fuck with that shit, honey," she told me, reaching for the pipe.

At another point I lost my crack pipe. I turned the entire hotel room upside down looking for it. I meticulously went over every square inch of the room, but could not find it anywhere. When I gave up, I flopped down on the bed and I felt it pressing against my back. It was in plain view, sitting on top of my bedsheet, the whole time. I began to wonder if someone sneaked in here and hid it from me, in an attempt to fuck with me. As I wondered about this, the phone rang. My mother. I knew instinctively that it had to be my mother. I considered letting it ring, but after what happened last time I relented and picked up.

"Jason?"

With a start I realized that it was Christian on the other line. He seemed tense, agitated. At first I thought he was going to try an angry-older-brother intervention on me, and then I realized that the agitated tone of voice seemed more worried than angry.

"What is it? What's wrong?" I demanded.

"It's Mom, Jason. She's sick."

My mind scrambled to process the information though the drug cloud. At first I took his statement at face value and imagined that she had a cold. My reaction was *Why is he bothering me with this?*

"Sick how?" I stammered.

"Sick. She's in the hospital. They think it's her heart!"

"What? But—but she's healthy . . . she . . ."

"She's worried about you, Jason! She hasn't been sleeping. She paces . . . in tears, hysterical! I mean, Jesus, is this surprising to you? She's an old woman! She can't be dealing with this shit! Anyway, the chest pains started an hour ago. We drove her to the hospital . . . I don't know, Jason. She's having tests."

"Fuck! Fuck!"

I sat there, trembling. Had I killed my own mother? I felt nauseous, weak. Or was this a lie? An elaborate plot to emotionally blackmail me into getting treatment? I didn't know how to feel. How to react. I needed more drugs. I needed not to feel. I needed something—anything—but *this*. My hand gripped the receiver so tight that I felt that it could turn into dust. My mind felt fragile; it screamed and squirmed in my skull, and I had to struggle to keep myself from losing it to anger or hysteria.

"I'm coming. Tell her I'm getting a plane."

"What! Jason, fuck that! She doesn't want you at the hospital! She wants you in fucking rehab where she knows you're safe, man! Jesus!"

"OK!" I screamed. "OK! Tell her I'm on my way to the hospital. I'm calling Heidi right now! I'll call you back."

I walked into the bathroom and looked at myself in the mirror. I looked fractured. My face didn't seem to fit together right. It was my jaw, my lips, my eyes, my nose, my forehead, my cheekbones, but somehow it didn't all fit together the way it should. A part of me was dying, I could see it right there.

"This isn't just fear anymore," I told myself. "You're scared. You're scared you can't do this."

I looked at myself, right in the eyes.

"Fuck you," I hissed. "I'm not scared. I'm not scared of shit."

I laughed at the absurdity of it, talking to myself in the fucking mirror. Jesus Christ. But as I gathered my belongings and disposed of what was left of the drugs, I knew that there was something fundamentally true about what I had said. I did feel fear. The same kind of fear that I felt before going up against a good opposing team, but also something else: a little of the old excitement. A little of the old exhilaration. It was a minute feeling, but it was there. I knew that if I could just hold onto that fragment of excitement, then I would make it.

Every scar on my body told a story. They reflected the bathroom light like marble. Each one brought back memories of a collision, the snap of bone, and the long convalescence from the surgeon's knife. There were other scars, the ones that people couldn't see, and they hadn't healed properly yet. In fact, they festered inside of me, poisoning me slowly from within. I dressed deliberately. I brushed my teeth until I retched into the sink. Then I stepped out, walking to the elevator.

It was game time.

ALONE
WITH THE
BADDEST
MOTHERFUCKER
IN GOD'S OWN
UNIVERSE

MY RAGE AT BEING LOCKED OUT OF BEAU MONDE
gradually dissipated as the drugs worked their way out of my system.
Walking into the place for the first time I was astonished by what I
saw. It was beautiful. I mean literally, jaw-droppingly beautiful. I felt
as if I was walking into an exclusive hotel instead of a treatment
center. Heidi greeted me warmly, my transgressions of the other
night forgotten. I felt more tired than I had ever felt. I had the sense
that I was walking into a sanctuary, a quiet place of safety, and all
of the abuse I had been heaping onto myself, all of the worry, the
pain, the stress began to drain out of me.

The staff was busy checking a former child star out. I recognized him vaguely from a television show of my youth. I grabbed
someone and asked where I should go.

"We'll be with you real soon," they said.

"Should I sit over here?"

They smiled and suggested, "Why don't you go hang out by
the pool for a little while?"

I thought: *The pool! Of course. Jesus Christ!*

"Are you hungry? Would you like us to cook you something?"

"Ah, no, no . . . I—uh." I was grinding my teeth like crazy, still
wired as hell.

"Ah yes. I see. Well, maybe later."

After I had checked in, I was shown to my room. It was a

stone's throw from the indoor pool. I would be staying in a master bedroom with its own bathroom, and French doors that opened up right to the poolside. I was completely freaked out by the luxury I was surrounded by. There were gleaming, hardwood floors throughout the house, and the place was situated on a hill, giving an unrestricted view of Balboa Island—and it was quiet! Nobody was cursing at the staff, or begging for painkillers, or threatening to kill each other. It seemed that besides the staff themselves, I was the only other person here.

While I originally intended to stay for only thirty days, I would wind up staying in Beau Monde for one year. Instead of having me sit in meetings with a bunch of other addicts to talk about my problems, all of my treatment was done one on one. I told them at the start, "I don't believe the twelve-step program is for me. I don't want to attend AA meetings." Instead of a lecture on how this was my disease talking, I was told that this was perfectly understandable and that a personalized treatment plan would be worked out with my full cooperation. Feeling that I had a measure of control over my treatment gave me renewed faith that this time I could really make a change.

I slept and ate for the first ten days, before slowly getting into a routine of meetings with a life coach, doctors, therapists, and specialists. The detoxification process was nowhere near as extreme as it had been in the past. By the time I checked into Beau Monde I was almost entirely opiate free, and as part of my treatment there I began taking a drug called Suboxone.

Suboxone is what is known as a partial opiate agonist. It comes in the form of small, orange tablets to be dissolved under the tongue each morning. In the United States, the favored method of maintaining and treating opiate addicts is with methadone. Methadone is basically a long-acting opiate, which is taken orally and replaces heroin in the body. Methadone is as addictive as heroin, and the withdrawal from it is a much more protracted process. In my prior rehabs I met plenty of people who were coming off of methadone and swore that kicking dope was easier. Suboxone, like methadone, replaces heroin, but it also blocks the opiate receptors so that if you do relapse and use street dope, you would not feel a thing. You would have to wean yourself off of Suboxone in order to be able to get high on heroin. Because it is an opiate, it was also useful in providing pain relief without my having to resort to problematic painkillers.

With my body stabilized on Suboxone, I threw myself into life at Beau Monde. For the first two months I lived on site, but instead of being treated like an inmate, I was allowed a lot of freedom. I was free to come and go, so I could catch a movie or sit in a coffee shop for a few hours. This level of trust in turn inspired me to start trusting the staff. Of course, I would be regularly tested for street drugs, but without an atmosphere of suspicion I felt an obligation not to let the staff down.

After two months I moved to a less supervised house with no one but other clients living there, and from there graduated into a sober living house with a roommate. My family, for the first time in many years, was completely happy. My mom recovered from her heart scare—which turned out not be a heart attack, but a stress-induced incident—and told me how proud she was of me.

"But, Ma, I miss you. I feel that I should be close to you."

"Jason, I want you to stay. I want you to spend as long as it takes over there. You are close to me. I think about you every moment."

After the honeymoon period, I started to get antsy. Thinking about what was waiting for me outside of Beau Monde filled me with terror. I thought about my apartment. I thought about the financial ruin I visited upon myself. I thought about the people I had let down. I thought about Grant, how I had ignored his calls so many times that he simply did not try to contact me anymore. I thought that maybe he hated me. That I had ruined one of the most meaningful, truest friendships of my life. I had chosen drugs over my blood brother. When I focused on these anxieties the urge to get high was almost overwhelming.

When the urge came, however, I was able to talk to someone about it straightaway. The one-on-one counseling helped me in immeasurable ways. Going into those meetings was like the pregame pep talks I gave in Nebraska. I would walk out of there full of determination and fire. I wanted to succeed.

After I had been there for two months, I got into the routine of waking at 7:00 A.M. with one of the recreation counselors and driving down to the beach to surf. I found something profoundly moving and inspiring in starting the day off in the perfect, unblemished water of Newport Beach while dolphins swam sometimes as close as ten feet away. The life that I had embraced, the drug life, a life locked away from the sunlight, from love, from nature itself, seemed all the more barren and ugly from this position. I sometimes experienced a rush as dizzying and gratifying as any produced by the crack pipe.

One morning the doctor who was treating me approached me with a proposition. HBO had contacted him because they were doing a special on athletes who abuse pain pills. They wanted to know if he knew of any athletes they could interview for the piece.

"Is this one of those bullshit exposé things?"

"No. This is HBO, not *Maury*. It's a serious piece. They just want to shed some light on the issue."

I was two months clean. When you are newly clean, your moods can be extreme. When you are happy, it is as if you are experiencing happiness for the first time in your life. This is where I was at. I wanted to change the world, I wanted to cure cancer. I had even been thinking of opening up a treatment center once I got clean. I was full of all kinds of complex, optimistic ideas like that.

The HBO special seemed like a perfect opportunity to do some good for once in my life. I thought about if for a few hours, and then told my doctor, "OK, I'll do it."

The show was *Real Sports with Bryant Gumbel*. The interview was done over the course of a day, and the interviewer was Bernard Goldberg, a gray-haired journalist who had done a negative piece on Nebraska for CBS back in the nineties. So when I saw him face-to-face I got a little tense. The filming was done inside of Beau Monde, and as I was put in makeup and sat down for the first interview, panic started to rise in my chest. I was really going to do it. I was about to stand up and say in a public forum that I was a drug addict. I knew that as soon as I went through with this, everything was going to change.

The interview was a nervous blur. In between takes, Bernard did not talk to me. We sat in silence, as the camera crew and the director would line up the next shot. It was awkward. I did not hold back. I talked about it all. The painkillers. The heroin. The crack. I felt as if I was purging, letting all of the vile shit from inside of myself out into the open.

At one point, Bernard came right out and said it: "You were a junkie!" and I had to answer, "Yes."

People get funny ideas about addicts. I knew that my image was about to transform—outside of the people I used drugs with and my close friends and family, nobody knew about my personal problems. Now it may be the first thing that people think of when they hear my name. That was going to be a harsh reality to deal with. But fuck it anyway.

When the piece aired, I watched it inside of Beau Monde with Heidi. She reassured me that I would really help people by going public. I wasn't so sure anymore. A part of me wanted to run and hide, lock myself away, smoke crack until my eyes bled and wait for the world to finally vanish. But seeing myself on the television, hearing myself speak, was a quiet revelation for me.

"I couldn't get out of bed in the morning. My eyes . . . half open. No joy. No sadness. Nothing."

"Recovery, trying to stop . . . It's the hardest thing I've ever had to do. There are still times now—and I've been in here six weeks—that I sit outside and cry. I just think: I CAN'T STOP. I could easily jump this fucking wall . . . and be outside using dope and smoking crack again."

"It's miserable to have something run your life . . . and you're not going to get better sitting in your apartment taking pill after pill, smoking crack

and taking heroin. That's not what the answer is if you want to live. If you want a life."

I was pretty shaken up by the time the broadcast was over. I sat there in silence.

"You did good," Heidi said to me eventually.

"Thanks."

I was lost in thought. I knew that there was no going back. I knew what an abject failure I would have really been if, after saying those words on television, I were to relapse and go back to doing the same shit. I finally saw a way that my catalogue of failures and let-downs could have been made much, much worse. I felt that I had finally made a definite decision. I remained quiet for the rest of the night, mourning the passing of a way of life.

The next day, I was waiting in line at a Fed Ex office. The guy behind the counter kept giving me funny looks. I had once been used to this, especially in Nebraska and Charlotte at the height of my career, but in California this was a pretty unusual thing. I checked my zipper, but it was up. It was my turn, and I brought the package over to him.

"You're Jason Peter, right? The football player from Nebraska."

"Yeah, that's me."

"I saw you on Real Sports last night."

"Oh yeah?"

"Yeah! You did a real good job. I think it's great that you were willing to talk about that stuff."

I smiled, awkwardly, and completed the transaction. It wasn't until I was out of the office and back into the midafternoon sunlight that I pondered the encounter and started to feel good about myself. There would be a follow-up show, and the next time I met Bernie, he was friendly and affable. The first thing he said to me was "I'm glad to see you're doing so well. You look really great." We laughed and joked in between takes, even walked along the beach after the interview was done to shoot the shit about football and recovery. We would actually become friends after the second interview.

For now, such things were off in the future. Not the far future, and not a future that was unimaginable to me anymore.

A chapter had ended, and something new, possibly wonderful was beginning.

I watched the tape again recently and noticed something that had escaped me the first time I saw it. It was something in my eyes, as the interview ended. On camera, Bernard leans across to me slightly and says, "I hope you make it."

My eyes, which still looked dead to me, drowsy and haggard . . . Well, they lit up for a second, animated with real honest-to-God life. On screen, I watch them as I say: "Thank you. I think I will this time, Bernie."

And there it is, suddenly clear to me for the first time. *Hope.* For that briefest of moments, up there on that television screen and for the first time in years, my eyes glowed with *hope.*

THE SUBSTANCE OF THINGS HOPED FOR

THE FIRST TIME I MET SARAH, EARLY IN 2006, I was due to go meet another girl for coffee. As I was getting ready, I got a call from Kimmie, my masseuse.

"Jason? I have a friend in town who you just have to meet."

"Oh hey, Kimmie. Listen, I'm actually meeting someone later, but—"

"No, no seriously. You have to meet this girl. We're coming by."

"What? Ah, shit. OK. OK."

So I sat around waiting for them to show, and pretty soon I heard Kimmie's car pulling up outside. Kimmie was a professional volleyball player, strong as shit, and had become a good friend over the months I had known her. I wasn't sure if this was her attempt to set me up on a date or what, but in my experience such things usually don't turn out well. I was getting fidgety about the time, and the coffee date I had with this other girl, but when she walked in with Sarah, well, none of that stuff seemed so important anymore.

I wasn't looking for a relationship. Since coming out of Beau Monde I'd had a few short relationships, and that initial urge to be involved with someone after a long time alone was out of my system. I was feeling much calmer, in control of myself these days. Jesus, had I matured? I hoped not.

But Sarah! Well, she was undeniably beautiful. I have known a lot of undeniably beautiful women in my time, but Sarah was something else. I introduced myself, and had everybody sit. We sat around talking for a while, and Sarah started telling me about her recent trip to Colorado. The thing that caught my attention was that all of the stories she told me revolved around her hanging out with her family. This was unusual because most of the girls I knew who went to hang out in Aspen were there for one of two things: to get fucked up or to land a rich husband so they never had to work another day in their lives.

I suppose hanging out in a certain group, with drug users, starfuckers, football groupies, had warped my perception of people a little. The value of family was something that had been on my mind a lot recently. Being stuck out on the West Coast after my stay in Beau Monde was beginning to get to me, and I was longing for a return home to once again be a part of the Peter clan. Just thinking of the things I had put my parents and my siblings through with my addiction was enough to bring me to tears sometimes. Hearing Sarah talk about her family with such . . . well, the only way I can describe it is with such *love* . . . it really touched me.

Just then Hank jumped up on her lap.

Hank is my puppy. He's an eager, kinda spastic basset hound. Not only did Sarah have to put up with Hank's attentions, but also she had Kimmie's German shepherd, Kanoa, to deal with. She was dressed nice, obviously ready to go out, and I knew that one thing that girls who came over to my place really hated was when Hank got all amorous and started shedding hairs on them and trying to lick their faces. I went to pull him off, but she said, "No! Leave him. He's a sweetie!"

I watched silently as Sarah ruffled first Hank's, then Kanoa's fur, bending down to allow them to lick her face in turn, and I smiled. Wow, this woman really loved dogs. I looked over to Kimmie, who was grinning at me as if to say, "I told you so."

I've always been a dog lover. My parents had dogs and even in my most chaotic, darkest moments, those big bastards brought me peace of mind and comfort on the rare occasions that I managed to drag my gasping shell over to my family house for a few guilt-ridden hours. I had dogs of my own in New York—a Rottweiler and an English mastiff—and they had to return to my parents because I knew that I was neglecting them badly. I couldn't even take them for walks.

When I had been in Beau Monde for roughly six months, I got Hank. I was living alone in my sober living home and feeling pretty lonely. Walking through the Beverly Center one day I saw Hank, barely squeezed into one of the glass cubicles where puppies for sale are kept. Something inside of me told me that this was the dog for me, and I went over to buy him. As this thought surfaced, a cold trickle of fear piped up, too. By buying this dog I was making a promise that I would be together enough to love him, to care for him. Buying Hank was as big a deal for me as deleting my dealers' numbers from my cell phone had been. Of course, I knew that I had paged my heroin connection so often that the number was indelibly etched on my brain, filed away with my date of birth, social security number, and my mother's birthday. Even now, as I think about this, I could recite that fucking number by rote without having to pause for thought. But still, something about deleting the numbers felt final. And something about paying for Hank and taking him back to my place felt final.

As he licked at me, and panted, and barked happily, I felt something painful inside; here was a living thing whose life now depended entirely upon me. I'm not an animal lover—I'm a dog lover—and I loved that little bastard from day one.

The first time Hank saved my life was maybe one month later. I was in still in Beau Monde, undergoing physical therapy. I was living in a halfway house, and had nearly complete freedom. My roommate had recently left the program and relapsed, and Hank and I were living in the house all by ourselves. When I woke up that morning, I didn't feel any different. I was following the program. I was taking instruction. The dreams were not as frequent, as vivid any more. The depression was lessening. I was in a routine that didn't involve being high before noon. I was doing what I had to do.

Nothing bad happened. I didn't receive any terrible news. I didn't switch on the TV and happen to see the scene in, say, *Drugstore Cowboy* where Matt Dillon shoots up in the back of the car after robbing the pharmacy and suddenly the air outside of the car turns rosy, and everything seems to move in slow motion, and looks like a junked-out Norman Rockwell picture floating in a sea of liquid ecstasy.

My shoelaces didn't snap. Nothing, nothing, nothing dramatic happened.

I just thought: I want to get high.

As soon as I thought it, as soon as I allowed the thought to articulate itself, my mind fell away from all of the good work it had been focused on and within fifteen minutes I was obsessed. Despite being clean for months, my hands felt clammy. My heart rate quickened. I could feel the beginnings of a serious bout of opiate withdrawal. Logically, I knew that this was all in my mind, a psychological craving, they call it, but my body was in full fight-or-flight mode. Every cell in my body was yearning for drugs. I went to the bathroom unsure of whether I needed to cry or scream. I splashed cold water over my face and thought, "Oh Christ, will this ever be over?"

Right there I gave in to the part of my brain that wanted me dead and I said to myself in the mirror: "Fuck this. Then get high. You're a grown man. Go get high!"

For the next hour I was a junkie again. I was having junkie thoughts, I was operating on junkie logic. My family had evaporated, my concerns for my health, for my future, for my happiness had gone into the ether. All that mattered was that I have drugs today. It was the most overwhelming craving I had had for dope, and it was happening a good six months after I detoxed, as if the dying monkey on my back was waging one final, desperate attempt at wresting control of my soul.

That day it was Hank who saved my ass.

When I got back to my house, with the full intention of checking out of Beau Monde silently, without a word to the doctors or the staff, without a plan beyond the fact that I was going to get into my car, I was going to make the call, I was going to be high within the hour—it was Hank who jumped up at me, full of joy and innocence, his eyes wet and burning with life, his tongue hanging from his mouth. I stopped and looked down at him. I knew that if I walked out of Beau Monde I would never come back. And I knew that if I did walk out of Beau Monde and never came back, it would be better for Hank if I didn't take him with me, because what was about to happen next would involve shit that might lead to his neglect or death, my throwing him away in the same reckless, unfeeling way that I had tossed aside my family and my own self-respect. I knew that if I walked out of Beau Monde, the best thing that was going to happen to Hank was that he was going to the pound. The worst thing was beyond contemplation.

That moment wrested my mind away from my overwhelming cravings and back to my self-control, and I lay down on the bed and breathed and tried to find a quiet place in my mind. Hank came to me, jumped up, and lay across me, as if to say, "You aren't going anywhere," and I listened to his solid, steady breathing. Thirty minutes later it was over, and I was OK again. I called my counselor and told him that I didn't want to live alone anymore. I was back in the main house that same day.

With that came the realization that I was no longer the center of my own universe any more. In reality I never was, but I acted as if I was. The drugs fueled that. The game fueled that. My college days, and the adoration, fueled that. The kind of skewed reality I existed in had warped me. I was a false God, but I didn't realize it. When the narcotic of sporting adoration was no longer fueling this delusion, it was actual narcotics. My mother's tears were as unreal and disassociated from me as the idea of planets adrift in unknown galaxies. Nothing could penetrate my core. My insides were ice, and my need for drugs was everything in the world.

Here, six months on, an animal had licked my face, looked at me with guileless adoration, and I had had my first real, honest-to-God attack of conscience since this whole mess had started.

That's when I knew I was going to make it.

When the time came that Sarah and Kimmie had to leave, I was in something of a daze. I remember thinking, without irony, "That is the kind of woman that you marry." Then I went out on my date.

I sat staring at my coffee and thinking of Sarah, and when I looked up I realized that my companion's voice had gone up expectantly, as if she had just asked me a question, but I hadn't heard a word of what she had said. My mind had been drifting back to Sarah. I fumbled my answer, kept it vague, and the date progressed slightly awkwardly, with no real enthusiasm, until we kissed each other on the cheeks and went our separate ways. I went back home, and lay back in my bed, slightly breathless and giddy. You know, it was something about her. I got up and paced around a little. I had that fluttery feeling I used to get in my stomach before my dealer would show up with an eight-ball. I sat down. I flicked the TV on. Channel hopped. Flicked it off. Goddammit. Lay down. Got up. Then I picked up the phone and called Sarah, immediately thinking that she would consider me a goofball, overeager. But when she picked up the phone, it was as easy and as comfortable as our introduction had been earlier in the day. It wasn't a trick of the mind.

"Hey, Sarah. It's Jason."

"Hi!"

"Listen, this might seem kinda . . . well, look, I know we only just met."

Oh great. I was sounding like I was back in school, stumbling over the words of an English report. Play it cool, motherfucker!

"I mean, would you like to go grab coffee sometime?"

"Sure! Sure, but—"

Argh! This was it! The moment it would all come crumbling down. I already started playing out the possibilities in my head: *Sure, but I'm kind of seeing this guy at the moment—and it's complicated.*

Sure, but listen, Kimmie told me a little about you and you SEEM like a really sweet guy—but I'm just not ready . . . kind of thing . . . friends . . .

I stopped my mind from destroying everything for once, and asked her, "But what?"

"Oh, it's nothing really. I'm heading out of town this weekend. But I'll be back Sunday night. Can I call you on Monday?"

"Sure! Great! I, uh, mean, yeah, whatever's cool with you, you know?"

The weekend dragged by. I looked at Hank at one point and snarled, "This is your fault, you know?" He didn't seem to get it. The stars must have been in alignment, because she did call on Monday, and we have been inseparable ever since.

On our second date, I talked about my drug problems. I wanted to beat to the punch anyone else who might want to inform her of it. After the HBO special, information on my addiction to painkillers was just a Google search away. I knew that this could be a deal breaker, but I also knew that the longer I left it, the more this information would fester and have the potential to kill this relationship dead.

So I told her. I told her everything. She was quiet for a very long time. Then she said: "And are you sure you're done with all of that?"

It's funny, when I had my counselors ask me that question I would always add a "but" in there. "I'm done with heroin. I just know that I have to have cocaine in my life . . ." "I'm done. Well, I mean, I'm done for now." That kind of thing. But when Sarah asked me that very simple, very direct question I was able to say, without faltering or doubt, "Yes. I am done with all of that."

Sarah's family was a bigger concern to me. It's one thing for Sarah to be OK with my past as a drug addict, but it's another thing for someone to allow a daughter to date an ex-junkie. Something that muddies the water slightly is the fact that I still take Suboxone. Twice a day I dissolve a 4 mg tablet under my tongue, my insurance against relapse.

Still, even knowing these facts about Suboxone, there is a part of me that doesn't feel "really clean" sometimes. If I skip the drug for more than a couple of days, I will start to feel withdrawal. Not the full-on puking and shitting withdrawal of heroin, but still enough that I will not feel comfortable. But if I wanted to take heroin, I would have to come off of the Suboxone for a couple of days before I would feel its effects. Relapse is something that happens in a matter of minutes, not a matter of days. As infuriated as I can still occasionally feel at being dependent on a state-mandated drug in lieu of a street drug, the insurance against relapse that it affords me is priceless. Every day without crack or heroin makes it less and less likely that I will go back to it. The more alien that lifestyle becomes to me, the better.

For a person who has never been an addict, the suspicion must persist that someone who is still taking a drug every day is not really "clean." I understand that. So it was with a little trepidation that I approached Sarah's family, when the time came. Thankfully, my fears were unfounded.

One of the major things that Sarah and I have in common is our love of family. My time as an addict reaffirmed my belief in the importance of family. Even in the years when I was continually hurting my mom and dad, ignoring my siblings' pleas to stop killing myself, disappointing them and blowing repeated chances, my family never gave up on me. So after emerging from Beau Monde, my belief in the power of family was stronger than ever. I knew I was going to be alright with Sarah's family after she told her mom about my past. I was expecting the reaction to be something along the lines of "Sarah, are you sure this is such a good idea?" Instead, her mother just shook her head and said, "His poor mom! What she must have gone through!"

I built our relationship through time spent with her family. From the very beginning we did a lot with her family, and whether it was showing up at her nephew's baseball games, or all of us going out to dinner, I made sure that I showed up and proved to them that

I could be trusted with their daughter. And when talk of my sobriety came up, I was able to talk about it without embarrassment or shame, because I was secure in the knowledge that life was radically different now than it once was for me.

When the first time came that I looked Sarah in the eyes and said, "I love you," I knew that I wasn't telling a word of a lie. When she told me that she felt the same way, I suddenly realized that in this world—no matter what damage, wreckage, or misdeeds you have committed in your past—second chances really can happen.

I know that there is no silver bullet that cures addiction: not substitute drugs, not God, not AA, not prison, not even the love of a wonderful woman like Sarah. But with Sarah at my side I knew that this battle that I would be waging within myself, against my very nature, was now a winnable one.

And you know that I like to win.

HAPPY ENDINGS: WHERE THE HERO GETS THE GIRL (AND VISITS A MEXICAN PHARMACY)

I NEVER THOUGHT THE DAY WOULD COME THAT I, Jason Peter, would tie the knot, but just like the day that I quit smoking crack and stopped trying to kill my brain, it happened. I mean, sometimes in my darkest moments I'd think I was cursed with women, the wrong women. I'd think that my career made it impossible for me to ever find a woman who would truly want me for the person I am, not for the team colors that I wore. Back in my days of professional football, it was what players called the Jersey Jumpers—the girls whose life ambition it was to fuck a professional football player—that made up the bulk of my experiences with women.

Some guys would even marry 'em.

They'd think it was cute that their women knew all of the stats of their particular team, that they knew the entire lingo of the game, that they knew how many passes and touchdowns their man had made going back four seasons. The women got off on walking into a trendy restaurant with a professional player on their arm, or walking with their guy from the stadium after a game. But man, as soon as that poor bastard was no longer in the spotlight, that shit didn't last. Those women were off to the next player, the next round of wish fulfillment.

I mean, if you marry a starfucker, what are you gonna do when you aren't a star anymore?

Once there was this girl who attended college at Nebraska with me. I had never met her while I was there; I found this all out later. When the Panthers drafted me, she moved out to North Carolina. The first inkling I had that something weird was going on was when the head trainer came up to me and laughed.

"You're quite the secret agent, Jason!"

"Huh?"

"Your girlfriend! How come you didn't tell me you are in a serious relationship? Scared to blow your rep?"

"But . . . I don't have a girlfriend!"

He frowned a little. Maybe he thought I was jerking him around.

"Well, there's a girl works over at my wife's office, she's been telling everyone who'll listen that she's your girlfriend and how you two are an item."

"Not me."

"Hm."

I blew it off at the time. Just another quirk of being in the public eye. Four months later, the same trainer came up to me and asked, "How come you didn't tell me you were getting married?"

Now I thought that he was trying to kid me, so I laughed. At this point, I still didn't even have a steady girlfriend. The idea that I was getting married was preposterous.

"Shit, Jason, I'm serious! That girl at my wife's office is sayin' that you two are getting married! Shit, she gave my wife an invitation! Are you sure you don't know this girl? I mean, Jason, getting married isn't the end of the world! Look at me and my wife. We've been together for ten years now, and still going strong!"

"Can you bring that invitation in for me?"

"Sure thing!"

The next day, he brought the invitation. Looking it over, I got a chill down my spine. There I was—Jason Peter—and some woman whose name I had never even heard before, cordially inviting people to our impending nuptials. I gave the invite to the head of the Panthers security, and tried to put it out of my mind.

Months later, I was at the stadium opening fan mail. Fan mail could consist of anything and everything from adoring letters from football-crazed ten-year-olds who want to grow up to be just like you to lonely housewives who send nude Polaroids of themselves and long descriptions of what they'd like to do with you "if you'd only call me up on this number."

One envelope looked pretty serious. It was from a school official in the Northwest. Inside was a full-page typed letter:

Dear Mr. Peter:

As you can well imagine, I was both shocked and disappointed at your no-show at the wedding this past weekend. My wife and I spent a lot of money ensuring that our daughter's big day would be everything she's always dreamed of, and your reckless, heartless decision has—I fear—broken her heart . . .

Goddamn. This was getting freakier and freakier. I realized then that I had a crazy on my hands, and immediately turned the letter over to security. As soon as the authorities got involved, the whole story started coming to me in bits and pieces. It turned out that this girl had been telling her entire family that she had been dating me for years. She had gleaned many details about my family through the press, and would pepper her conversations about our fictitious relationship with enough innocuous details as to keep it convincing. The whole charade culminated when she had her entire family fly down to Charlotte for the "wedding" that—of course—I didn't show up for. The story she told her father was that Christian had come to my house the morning of the wedding and we had split town together.

Of course my first question was, how could the family believe this shit when they had never even met me?

Well, the answer came back, every time the family came into town she had an excuse lined up why I couldn't be there. I was out of town on team business. I was seeing the doctor for an injury. I was visiting my family. I guess no one really wanted to believe that she was a fantasist, and the whole story culminated in her entire family sitting in a church in Charlotte wondering where the fuck I was.

Even once the authorities got involved, the girl's father didn't want to believe that his daughter had fabricated the entire thing. But when the truth could no longer be denied, the poor girl was committed to a psychiatric hospital.

After my football career ended, Diane was the closest thing I had had to a real relationship in my drug years. But it was no healthier than my relationship with my crack pipe was. Over time I came to care about her, to care what happened to her, of course. I wouldn't have been human if that wasn't the case. But never, in my darkest and most drugged-out of fantasies, did I see myself growing old with her. It was the very idea that she might have become accidentally pregnant that sent her out on to the fire escape that night—and me into treatment for the last time.

In Sarah I had found a woman who didn't know the difference between a first down and an extra point, and I liked that. She had grown up in Pasadena, California, and spent her summers at Newport Beach. Her career is in television—she has worked as a director on reality shows such as *The Osbournes, Newlyweds: Nick and Jessica*, and *House of Carters*. Since I started coaching the football team at Edison High School in California, Sarah has attended all of the games with me, even though she isn't a big football fan. I think of us as one of those "opposites attract" type of couples. I do my best to get her into sports, and the most successful I have been—funnily enough—is with *Ultimate Fighting*. Sarah likes *Ultimate Fighting* so much that she keeps bugging me to take her down to Vegas to see it live. But it's not all me imposing stuff on her; Sarah has opened my eyes to new things as well. We've taken in art galleries, Broadway shows, and museums together.

I swore that I wasn't going to cry at our wedding. Sarah tends to be the emotional one, and I figured that she'd be the one to cry.

But even in the buildup to the day, seeing all of those old faces—Coach Charlie McBride, his face with a few more wrinkles, his silver hair combed back neatly, but still the same Coach McBride, his yells from the sidelines still echoing down the years; Grant Wistrom; and my own brother, newly retired from the NFL, his body shrunken down to civilian size again, greeting me with a warm embrace and the ease of ex-comrades in arms—all of that started to get to me.

It was as I was standing by the altar, as Sarah entered the church, wrapped in the flowing ivory of her dress, that the tears started to come. It was as if all of the trauma and all of the hurt of the last several years were finally released from me. I could see my mother, my father, my aunt Lee looking at me, and I thought of the hurt I had inflicted on all of them. The tears were good, they were cleansing, and although a part of me wondered what in the hell I had done to deserve a woman as beautiful, as loving, as caring as Sarah, I knew that what was happening here today was what was meant to happen. I had survived. Jesus, like in some cornball movie I had got the girl, too. And here I was, watching my wife walking down the aisle, the luckiest bastard on the earth it seemed, about to finally fulfill my squandered promise.

As we exchanged vows, I managed to get my emotions under control. When the exchange of rings happened, when Sarah placed the wedding band on my finger, the importance of this moment in my life really hit me. I'm not a guy who wears a lot of jewelry. I have four rings to my name. Three are the national championship rings that I never wear. I keep those in a top drawer at home. The other is this wedding ring that I will now wear every day of my life. All of these rings are sacred objects. The first three were achieved not long before my descent into addiction and despair and the other was not an achievement but a blessing, a testament to my bond to Sarah and my drug-free life with her.

Driving the dirt roads to Grant's house in La Paz, Mexico, where we would be spending the first five days of our honeymoon,

I noticed all of these little makeshift graves by the side of the road. Grant had told me about them. They marked where people had been killed in auto accidents, and local practice was to just bury them where they lay. Grant's place, once known as Bahía de los Muertos ("The Bay of Death") was now known by the slightly friendlier moniker of Bahía de los Sueños. I ain't the superstitious type, but still the Bay of Dreams has a much nicer ring to it. One of the leading causes of automobile accidents on these dirt roads— apart from the suicidal driving style of the locals, who barrel around, seemingly navigating on a prayer and gut instinct—is the cows that sometimes wander out onto the roads. We came across a few of them. The looked mangy, ill, with their ribs sticking out of their bodies and legs, which looked like they would snap under the weight of their own frames. They looked something like crackheads.

At the Mini-Mercado Sarah and I navigated past the two men who were passed out drunk at a table at the front of the store, and in my eighth-grade Spanish I managed to purchase a jug of drinking water and potato chips. A tired fan did its best to keep the dry heat at bay. My shirt soaked through with sweat, I got back behind the wheel and we carried on to our destination.

Following Grant's instructions, we stopped at the only other building on this road, a restaurant called the Giggling Marlin. We ordered food while the owner called Sergio, the guy who looked after Grant's place and would take us the rest of the way. We trailed Sergio along winding dirt roads, and it was not until we pulled up to the house that I finally started to relax. Sarah and I sat in awed wonder for a moment looking at this magnificent building.

"Oh shit," I breathed after a moment. "This place is incredible."

For the next five days we did nothing but hang out together, enjoy the infinity pool, which literally looked straight down a cliff into the sea below, fish off the rocks, and bask like lizards in the sun. Grant's neighbor was a guy I knew from the NFL, Kyle Turley. He had just

left for the States, but allowed us to use his ATVs and off-road vehicles. The days seemed to fly by. When the fifth day came around, we
left for the Palmilla Resort in Cabo San Lucas. The seclusion of
Grant's place was incredible, but we were both looking forward to
being able to order a cocktail by the pool.

The first night in our hotel, I was lying on the bed and Sarah
was standing on the balcony, overlooking the ocean.

My mind drifted back, for a moment, to another balcony, or
rather a fire escape, another city, a different woman, another lifetime.
I thanked whatever force of the universe that had saved my ass and
delivered me here.

There are certain rumors you hear when you are a junkie.
Some of them are true, some of them are false, but they remain
pretty constant. One is that if someone ODs on heroin you should
shoot them up with saline solution. That one I know is bullshit. Another is that if you don't burn the chemicals off of aluminum foil
before you smoke heroin off of it, you can fuck your lungs up real
bad, too. I've read that one is an urban myth, too. Another is about
Mexican pharmacies that dole out painkillers, no questions asked.
That one I had to go discover for myself.

One day, shopping in Cabo, as I sat outside on the sidewalk
while Sarah tried on a dress, I found myself staring into the window
of a backstreet Farmacia. I looked back through the window of the
shop, and Sarah was still in the changing room. I debated with myself for a few moments before walking across the street.

I pushed open the door, and a bell tinkled softly. Inside, it was
dark and cool. Unsure of what the fuck I was doing here, I walked
in slowly, and the pharmacist came out of the back to greet me.

I don't know if it was something about the way I looked, my
tattoos, or whatever, but before I could even say, "Cómo está?" she
had pulled out two boxes, one containing Vicodin, and one Xanax. I
froze. Then I smiled, shook my head in the negative, and I cut out
again.

When Sarah emerged from the shop and I told her about the

pharmacy, she shook her head in disbelief, asking, "Why did you feel the need to do that?"

I shrugged my shoulders and grinned.

"Just like to know I haven't lost the magic touch."

I have to admit I had some of that anxious, Christmas Eve anticipation in my stomach when I saw those boxes. In reality I knew that there were much more complex reasons for my checking out the pharmacy. Part of it was just to experience—however fleetingly—the vicarious thrill of going to score again. Part of it was the ten-year-old still inside of me, who lived for summers spent dive-bombing from diving boards, letting me know he was still around. Part of it was to prove something to myself, to show myself that I should not be afraid anymore.

HERO OF THE UNDERGROUND

THE DREAM IS ALWAYS THE SAME.

I am seven years old, and my family and I are at a circus. This isn't your Barnum and Bailey or Big Apple type of circus—this is one of the traveling fairs that used to take up residence in the parking lot of the local mall, a park in Fair Haven, New Jersey, or whatever. But in the dream, I am not interested in the collection of half-assed attractions, the rusting thrill rides, the sweet smell of the cotton candy machines, the barkers screaming, "A dollar buys you three chances to win! Pick any toy from the top row!"

No, in this dream I am being drawn, inexplicably, toward a dark cage that seems almost totally ignored by the rest of the crowd. My family, and indeed the entire crowd, seems6 to dissolve around me as I walk toward this abandoned place. The deep, throaty purrs of a big cat are emanating from within the shadows of the structure. Inside, the faded, peeling sign promises I will see the King of Beasts, but as I nervously approach, all I can see is a limp-looking form lying on a bed of wet straw. As I continue toward it I can sense—in the way that one can in dreams—that the animal inside is old, sick, and neglected. As each breathless step takes me closer, closer, I can make out visual clues that confirm this: the animal's lank, mottled fur, which is missing in patches, the contours of the ribs, which are clearly visible through parchment-thin skin, the colorless, dried-out texture of the beast's skin, the infected watery eyes, which gaze upon me with only a shred of the threat and authority they no doubt once exuded. The face, shriveled up like that of an old man, teeth that seem too big for the mouth, the mane covered in drool and rotting food.

Even as I notice all of this, fear still wells up inside of my chest. For I know that if this animal somehow got loose, even in this beaten, weakened state, it still could snap me in two with its mighty jaws. Even neglected, starved, aged, this animal still holds the power of life and death within it.

The animal's foul smelling breath comes out of it unsteadily, in ragged huffs.

I step up to the bars, and place a hand quietly on the metal.

Our eyes meet.

And I jerk awake, gasping for breath.

Waking from this uneasy dream, walking down corridors I have long tried to forget, in the comfort of my own bed, with the warmth of Sarah next to me as she, too, begins to dreamily stir, I know that something indefinable has shifted within me. Today I wake up, newly married, no longer a multimillionaire, no longer a professional football player. Today my life will consist of the routine, the mundane, the things that were once so terrifying, so alien to me.

I open my mail. I read the bills. I place things in orderly, neat piles, and I brew coffee and place the bread in the toaster.

I did not know, when I sucked on my crack pipe in the Four Seasons, that that would be the last time that I would get high. How could I know? In the end, an event as profound and life-changing as that first hit on the pipe all of those years ago—or being drafted into the NFL, or taking home the 1997 national college championship—simply passed without a murmur. It was just another instance of me getting high, buried within countless other, desperate moments.

Ask any former drug addict, and rarely will they be able to recall with perfect clarity the last time they used drugs. Some will say, "No more! I'm done!" get high one last time, and then stop forever, but those are a small minority. The rest of us will approach our last attempt at getting clean with no more sense of finality than we approached our many previous, futile attempts.

It is as if the act of getting clean were not even our own doing. We did not quit. Something in the universe around us shifted, and we awoke gradually from a bad dream of our own devising. One day of abstinence became a week, one week a month, one month a year, and one day we find ourselves standing in our kitchen, buttering our toast, and we realize that we are clean.

How did that happen?

The only answer is: Slowly. In imperceptible steps. Sarah did not materialize from the skies to Save Me. Once I realized that I had enough of myself to give to her, I knew that I had already been saved. I did not look up to the blue skies above Beau Monde one day and make a pact with God. I did not fall down and weep and beg for forgiveness.

America cultivates, worships, hates, and fears its beasts in equal measure. The beast that society seems to worship—the football warrior, the All-American, the baddest motherfucker in God's own universe—is still a part of who I am. It shaped, and continues to shape, my life, even off of the football field. The beast that society seems to abhor—the drug addict, the nihilist, those who lie and cheat and break the law to secure their next fix—is still a part of who I am. The two extremes of my being have at last forged an uneasy ceasefire, but in every aspect of my life I carry the memories, the sensations, the tastes, sights, and smells of a life lived as a challenge to God.

I am part Hero, standing under the long-ago lights of Memorial Stadium, a sea of red surrounding me, 78,000 voices chanting my name . . .

I am part Underground dweller, hidden away in darkened rooms with the curtains holding the world at bay, locked into a drug-fueled death match with myself . . .

In the next room, I hear Sarah moving from the bed, grabbing her robe, walking out to the kitchen, and I don't turn. I wait until I feel her hands on my shoulders and she says, "Morning, baby."

I know that I am at the farthest possible point from where I once was, from walking the midnight streets of New York, seized by paranoia and drug need, from the cold, nocturnal world of the junkie. The Beast inside of me remains chained up, locked away, and every instance of goodness, of love, of warmth, of joy in my life is one more blow to It. It remains like the lion in my dreams: biding its time maybe, but for now strictly contained. Maybe one day there will be nothing left in the cage but the fossilized remains of What Once Was.

Once, I could never have enough. There was never enough money, there were never enough women, and there were never enough drugs. I was the American dream all right, the dream that consumes and consumes until there is nothing left for it to do but swallow itself whole.

At Sarah's touch I turn, and smile, and say something banal, like "The coffee is on," and I look into her eyes, her devastating hazel eyes.

And I know that this is enough.